SPEAK YOUR MIND

ALSO BY DR. EMERSON EGGERICHS

Love & Respect

Mother & Son

Love & Respect in the Family

The 4 Wills of God

The Language of Love and Respect

Living Above the Bar

The Love & Respect Devotional

SPEAK YOUR MIND

Evaluating and Unleashing Your Communication Strengths

EMERSON EGGERICHS, PHD

W Publishing Group

An Imprint of Thomas Nelson

Speak Your Mind

Some content has been adapted from the previously published title *Before You Hit Send*.

Published in Nashville, Tennessee, by W Publishing, an imprint of Thomas Nelson. Thomas Nelson titles may be purchased in bulk for educational, business, fund-raising, or sales promotional use. For information, please email SpecialMarkets@ThomasNelson.com.

The author is represented by Joy Eggerichs of Punchline Agency.

Italics and other emphases added to Scripture quotations are the author's own.

Names and facts from stories contained in this book have been changed, but the sentiments expressed are true as related to the author through personal conversations, letters, or emails. Permission has been granted for the use of real names, stories, and correspondence.

Interior design: Kait Lamphere

ISBN 978-1-4003-3859-7 (audiobook)
ISBN 978-1-4003-3858-0 (eBook)
ISBN 978-1-4003-3857-3 (SC)

Library of Congress Control Number: 2024944748

Printed in the United States of America

25 26 27 28 29 LBC 5 4 3 2 1

CONTENTS

PART FOUR:
Speak Your Mind Clearly

TO GET THE MOST FROM THIS BOOK

Do you want to improve your communication skills and become more persuasive in speaking your mind? Would you like to strengthen your relationships, prevent misunderstandings, and express your thoughts and ideas effectively? If so, this book will help you discover and harness your communication strengths while you recognize and tame your weaknesses.

You have communication strengths—you really do. But since you're reading a book about speaking your mind, I assume you are like me in that you tend to say, or want to say, things that shouldn't be said or should be said more wisely. You may even have underlying issues affecting your communication that you aren't aware of yet.

The goal of this book is simple: to help you speak your mind by unleashing your communication strengths and silencing your communication weaknesses!

In the introduction, you'll learn the four critical questions for effective communication, which provide the foundation of this book.

In the prologue, you can take the *Speak Your Mind* communication self-assessment to discover your strengths as a communicator. At the same time, you can identify any weaknesses that may be hindering your effectiveness as a communicator. To benefit the most from this book, I encourage you to set aside enough time to answer these eighty questions honestly and thoughtfully.

After you complete the *Speak Your Mind* communication self-assessment, you will be ready to dive into chapters 1–21, where you will explore in depth how to speak your mind based on the findings from the assessment. In these chapters, you'll discover specific ways to harness your communication strengths while you tame your weaknesses. The self-assessment allows you to turn to those pages in the book and go to work immediately.

These chapters will also give you insight into how the people you interact with communicate. It's my hope that the insights you learn in this book will give you wisdom and grace as you seek to communicate with all different kinds of people.

This book is like an encyclopedia of communication strengths and weaknesses. Don't be overwhelmed by all the information. You don't have to master all this content; however, I would encourage you to keep this book around for a reference and refresher—and give yourself a break when you make a mistake. I've written this book, yet I still make communication blunders more than I wish!

Are you open to improving your communication? Are you ready to become more persuasive in speaking your mind? Do you hope to earn a reputation as someone who seeks to understand and listen more than to be heard and be right?

If your answer is yes, I invite you to turn the page to begin your journey of discovering where you can increase your knowledge about communication and improve your skills.

INTRODUCTION

TRUE, KIND, NECESSARY, AND CLEAR

Since you're reading a book about speaking your mind, you may relate to one of the following common communication struggles:

- You have been holding back your ideas, only later to regret not speaking up.
- You tend to blurt out your thoughts and feelings but later are sorry you didn't think before speaking.
- You are a fairly good speaker but haven't yet become the master communicator you know you could be.

In this book, you will uncover why you tend to refrain from speaking up, succumb to communication disasters, or feel stuck as a merely average communicator. You'll also learn how to harness your communication strengths. And, perhaps most importantly, you'll learn the powerful four-part strategy that has successfully guided and guarded my speech and writing for the past five decades.

THREE RULES OF COMMUNICATION . . . NO, FOUR!

As a college student, I sat in a chapel service at Wheaton College and heard a speaker make the following statement: "All of us must ask three questions before communicating: Is it true, kind, and necessary?"

I don't remember the name or face of that speaker, but I remember that advice as though it was given yesterday. It rang true for me immediately. That brief sentence struck a chord and stuck in my brain, and it has chaperoned my thinking for the last five decades.

Many have credited the fifth-century BC philosopher Socrates with originally asking, "Is it true, is it kind, or is it necessary?"[1] No one knows, however, who first penned the question. Regardless, in that chapel service I came into the possession of a rule of communication that has worked well for me—and I'm confident it will work for you too.

These three qualifiers pulsate throughout the Bible as well. As a pastor for nearly twenty years, I often heard Ephesians 4:15 quoted by folks in my congregation: "Speak the truth in love" (NLT). This verse emphasizes the importance of truth and kindness in our communication. Or who hasn't heard it said that there is "a time to be silent and a time to speak," originally written by the wise King Solomon (Eccl. 3:7)? This verse reveals that some things are not necessary to say, while other things are.

Bottom line: We intuitively know that we ought to speak the truth in love at the appropriate time. This foundational aspect of interpersonal communication rings true for all of us.

These three rules of communication appealed to me since I wished to be a person whom, when I spoke or wrote, others would view as accurate, goodwilled, and helpful. I had a desire to be competent, trustworthy, and effective. I wanted to be a good communicator. I wanted to be confident that when I spoke my mind, the words I said were true, kind, and necessary.

I believe the same can be said about you! If you didn't see the value in becoming an effective communicator, you wouldn't have picked up a book called *Speak Your Mind*. You, too, likely wish to take control of your speech. It's a beautiful thing to learn how to communicate in a way that touches others' hearts and allows them to know ours as well.

ONE MORE TO ADD TO THE CHECKLIST

Since that day in the chapel service, I have come to the conclusion that a fourth checklist item must be added: "Is it *clear*?" What we are communicating to another must also be clear.

There have been many times when I knew what I said was true, kind, and necessary, but I later found out that I had been unclear in how I had communicated it. Can you relate? For example,

- I wrongly assumed others knew all the facts—the whole truth. But if they were not fully informed, they felt confused about what I communicated.
- I assumed people understood when I was being silly in a comment, not unkind. Instead, they thought I belittled them.
- I assumed readers or listeners appreciated all the information, but I found out they deemed some of it unnecessary if they had to ask, "What exactly is your point?"

The Bible also speaks of our need to be clear when communicating. In 1 Corinthians 14:9 the apostle Paul asked, "Unless you utter by the tongue speech that is clear, how will it be known what is spoken?" This is a universal rhetorical question.

With the addition of "clear," we now have four questions we must ask ourselves before communicating:

- Is this communication *true*?
- Is this communication *kind*?
- Is this communication *necessary*?
- Is this communication *clear*?

These four questions have stood the test of time as a proven framework for communication. In speaking and writing based on this checklist, we win many friends and influence many people.

As a Christian, I believe God intends for us to be truthful and kind people who speak what is clear and necessary. For me, that is all the reason I need to hold up these four checklist items toward every word I communicate. But even if you do not share my Christian faith, you likely recognize the importance of being a truthful and kind person who speaks what is clear and necessary. Would any goodwilled person disagree?

When we apply these four pillars of effective communication, we will be able to change our world one conversation at a time. What joy it is to learn how to winsomely affect the hearts and minds of others! Are you in?

IT'S NOT ONLY ABOUT SPEAKING LESS, THOUGH

You may be saying, "But Emerson, some things just have to be said, even if the person may not like it. I have to be able to speak my mind!"

I agree. That's why you are holding this book in your hand. Back in 2017, I wrote *Before You Hit Send: Preventing Headache and Heartache*, which served as the source material for much of this book. However, I knew that not all communication problems can be solved simply by refusing to "hit send"—or by choosing not to speak your mind. Eventually, many uncomfortable but necessary conversations need to be had.

Speak Your Mind is not only about holding back communication; it will also give you the clarity and confidence you need to speak up more often, even though it may be uncomfortable. In these situations, how can someone best speak their mind?

How do you "speak your mind" to your spouse when you feel unloved or disrespected?

Or to your coworkers when they're not pulling their weight around the office?

Or to your friends when they're making decisions you don't agree with?

Or to your family members who have different political views than your own?

How do you skillfully, honestly, and lovingly speak your mind when you have a truth to share with another—a truth that will be tough to hear?

As you read this book, I hope to serve you well by providing a little know-how on how to speak your mind *truthfully*, how to speak your mind *with kindness*, how to speak your mind *only when necessary*, and how to speak your mind *clearly*, even when you need to share a challenging and uncomfortable truth. In the pages to come, we are going to discuss in detail what it truly means for your communication to hit all four checklist items.

Will you join me as we look closely at these four concepts? We will answer the following questions:

- Is what I'm about to say the truth, the whole truth, and nothing but the truth?
- Is it loving and respectful?
- Do I know if it should be said now instead of later or not at all?
- Will what I say be clear to me and to the other person?

When the answer to all four is yes, let's speak our minds! Remember, mastering the art of communication isn't just about speaking less but rather about communicating with confidence, purpose, and effectiveness.

I invite you to join me on this journey of learning when to speak less and when to speak up. These four distinct dimensions act as guidelines and guardrails for effective communicators. They allow us to move forward with confidence, purpose, and effectiveness.

First, though, do you know where your strengths lie regarding these four dimensions? Do you have ideas about where you could stand to improve? In the prologue, you'll begin with a self-assessment of your current communication. I urge you not to skip over this important first step in becoming a master communicator. Before you can get to where you want to be, you need to first know where you are.

So turn the page to find out!

SPEAK YOUR MIND COMMUNICATION SELF-ASSESSMENT

Before you begin this study of how to improve your communication with the four qualifiers—*Is what I am about to communicate true? Kind? Necessary? Clear?*—it would be beneficial for you to be aware of your starting point on this journey.

Every person has specific strengths and weaknesses when it comes to communication. For example, someone may usually speak the truth but not be aware that much of the truth they speak isn't particularly necessary to share. Or maybe someone is rarely ever a verbal bully, but does their impatience sometimes lead them to snap back with unkind words?

For this reason, I want you to begin your journey toward becoming a great communicator by assessing yourself accurately. While we may have a general idea about our communication abilities, we may not have considered subtopics in the four categories. I will highlight these subtopics to reveal to you where you possess strength but also where you can improve as a communicator. And, by the way, you can still be a great communicator while strengthening areas that may have weakened! No one is perfect all the time, but that does not mean you cannot communicate effectively most of the time.

None of us is beginning at the same starting point, either, and it would be unwise to pretend we are. The assessment that follows will introduce you to twenty subtopics each of true, kind, necessary, and clear communication. By honestly answering the questions, you will learn not only what your strengths and weaknesses are among the four communication qualifiers of true, kind, necessary, and clear, but where in each of them you rate the most positively and, perhaps more pertinent, where you would be wise to address specific communication weaknesses that have potentially caused fissures in even the dearest of your relationships.

As you proceed, do your best to answer honestly the questions in each section about yourself. Do not rush through but take the appropriate time to assess yourself accurately. After you are finished, you will have a much better idea of your starting point on this journey. My hope is that having a more accurate idea of where you currently stand will help you direct your focus in the proceeding chapters as we break down in detail all the ways to speak your mind truthfully, with kindness, only when necessary, and clearly.

In the introduction, we discussed three possible categories you might belong to (listed below). Please keep these questions in mind as you proceed in your assessment:

- Where have you been holding back your ideas and opinions, then later regretting not speaking up?
- In what ways do you tend to blurt out your thoughts and feelings, only to later regret not thinking before speaking?
- In what areas are your communication skills only average, but you want to learn to be a master communicator?

The journey to learning these answers begins here!

PART ONE: SPEAK YOUR MIND TRUTHFULLY

Instructions: For each pair of adjectives, circle a number on the scale that best represents your current communication style.

SECURE IN THE TRUTH

1	2	3	4	5

Fearful
Because of fear, I hide my missteps to avoid the consequences of past mistakes.

Brave
Despite my anxiety over the consequences, I choose courage by confessing my misleading comments and committing to honor the truth confidently.

1	2	3	4	5

Evasive
If others don't know what I did wrong, there will be fewer problems all around.

Straightforward
I am assured that being open, direct, and truthful builds trust and meaningful relationships, since honesty is the best policy and prevents the heartaches that can result from being evasive and misleading.

1	2	3	4	5

Chameleonlike
To avoid conflict, I blend my beliefs to fit my audience, which pleases them.

Unwavering
In social settings, I am comfortable in my skin in resisting the pull I feel to blend in as a compromising and conforming people-pleaser by expressing my values honestly and wisely when necessary.

1	2	3	4	5

Protecting
I feel responsible to protect another's interests even if I have to lie to do so.

Morally Grounded
Though I feel genuinely responsible for protecting those I care about, I will not advance their interests by lying, since I am centered on and bound by a moral code that grounds and guides me in my service to others.

TRANSFORMED BY THE TRUTH

1	2	3	4	5

Self-Deluding
Some claim I lie to myself. But that's a lie. I'm 100 percent honest with myself.

Self-Aware
I wish to be more cognizant of my shortcomings that hinder the best version of me as a truthful communicator, so I examine myself to reduce my bias and blind spots that work against my good reputation and healthy relationships.

1	2	3	4	5

Chronic
I've always lied even when the truth was better. Something comes over me.

Resistant
While I used to battle chronic lying and the allure to deceive to gain something or get away with something, now I resist these tendencies and choose honesty, recognizing that it is the best and most empowering policy.

1	2	3	4	5

Ashamed
Out of embarrassment for the bad stuff I have done, I lie to appear good.

Confessing
I value the renewal I feel when being truthful and transparent, since this is the right thing to do. Nothing compares with a clear conscience and the inner peace that results from choosing confession over shame.

FORTHRIGHT WITH THE TRUTH

1	2	3	4	5

Expedient
I lie, since it is quicker and easier for me at the moment.

Up-Front
Though lying about something that might go wrong can be practical, I now sincerely reveal a potential problem ahead of time; speaking half-truths and falsehoods about a possible inconvenient truth is no longer an enticement—especially since most people want to hear the truth, no matter how difficult it may be.

1	2	3	4	5

Brainy
I'm smart, retaining both the lies and the truth. It's easy to get away with lying.

Wise
I stopped lying, though I am good at it, and am honest and plainspoken because I realized that it's foolish and arrogant to think I could outsmart and outrun God with my human expertise in deception.

1	2	3	4	5

Wordsmithing
I find it easy and fun to twist words, using double meanings that mislead.

Well-Spoken
In the past, I used my ability to be an effective communicator to twist the truth cunningly, but now I use that ability to be persuasive, eloquent, direct, and clear so my speaking and writing can be a positive influence.

MORAL WITH THE TRUTH

1	2	3	4	5

Entrapped
It's not my fault. I was lured into swearing secrecy and facilitated a lie.

Integrous
Though lured by others into swearing secrecy to facilitate a lie, I refuse to be entrapped, since I have a moral compass about walking in integrity, and will not compromise even when others claim I do not care about them and try to guilt-trip me to do what they want.

1	2	3	4	5

Copycatting
I'm not really interested in lying, but everybody else lies, so I do too.

Individualistic
I stand alone on my values and principles, strong and independent in telling the truth, even when those around me have a mindset to lie and expect me to copy them and shrewdly deceive others for personal gain.

1	2	3	4	5

Perpetuating
I lie to stay ahead of other lies I have told, not concerned that lies beget lies.

Self-Correcting
My previous strategy of lying to stay ahead of exposure—having to lie about lies—not only was exhausting but impeded healthy relationships, so I amended my ways and changed course by prioritizing the moral value of honesty, and I am much happier.

INFORMED OF THE TRUTH

1	2	3	4	5

Emotional
If it feels true, I say it; I don't need all the facts when I feel I'm right.

Factual
When I feel something is true or right, I fight against saying it or acting on it until I have all the facts; otherwise, I can jump to wrong conclusions based on my emotions or impulse.

1	2	3	4	5

Inattentive
I didn't know that what I said was inaccurate; everyone makes mistakes.

Observant
When I am inaccurate in what I say, I try to be attentive and set the record straight when I learn the facts. Previous ignorance is no excuse nor self-justification for perpetuating an untruth.

ALTRUISTIC ABOUT THE TRUTH

1	2	3	4	5

Selfish
What can I say? Lying works to my advantage, advancing my agenda.

Unselfish
All people are made in God's image and have equal value, which requires fairness and win-win solutions. Therefore, I consider the just interests of others and not solely what benefits me at their expense, even if lying may work to my advantage.

1	2	3	4	5

Prideful
I need to look better than I am so others will feel good about me and like me.

Humble
Striving for authenticity and sincere, respectful relationships, I resist the temptation to lie about being better than I am to feel good about myself and to gain approval. As I will not lie about my inadequacies to prevent rejection, I have ceased projecting a false image at the expense of the truth about who I am.

1	2	3	4	5

Flattering
I want to be truthful and tactful, but insincere praise works better for me.

Genuine
Though flattery or false praise may work in the moment, people eventually see through the insincerity, so I have committed to affirming what is true about others without exaggeration.

1	2	3	4	5

Oath-Making
I admit that when hedging, I sometimes swear to God so others believe what I'm saying.

Reverent
In my communication, others need me to be trustworthy and competent; they do not need me to coerce them into believing I am credible and truthful because I say "Honest to God" or "I swear to God."

1	2	3	4	5

Self-Amusing
Frankly, I view tricking others as an exciting and entertaining game.

Mindfully Humorous
In the past, I might have used inappropriate, disrespectful, and offensive humor to amuse myself, but that hurt others, so I decided to get serious and sincere to help others with problems by using my quick thinking to assess the truth and creatively find innovative solutions. I now try to use only good humor for comedic relief.

A WORD OF PRAISE!

You're off to a great start, but let's take a quick pause.

If you answered 4 or 5 on any of the descriptors, then you need to be saluted. You are a truthful communicator. Even when you feel threatened by possible unpleasant outcomes, you tell the truth. Though you might have personal issues and troubles from the past, you do not use those as excuses to hedge on truth or to lie. In many situations you could be crafty and use both the lie and the truth to your advantage, but you reject such craftiness. You have avoided the traps of getting yourself obligated to others in protecting them with a lie and have not given in to the idea that you're obligated to keep on lying once you have lied. You don't presume you know the truth just because you feel a certain way, and you make sure you are aware of the facts before communicating. And though you care deeply about your own interests, you do not give into a self-serving mindset that says lying is justified if it advances your agenda.

Bottom line, you are a person of integrity and you need to be applauded. This has not been easy, but you have resolved in your heart that you will be a truthful communicator. So let me exclaim: Congratulations! You have countered what is difficult for many of us, doing so with courage and integrity. I admire your honesty and commitment to do the right thing!

Also, you need to be encouraged if you used to be a poor communicator but have changed for the better. This assessment tool will help you see these changes and motivate you to stay the course. This tool, assessing all four dimensions, can help you realize your propensity to default to being untruthful, unkind, unnecessary, or unclear unless you keep taking these new steps to guard against that. So, though you struggled in the past, don't worry. It is a new day! We all have fallen short at communicating in ways that reflect the best version of ourselves. But we can take steps to improve, and that will be worth celebrating.

However, please understand that we all have a tendency to be biased in our own favor. Some of us focus on our positives and block out the negatives. Yes, in general we could be truthful communicators, but we also overlook those moments when we consciously and willfully mislead people with untruths. We suppress our lies because we do not feel lying is something we do in general. But that's comparable to the bank robber declaring, "I am no thief. I only robbed one bank."

As you take the remainder of this assessment, you might find that you are 90 percent stellar. However, what about that 10 percent? Is that 10 percent poisoning your effectiveness as a communicator? Do you need to be honest with yourself about how others are interpreting you? The goal here is not to shame you but to improve your effectiveness as a communicator. For this reason, seek to be as honest as you can in your self-evaluation so you can strengthen yourself and not give in to your weaker moments.

On that point, if you answered 1 or 2 on any of the descriptors, then allow me to stop and applaud you for being honest about your dishonesty! Bravo! Being honest with yourself is the first step toward making a change in your communication patterns. I would strongly recommend that you now tell a trusted person in your life what you are recognizing about yourself and see if they can help you get to the "why" behind your dishonesty. Once you understand that, you will be much more equipped to choose honesty going forward. The same applies for the next three parts of this assessment.

The rewards are worth the application of this information! Not only will you feel good about yourself, but you will also build trust and respect in your relationships. You will find greater success in every facet of your life—success that is significant, satisfying, and far-reaching.

PART TWO: SPEAK YOUR MIND WITH KINDNESS

Instructions: For each pair of adjectives, circle a number on the scale that best represents your communication style.

CARING WITH YOUR WORDS

1	2	3	4	5

Bullying

When I am mean-spirited, it works. When I intimidate, I get my way.

Gentle

My gentle demeanor and kind words can break down others' walls, encourage teamwork, prove winsome, and maintain my good reputation. Therefore, I do not use bullying and intimidating tactics.

1 2 3 4 5

Retaliating

I'm mean only when others are unkind to me; it's an eye for an eye.

Benevolent

I choose to be a kind person who returns good for bad, which allows me to speak the truth about another's lack of kindness rather than stooping to their level with tit-for-tat vindictiveness.

1 2 3 4 5

Vanquishing

To win, I'll lie and dishonor my competition. My end justifies my means.

Affirming

As a secure and value-driven person, I kindly compliment others' achievements, even when they outshine mine, and though this praise could contribute to their advantage over me, I am comfortable being truthful and validating about their character and diligence.

1 2 3 4 5

Intolerant

I detest and cannot stomach those who hold beliefs at odds with mine.

Tolerant

I recognize that differing opinions are a reality, and though I might hold contrary convictions and will not compromise them, I treat those who reject my beliefs kindly, with a spirit of tolerance.

1 2 3 4 5

Abusive

I'm not abusive, and whatever idiot says that better watch their backs.

Peaceable

I used to react with aggression, combativeness, and threats when mad, but this damaged relationships, caused shame, and pushed God away, so I strive to be conciliatory by actively listening, speaking calmly, acknowledging goodwill, and finding common ground—and this works!

SENSITIVE WITH YOUR WORDS

1 2 3 4 5

Unempathetic

I'm no teary-eyed hand holder. The feeble need to toughen up.

Empathetic

I understand others' struggles and approach them with consideration and kindness, not dismissive judgmentalism, when addressing the burdens and shortcomings that they are navigating.

1	2	3	4	5

Impatient
I don't have time for polite greetings but need to get to my point.

Polite
I am patient and warm when communicating a difficult but necessary truth with another, and I refrain from hurrying the conversation, interrupting, or making it too brief.

1	2	3	4	5

Unmindful
Truthfully, I am preoccupied and don't have time to think about how others might be inadvertently hurt by my neglect.

Aware
I am sensitive to the needs of others and am attentive to showing kindness by immediately responding or rebounding when I innocently overlook their concerns.

1	2	3	4	5

Unintentional
I didn't mean to be insensitive or coldhearted; I was just upset.

Amending
I humbly acknowledge that I meant no ill will, though I reacted unkindly, and I will change my ways and make things right.

1	2	3	4	5

Oblivious
I think others are hearing things; I don't hear unkindness in my voice at all.

Reflective
I strive to be a self-examining individual who is not only conscious of the impact of my unkind words on others but open to feedback on how I may not always hear what another is trying to say so I can improve my interactive communication.

RESPONSIBLE WITH YOUR WORDS

1	2	3	4	5

Blunt
I'm not harsh but brutally honest in telling others what they don't want to hear.

Thoughtful
Being brutally honest can come across harshly, so I responsibly think about the time, place, and way to kindly and tactfully share my opinions on an inconvenient but necessary truth.

1	2	3	4	5

Resentful

I have been dishonored and treated unfairly. I'm infuriated and gruff.

Gracious

I am composed when dishonored, responsibly controlling my anger, and then as best I can, I kindly assert that I have boundaries against such mistreatment as I seek a peaceful solution, going more than halfway in extending unmerited favor.

1	2	3	4	5

Conditional

People who don't earn my respect don't deserve it. Period.

Unconditional

I refuse to treat others with contempt because I feel they haven't earned my respect; instead, I am a kind and respectful person regardless of the conditions.

1	2	3	4	5

Trendy

People need to get over it and get with it. This is how we talk and text now.

Time-Tested

Not everything from the past merits continuation if it is outdated; even so, I am committed to conserving proven and universal virtues like kindness, responsibly accepting these as immutable truths.

1	2	3	4	5

Family-Bred

People need to chill out. This is how my family of origin reacts in conflict.

Accountable

My upbringing instilled in me unacceptable patterns of talking, such as yelling, pouting, and stonewalling, but I take responsibility for correcting these negative communication patterns and refuse to blame others for being thin-skinned when I am answerable to God for my unkind and ugly discourse.

RESILIENT WITH YOUR WORDS

1	2	3	4	5

Defeated

Showing kindness doesn't return kindness. It backfires. It must be me. I must be to blame.

Empowered

I will not let others' unkindness toward me define who I am, as though I have no worth; instead, I will be confident in God's love for me as His beloved child and act on this. I will be kindhearted even toward the unkind and will not change my course of action or belief that this best enables me to influence people.

1	2	3	4	5

Envious

Life is unfair to me. I don't have what others do.

Grateful

Even though I have less than others, I have more than most; therefore, I will not begrudge those better off but will give thanks from a heart filled with gratitude for all my gifts received and treat with kindness those who have more.

1	2	3	4	5

Rebellious

I can't stand rules like being told to be kind. I'll be any way I wish to be.

Cooperative

I affirm healthy autonomy and strongly resist blindly adhering to convention, but bemoaning and rebelling against social virtues like kindness just because others urge mutiny against it is not productive in achieving long-term cooperation, which requires a steadfast commitment to working with people, not against them.

1	2	3	4	5

Antisocial

I want to be left alone, so I push people away. I don't want to be bothered.

Friendly

Though people may fall short, I recognize the value of every person created in God's image and strive to be approachable and kind like Jesus, an enduring friend of sinners, while still maintaining healthy boundaries and alone time.

1	2	3	4	5

Self-Hating

Stressed out, underexercised, and overeating, I react. I don't like myself.

Self-Accepting

When overwhelmed with life's responsibilities, I do not let myself edge into self-loathing, since hatred of self makes me appear unkind and hateful of those around me. Therefore I call a time-out and revisit God's love for me and meet with someone for guidance and inspiration to be resilient spiritually, emotionally, and physically.

A WORD OF PRAISE!

If you selected 4 or 5 on any of the descriptors, then you need to be saluted. You communicate kindly to others. You have refused to be a cruel individual who is mean-spirited and uncharitable in your conversations. You feel what other people feel; you are not unaware or unfeeling when it comes to their concerns as you converse with them. When you do give into those rare moments of unkindness, you take ownership of your words and never blame others to justify your inconsiderate remark. And though life and circumstances mistreat you at various times, you do not bemoan your plight with "woe is me" in a juvenile way to solicit pity. Bottom line, people enjoy talking to you because you are truly kind toward them and focused on them.

I have to say, you are impressive.

However, none of us arrives at a place called "perfectly kind." This is a journey, not a destination. Give yourself some mercy and grace where you have come up short. Be patient with yourself. This exercise is for the purpose of self-improvement, and that entails time. Change does not happen overnight, just as Rome wasn't built in a day. But with God's help and encouragement from others, you can grow as a kind communicator as you do your part and put in the grind.

However, please recognize the proclivity to convince yourself on occasions that you are kinder than you are at those moments. Some of you block out those unloving and disrespectful reactions that appear hostile and contemptuous. Because you prefer to see yourself as kind, you conveniently forget the harsh and disdainful words. When you do see yourself reacting negatively, you claim, "This isn't me but my reaction to who they are. They caused me to react unkindly."

However, as I share in my marriage book *Love & Respect*, "You must get to the place where you can say, 'My response is my responsibility.' In my own marriage, Sarah doesn't cause me to be the way I am; she reveals the way I am. When my reactions to her are unloving, it reveals that I've still got issues."[1]

What if you are unkind only 10 percent of the time? Is that 10 percent undermining your effectiveness as a communicator? The goal here is to express your communication in ways that sound dignified and caring—all the time. For this reason, be as honest as you can in your self-evaluation.

If you answered 1 or 2 on any of the descriptors for this part, then it would also be right to applaud you for being honest with yourself about unkind communication! Honesty is the first step toward making a change in your communication patterns. I strongly recommend that you now tell a trusted person in your life what you are recognizing about yourself and see if they can help you get to the "why" behind your unkind remarks. Once you understand that, you will be much more equipped to choose a kinder and gentler form of communication.

You can turn a past misspeak into a pivot point to communicate more kindly. The best communicators were not born with exceptional skills but reflected on their less-than-best expressions and turned that reflection into a challenge to convey content more kindly by acquiring a bit of know-how. See yourself joining their ranks as they wave at you to come over to their side. Be uplifted as they tell you, "Hey, we once stood where you stand."

PART THREE: SPEAK YOUR MIND ONLY WHEN NECESSARY

Instructions: For each pair of adjectives, circle a number on the scale that best represents your communication style.

PRUDENT WHEN NECESSARY

1 2 3 4 5

Untimely
What I said was true; it doesn't matter that it was the wrong time and place.

Pertinent
I appropriately communicate thoughtful, applicable, and germane information and avoid unnecessary intrusions.

1 2 3 4 5

Nonlistening
My style is to listen until I know what I want to say and then say it.

Contemplative
I listen first to understand the need, then contribute to the conversation what is wise and edifying for the moment's need in the way Christ would.

1 2 3 4 5

Mothering
When others aren't listening to me, I say it anyway because I care.

Diplomatic
Though I care for others and would love to put in my two cents, I do not blurt out my opinion just because I care, since kindness without tactfully stating what is true is unnecessary and unhelpful.

1 2 3 4 5

Unprayerful
Maybe I should wait quietly in prayer, but I feel they need to hear it now.

Kneeling
I want to make sure the words from my mouth reflect the heart of God, so I go to Him first and ask for His wisdom, and sometimes He tells me, *Not now.*

COMPOSED WHEN NECESSARY

1 2 3 4 5

Volcanic
I have to vent my pent-up feelings; it isn't healthy to repress my negativity.

Processing
I can sort through my feelings inwardly before speaking so that I don't erupt but instead express accurate and necessary things that serve the other person.

1 2 3 4 5

Pity-Partying
I have sorrows, okay? I look for anyone who will listen to my burdens.

Discriminate
As I navigate the obstacles I am facing, I share my burdens only with those who contribute to my emotional or spiritual growth, and never to those who do not.

1 2 3 4 5

Exaggerating
Honestly, to ignite empathy and change, I jarringly overstate reality.

Matter-of-Fact
I refuse to exaggerate or jump to conclusions in an overly dramatic fashion to gain empathy but instead stick to the necessary facts in my speech, though not without feeling.

1	2	3	4	5

Grumbling
When I don't get what I want, I am unhappy and feel it's my right to gripe.

Accepting
When good things don't come my way, I do not give in to complaints that are unnecessary, despairing, and hysterical, but come to terms with difficulty—some of which is a normal part of life I must roll with—and give voice to constructive ways to move forward.

HONORABLE WHEN NECESSARY

1	2	3	4	5

Coarse
Admittedly, my words are off-color, but others shouldn't be such prudes.

Wholesome
I have committed and limited myself to speech that would not cause my grandmother to exclaim, "That wasn't necessary to say!"

1	2	3	4	5

Gossiping
I must be first to know and tell, though I suppose some of it isn't my business.

Good Neighborly
I believe it is not necessary to discuss problems that are none of my business, as that can be gossip among my network of relationships; however, if asked for help and input, I am willing to offer any necessary solutions to the issue.

1	2	3	4	5

Unfiltered
I unthinkingly speak unwarranted words, but there's no ill will.

Thoughtful
I value contemplative, cautious, and purposeful communication, since I do not like the damage my mindless, careless, and useless words cause to other people.

1	2	3	4	5

Spying
I don't see it as snooping but as monitoring their mistakes to help them improve.

Boundary-Respecting
I have resolved not to spy by secretly watching and listening, since that is a disrespectful invasion of privacy; instead, I operate within appropriate boundaries and I ask God to show me if there is anything I need to know.

RESTRAINED WHEN NECESSARY

1	2	3	4	5

Oversharing

I think I provide helpful information but some feel overwhelmed, so they say.

Judicious

I want to be sure not to share too much information that ends up being unnecessary and unhelpful, so I err on the side of caution and restraint as I use my best judgment in thoughtfully and purposefully communicating.

1	2	3	4	5

Rehashing

I've got to go over it again. I won't drop it and move on until I feel okay.

Succinct

I know when to state my exact concern once or twice and then stop the unnecessary repetition, since rehashing the issue wears out the listener and is unproductive.

1	2	3	4	5

Rambling

I dislike silence, so I fill it with whatever I am thinking at the time.

Reserved

I am comfortable in the silence and don't need to fill the air with chitchat to compensate for my nervousness and insecurities, since that has nothing to do with being friendly or setting others at ease.

1	2	3	4	5

Piling On

When upset, I think of additional stuff and say it; it's not off topic to me.

Focused

I no longer say, "And one more thing" when in conflict but state my single concern and let the truth about that one point carry its weight instead of piling on with other and unnecessary accusations, even though I have other unrelated burdens and the person is attentively listening.

OTHER-CENTERED WHEN NECESSARY

1	2	3	4	5

Prying

Not knowing the details, I have to meddle to enable me to advance my cause.

Considerate

Though curious and caring, I do not probe and meddle by asking intrusive questions to unearth confidential information that is unnecessary for me to know. Therefore I have committed to being a courteous person, honoring others' privacy and only acting in beneficial ways.

1	2	3	4	5

Interrupting
People tell me I interrupt them unnecessarily, but what I say is important for them to hear and understand.

Listening
Since I am other-focused, I first attentively listen to understand the concern.

1	2	3	4	5

Distracting
I refuse to be put on the hot seat, so I sidetrack others with unrelated stuff.

Transparent
I strive to be straightforward about myself and what is true, since this is necessary for the health of relationships, so I set aside the insecurities that tempt me to sidetrack the conversation with tangential and misleading information to keep me off the hot seat.

1	2	3	4	5

Limelight-Seeking
Other people are quiet or boring, so I take center stage with my interests.

Supportive
I have no desire to upstage anyone, especially when their needs are unheard. I ask questions and contentedly focus on their calling, interests, and burdens.

A WORD OF PRAISE!

If you answered 4 or 5 on any of the descriptors, then you need to be saluted. It can be said of you that you are very strong at communicating what is necessary. You refuse to be an annoying person who intrusively and insensitively interacts with others. You genuinely sense what is needful at the moment of writing or speaking. When flustered, you maintain self-control even when you are overwrought with emotion and feel tempted to say what you ought not to say. You are not improper, giving into words that are not becoming of you nor edifying to others. You are not verbose in the sense that you start talking for sake of talking and end up spouting things unthinkingly. And you are not egocentrically preoccupied with yourself; rather, you focus on the concerns and interests of others.

Again, congratulations! You have the wisdom to speak what is necessary. The ability to know when to say something and when not to say something is a marvelous trait you have gained. Although it's not always easy to know when something should or should not have been said, overall, you can have the confidence that you know what to say and when (or when not to) say it!

If you answered 1 or 2 on any of the descriptors, then it would also be right to stop and applaud you for being honest with yourself about communication that is unnecessary! I salute you! Honesty is the first step toward making a change in your communication patterns on this topic of necessary expressions. I strongly recommend that you now tell a trusted person in your life what you are recognizing about yourself and see if they can help you get to the "why" behind your unnecessary statements. Once you understand that, you will be much more equipped to halt unnecessary words.

PART FOUR: SPEAK YOUR MIND CLEARLY

Instructions: For each pair of adjectives, circle a number on the scale that best represents your communication style.

INTELLIGIBLE COMMUNICATION

(1 2 3 4 5)

Unaware
At times when communicating, I'm unaware that others don't know what I know.

Clarifying
I do not assume I am always clear or people are tracking with me, so I purposefully ask, "Does that make sense?"

(1 2 3 4 5)

Mystical
I know what I mean. I just don't know how to say it.

Articulate
Instead of saying, "I know what I mean, I just can't say it," I write or process my thoughts with someone until I have clarity about what I mean, and then I speak coherently.

(1 2 3 4 5)

Incomplete
Occasionally I leave out vital information, since I fail to answer who, what, when, where, why, and how.

Thorough
To be clear, I ask, "What needs to be said and why?" "Who needs to hear this, when, and where?" and "How do I best deliver the message?"

1	2	3	4	5

Indecisive
When undecided, my delay leaves others uncertain about my wishes.

Decisive
I provide clear and timely information about a required decision, since when I dawdle and stall, this leaves people uncertain and confused about my view and intent.

IMPROVED COMMUNICATION

1	2	3	4	5

Misconstrued
I didn't mean it as they interpreted it, but yeah, those were my words.

Revising
When people misinterpret me, though I think I have been clear, I take the initiative to improve communication by revisiting the matter and explaining myself better.

1	2	3	4	5

Snobbish
Others don't understand because they're stupid. It isn't me. I'm clear.

Simplifying
When misunderstood, I do not show condescension but improve my communication by making it simpler as I strive to reduce complexity, use basic words, give examples, create visuals, and stick to the main ideas.

1	2	3	4	5

Unfunny
I try to be funny, but others hear it as sarcasm and misunderstand.

Cultivating
While humor has its place, being sarcastic and abrasive at the listener's expense proves and improves nothing and fails to cultivate a better relationship or ensure greater open-mindedness so others will clearly listen.

AUTHENTIC COMMUNICATION

1	2	3	4	5

Fence-Sitting
I don't land on either side of an issue to avoid trouble with both sides.

Direct
Though life has moral ambiguities in the gray areas, I strive to be honest and straightforward about my preferences when a decision is required, since, as an authentic person, I need to be clear about my opinions without being demanding and unkind.

1	2	3	4	5

Relativistic
I'm unmoved by my contradictions. Truth is what I say it is at the moment.

Principled
I have moral convictions as an authentic person and will not compromise these to suit my selfish wants or appease those around me; otherwise, this inconsistency confuses people on what I say I believe at my core.

1	2	3	4	5

Intoning
The words I speak are sincere and clear, but my stern tone puzzles people.

Congruent
I ensure that my body language and tone coincide with my words when I talk, which is what an authentic person does, to prevent confusing my listeners with an apparent contradiction.

1	2	3	4	5

Hypocritical
My words ring hollow when my actions don't match my words.

Reliable
I do not overpromise and underdeliver, since that perplexes people, but do what I say I will do.

POISED COMMUNICATION

1	2	3	4	5

Unedited
When snubbed, I react instead of calmly editing myself to be clear.

Self-Editing
I take the time to consider things carefully and share thoughtfully; otherwise, I may speak in an unedited fashion, which only confuses others.

1	2	3	4	5

Provoked
When upset, I react in ways that appear unreasonable and confusing.

Temperate
When provoked, I remain emotionally self-controlled to avoid brash and unreasonable communication that only confuses and aggravates others and exacerbates the conflict.

1	2	3	4	5

Weary
I don't think or communicate well when I'm too tired, especially at night.

Rejuvenated
When worn out, I know my limits on trying to communicate, since I am physically and mentally fatigued, so I recharge my batteries with nourishment and rest in order to communicate clearly and kindly.

ORGANIZED COMMUNICATION

1	2	3	4	5

Spiderwebbing
I start out on one topic, but this can trigger a web of unrelated points.

On Point
I don't sidetrack others with confusing tangents and side notes but stick to the topic.

1	2	3	4	5

Disorganized
My communication is not always well-thought-out and well-organized.

Prepared
Before communicating, I thoroughly plan and organize my thoughts on the topic to guarantee a clear and coherent presentation that my audience can easily understand and follow.

1	2	3	4	5

Hasty
Yes, I'm hard to follow. I talk too fast and make impulsive remarks.

Well-Paced
I don't speak too quickly but use measured words so people can process and understand the information, because though the material is clear to me, too much information too fast gets lost for the listener.

OPEN COMMUNICATION

1	2	3	4	5

Willfully Ignorant
I sometimes talk while knowing I'm uninformed or misinformed.

Scrupulous
When talking, I don't fake it until I make it, but I take great care to verify information so I can be accurate, which enables me to speak with confidence, truthfulness, and clarity.

1	2	3	4	5

Falsely Humble
I don't wish to appear self-promoting, so I veil my competencies.

Learned
I have no interest in self-promoting to soothe my ego, but there are moments when I know what I know about what can be done, so I communicate with clarity and goodwill what I can competently do.

1	2	3	4	5

Overly Sensitive
Not wanting to hurt people, I hold back on what is clearly true.

Authentically Friendly
I am loyal and trustworthy but also honest and candid—a true friend—so while I seek to be sensitive, I won't give in to fearful silence that would deprive others of hearing about what best serves them.

A WORD OF PRAISE!

If you answered 4 or 5 on any of the descriptors, then you need to be saluted. You communicate clearly. You have taken steps in your life to be clear, not fuzzy. You are requiring yourself to be clear instead of finding fault with others for not listening or understanding. You have remained true to your convictions instead of being two-sided on issues and confusing those around you. Though you get emotional, you control your emotions so that you do not say things you should not say or leave people confused about what you mean. You do not like being disjointed in your thoughts, so you work hard at being logical, well-thought-out, and organized. And you do not suppress information so that people are left in the dark about what they need to know.

If you answered 1 or 2 on any of the descriptors for this part, then it would also be right to applaud you for being honest with yourself about the lack of clearness in what you communicate. Super! Honesty is the first step toward making a change in this communication pattern that contributes to confusion. I strongly recommend that you now tell a trusted person in your life what you are recognizing about yourself and see if they can help you get to the "why" behind your unclear comments. Once you understand that, you will be in a better position to talk so as to be clearly understood.

May I express my admiration for your clarity as a communicator? Your intentionality to be intelligible and precise sets you apart from many. You have the desire and commitment to make sense! You work hard to remove ambiguity and incoherence, a characteristic of a mature communicator. You serve others well by communicating clearly, which is not always an easy task.

You did it! Whew! All four dimensions!

You took the first step in assessing your application of true, kind, necessary, and clear communication. Thank you for willingly engaging these descriptors.

Recognizing your strengths as a communicator brings deep satisfaction, and I hope you let yourself enjoy those moments of self-discovery. At the same time, you had moments where you may have exclaimed, "Ouch!" However, this assessment arms you with a comprehensive overview of your communication style—the good and the not so good. The challenge is to maintain those successful traits as a communicator while tackling the topics triggering "Yikes!"

Because you completed the toughest assignment in the book, you have the willingness to diligently enhance your strengths, since we can all improve what we do well. But you are also ready to dive in on those areas that have revealed weaknesses that may be robbing you of effective ways to win friends and influence people.

Let's begin that now!

PART 1

SPEAK YOUR MIND TRUTHFULLY

Not long ago, my daughter Joy served on a grand jury. Their job was to interview people involved in the crime and take copious notes. Since it can be years before a case goes to trial, a grand jury's notes are vital during the trial. If what a witness says while on the stand during the trial doesn't match the testimony the grand jury recorded, then that witness is caught in a lie, and the court throws out that testimony. Who can believe a person who has been caught in a lie?

Sadly, unless sworn by oath under the penalty of perjury, many people are prone to lie. One person e-mailed me: "Seems everyone is lying these days. It's just easier not to tell the truth."

Some contend that it's okay to say something untrue as long as it's necessary and kind. However, a lie is a lie by any other name. No matter how compassionate you may feel in telling an untruth, eventually the lie will be exposed. It makes no difference whether your spin was compelled by compassion, hope for career advancement, or desire to suppress opposite positions; little good comes to you in the long run when you choose not to tell the truth, the whole truth, and nothing but the truth.

You may be thinking, *But telling the truth isn't always easy.* Yes, the temptation to mislead others can be enticing. But by reading this material and thinking about it, you are nobly announcing your intention to be truthful, transparent, and trustworthy. Your integrity as a person is admirable. Stay the course!

THE HEART OF COMMUNICATING WHAT IS TRUE

Jesus said, "The mouth speaks out of that which fills the heart. The good man brings out of his good treasure what is good" (Matt. 12:34–35). In other words, the mouth speaks what is good and honest because of a good heart. Though Jesus recognized every person's sinful condition and need to trust Him as Savior, He described some people as having a "good heart" (Luke 8:15).

On the other hand, lying points to a bad heart—our darker nature. In John 8:44, Jesus said to the Pharisees, "You are of your father the devil, and you want to do the desires of your father. . . . There is no truth in him. Whenever he speaks a lie, he speaks from his own nature, for he is a liar and the father of lies." According to Jesus, lying arises out of our sinful nature.

How do you know if lying is in your nature? Acts 5 tells the story of a man named Ananias and his wife, Sapphira, who lied about the size of their donation to the church to make a good impression on church leaders. Like Ananias and Sapphira, do you have a price? At what price would you compromise your integrity?

What if you did cross a line in the past? The past need not define you. How you rebound from the past newly defines you.

THE GOLDEN RULE OF TRUE COMMUNICATION

I recently spoke with a friend who learned from a mechanic that his vehicle had a major problem. The mechanic said, "If we do these repairs, people won't buy this car once it goes on Carfax. On the other hand, if we don't do the work, you can sell it without the buyer knowing the serious problem since there will be no public record of it." My friend asked me what he should do. I replied, "Well, the answer is easy enough.

If you were the consumer and someone withheld the truth about this car from you, you'd be up in arms when the car died on the highway during rush hour. I've found honesty is the best policy even if in the short haul it proves more costly."

The Golden Rule says, "Treat others the same way you want them to treat you" (Luke 6:31). Do you want to know how to communicate truthfully? Ask yourself, *Am I about to communicate unto others in the way that I would want others to communicate unto me?*

I find it fascinating that some people want to be treated with the Golden Rule of true communication but don't want to be bound by it themselves. These people are saying, "I have a right to lie to you, but you have no right to lie to me." Such a position is not only hypocritical but also lacks compassion toward another's rights. We damage trust when people cannot rely on us.

When telling the truth will cause you to lose something or not gain something, do you give wrong information to protect your interests? Do you hedge on the truth and mislead people? Do you buckle and compromise the truth? Do you fail to say what you know is the right thing to say? Or are you committed to telling the truth, the whole truth, and nothing but the truth, so help you God?

The difficulty is that many times we don't think before we speak. We want to communicate the truth, but we let other factors change our minds.

BACK TO THE ASSESSMENT

In this first part of the book, I invite you to consider more fully the twenty reasons people lie that were described in the *Speak Your Mind* communication self-assessment. Did any of those negative descriptions ring true to you?

As I studied more closely the twenty descriptors for those who are truthful, I noticed connections between many, or what I call *clusters*. In the following chapters, we will examine these twenty descriptors by looking at their clusters. To learn how to speak our minds truthfully . . .

- We must move from feeling threatened by the truth to being *secure in the truth* (chapter 1).
- We must no longer allow unresolved personal issues to leave us feeling troubled, but instead we should remove the unhealthy obstacles that block our truthfulness and seek to live a life *transformed by the truth* (chapter 2).
- Instead of being crafty with the truth, we must learn to be *forthright with the truth* (chapter 3).
- Instead of feeling obligated to repeat others' lies, we need to become people of integrity who are *moral with the truth* (chapter 4).
- If we've often been caught in lies as a result of being presumptuous, we need to take intentional, appropriate action to ensure we are *informed of the truth* (chapter 5).
- We must move from being self-serving to thinking of others above ourselves by being *altruistic about the truth* (chapter 6).

As you reflect on true communication, be encouraged by how simple this is. You need only ask, "If the roles were reversed, would I want that person to tell me the truth, the whole truth, and nothing but the truth?"

CHAPTER 1

SECURE IN THE TRUTH

It is only natural to fear the unpleasant outcomes that may result when telling the truth, the whole truth, and nothing but the truth. We feel threatened by what may happen if the truth is discovered, and as a result, we find ways to tweak the truth to avoid negative reactions or consequences.

Our goal is to avoid feeling threatened by the truth and instead focus on making our communication *secure in the truth*. That means in our communication we are brave, straightforward, unwavering, and morally grounded. We are courageously truthful, are open and direct, resist compromising the truth to fit in, and hold to a moral code despite the pressure to help another by lying for them.

Learning to become secure in the truth begins with simply believing that telling the truth produces the best positive outcomes in the end. With this as our foundation, we can bravely move forward in honesty, even when others encourage us to hedge on the truth to save face or spare hurt feelings. "A little white lie never hurt anyone," some would say. However, that still, small voice inside us does not agree. Of course, we are not talking about keeping secret a surprise birthday party. I believe most people recognize the difference between withholding knowledge temporarily so as to keep a fun surprise and speaking an untruth so as to protect one's selfish interests. As tough as it can be in these times, you need to speak what is true and necessary in a kind and clear way because you're confident that honesty is always the best path forward.

To begin your journey in learning to speak your mind truthfully, consider the following struggles we have when we're apprehensive about what may result if we tell the whole truth, as well as how we can discover both the freedom and security of telling the kind, necessary, and clear truth.

FEARFUL VERSUS BRAVE

Fearful: Because of fear, I hide my missteps to avoid the consequences of past mistakes.

Brave: Despite my anxiety over the consequences, I choose courage by confessing my misleading comments and committing to honor the truth confidently.

Oftentimes we fear that disfavor will come on us if we speak a truth that is negative, either about ourselves or someone else. As a result, we can remain silent about the truth or say something that is at odds with the truth to prevent our fears from being realized.

Let's consider how fear drives the following reasons for telling a lie:

- "I lied about the affair because I was afraid my spouse would divorce me."
- "I lied to my roommate about where I was last night because I knew she would disapprove, and I want her to like me."
- "I lied to my professor about why I skipped class because I was afraid I would fail if he didn't let me make up the pop quiz I missed."
- "I lied about my credentials on my résumé for fear they wouldn't give me an interview."
- "I lied to my boss on the report because I feared conflict with her."
- "I lied on social media about going on an exotic trip for fear that people would not find me important and happy if they knew only of my normal daily life."

There may be some good intentions at the root of these lies. Avoiding divorce, staying in good graces with the boss, and gaining new clients are all worthy goals. However, a lie is a lie, no matter who knows or what results from it, and lying is not the wiser choice even when it gains you a competitive edge at work or helps you get a job and salary your family desperately needs. In the end, the question is not whether you believe that to be the case, because most goodwilled people do. Instead, the question is, will you be brave enough to present the truth, no matter what it may be, even if you have good reason to fear the outcomes of doing so?

SPEAK YOUR MIND TRUTHFULLY:

Emerson's Checklist for Brave Communication

- ☐ Do I embrace the value of communicating the truth, since honoring the truth is the better and good choice?
- ☐ Do I communicate honestly, since others deserve the whole story and it is also in my best interest in the long-term?
- ☐ Do I recognize the negative consequences of past missteps and untruths?
- ☐ With courage (a virtue I intend to have in my life), do I overcome my fear of disclosing the truth about my past misleading statements?
- ☐ Do I understand the consequences of revealing my mistakes but am hopeful this leads to healing and reconciliation?
- ☐ Do I prize how my courageous truthfulness creates and maintains trusting and genuine relationships?
- ☐ Do I find new energy in being honest from the beginning, in every scenario?

EVASIVE VERSUS STRAIGHTFORWARD

Evasive: If others don't know what I did wrong, there will be fewer problems all around.

> **Straightforward:** I am assured that being open, direct, and truthful builds trust and meaningful relationships, since honesty is the best policy and prevents the heartaches that can result from being evasive and misleading.

Consider the following scenario: You did something that was neither good nor acceptable, such as using discretionary funds from the company to buy an expensive golf club driver. You conclude that if no one knows what you did, then it will be better for all involved. *What they don't know won't hurt them,* you convince yourself.

When someone asks you about the expenditures, you are vague and evasive. You perhaps even plead ignorance. Yet when a coworker comes into your office and says, "The CEO wants to see you," you break out in a nervous sweat. Because you didn't come clean on your misuse of those discretionary funds, you have an anxiety attack. You feel the evasion is over. You feel caught. Your mouth dries up. You conclude the CEO intends to fire you. But wait, maybe you can come up with an excuse. Maybe you can evade the truth again. You quickly formulate a lie that you intended to pay back the company for the money you used to buy the golf club but honestly forgot.

When you enter the CEO's office, he says, "Hey, thanks. I have a quick comment and request. Excellent job on the Macintosh account. Because of that, I want you to give a report on the account to the management team next Tuesday at 10 a.m. here in my office."

As you return to your office, your sense of relief cannot be measured. You got away with your evasive lying. But your conscience speaks loud and clear: *People who walk in truth don't experience heart palpitations like this.*

God provides your conscience, which whispers, *Change course. Be honest. Make things right.* The person who comes clean realizes it isn't just about them. As Khaled Hosseini wrote in *The Kite Runner*, "When you tell a lie, you steal someone's right to the truth."[1] The company has a right to know about the misallocation of funds.

"But, Emerson, when others aren't hurt by what they don't know, isn't it best to be evasive? Why risk upsetting them and harming my reputation?" Being evasive with the truth to save face or avoid trouble is not noble but an act of deceit, for we are told in Proverbs 12:17, "One who declares truth tells what is right, but a false witness, deceit." A difficult truth shared, even when uncomfortable, will always be better in the end than an evasive lie that deceives others and damages relationships.

SPEAK YOUR MIND TRUTHFULLY:

Emerson's Checklist for Straightforward Communication

- ☐ Do I buy in to the axiom "Honesty is the best policy"?
- ☐ Do I wish to be viewed by others as trustworthy and reliable because I remain truthful in all I do and say?
- ☐ Do I prioritize truth and genuine relationships over untruths and superficial relationships?
- ☐ Do I see the long-term headaches and regrets from my persistent mistreatment of others when I withhold the truth or state misinformation?
- ☐ Do I choose directness by being candid about what I did wrong, since my evasive tricks only temporarily keep lies in the dark?
- ☐ Do I accept the consequences of being honest about the past as a way of enabling me to begin anew, even if it means facing criticism or conflict?
- ☐ Do I detect the tendency to be evasive when feeling the embarrassing truth will be detrimental and remain committed to overcoming this propensity?
- ☐ Do I speak the truth when questioned and refuse to hide behind the false claim "I have no idea what the answer is to your question, since I am ignorant of the facts"?

CHAMELEONLIKE VERSUS UNWAVERING

Chameleonlike: To avoid conflict, I blend my beliefs to fit my audience, which pleases them.

Unwavering: In social settings, I am comfortable in my skin in resisting the pull I feel to blend in as a compromising and conforming people-pleaser by expressing my values honestly and wisely when necessary.

In order to make others happy, chameleonlike communication appears sincere by telling people what they want to hear. But the motive is to fit in at the expense of truth. This is not an accommodation in the gray areas but a compromise on black-and-white matters. For example, you are conservative with conservatives on Monday night (e.g., pro-life) and liberal with liberals on Tuesday night (e.g., pro-choice). Though you're trying to make everyone like you, everyone eventually sees you as lacking core convictions and integrity. Chameleonlike communication is a double standard, and the fallout undermines your credibility and good reputation.

A person who uses chameleonlike communication may rationalize, "I don't like tension and conflict." But this approach involves deception. A young man explained, "I don't support the political candidate my girlfriend expects us to vote for, but if I reveal my true voting preference, there will be a heated argument. It's easier to deceive for the sake of peace." A chameleonlike communicator changes colors—or adapts their stance—to align with the desires of another person or group, even though it contradicts their convictions or preferences.

SPEAK YOUR MIND TRUTHFULLY:

Emerson's Checklist for Unwavering Communication

- ☐ Do I approach social settings with a desire to engage others, know what they believe, and learn from them?
- ☐ Do I seek to understand where another is coming from in what they espouse?
- ☐ Do I acknowledge the concerns and convictions of others who differ from me without changing what I believe so they will accept and like me?
- ☐ Do I adapt in appropriate ways to the needs and concerns of people without compromising my values by conforming to what others expect at the expense of my convictions?
- ☐ Do I resist the compulsion to be liked as someone I am not?
- ☐ Do I stand firm on my convictions, since I will be true to myself even if rejected, though this rarely happens because people enjoy being around humble and honest folks?

☐ Do I have the confidence that when I am genuine and humble as I kindly communicate what is true to my values and convictions, most people are attracted to me as a person even when disagreeing with me?

PROTECTING VERSUS MORALLY GROUNDED

Protecting: I feel responsible to protect another's interests even if I have to lie to do so.

Morally Grounded: Though I feel genuinely responsible for protecting those I care about, I will not advance their interests by lying, since I am centered on and bound by a moral code that grounds and guides me in my service to others.

In the Bible, a woman named Rahab hid Israelite spies from the king of Jericho and received honor and praise from God for her bravery (Josh. 2; Heb. 11:31). Most of us would agree that there is some virtue in protecting others from those who intend to harm them. In times of war, when evil rulers intend unjustified violence against the innocent, a protective lie can be a noble thing. But apart from the evils of war or other such rare examples, can we justify a protective lie as noble?

For example, Lisa lies to protect a work associate. "Kelli is out sick today," she tells their supervisor. "I talked to her. She may have to see the doctor." But Kelli is with her boyfriend to resolve a big fight they had the night before, so she asked Lisa to cover for her. Lisa goes along with the cover-up, since it helps Kelli with her relationship and protects her job. In some odd way, Lisa feels responsible to cover for her friend instead of coming up with a plan to enable Kelli to take a vacation day or resolve the conflict after work.

"What's the big deal?" many ask. "It's just a white lie to help a friend with a personal problem." But when Kelli and Lisa lie to management, they are lying to other human beings. Furthermore, if Lisa became the manager and Kelli lied to her about Barbara being sick, Lisa would not see Kelli as acting responsibly to protect Barbara.

She'd say, "Look, get someone to cover for Barbara, but don't cover up for Barbara." We are back to the Golden Rule of true communication.

There is a slight shift from "I have you covered as my friend" to "I will cover up for you as my friend." There is a difference! Then it becomes a quid pro quo situation: "You owe me." Eventually, the other covers up, and now they've formed an alliance. Both feel duty bound to lie for each other.

Have you ever found yourself advancing a false narrative so another person doesn't get in trouble? Have they returned the favor? Rarely does this work out. In our example above, when layoffs came, who do you think were the first employees to be let go? Kelli and Lisa, of course. Word got out that they were not trustworthy.

Before moving on from the idea that "a little white lie won't hurt anyone," we would be wise to take notice of how quickly a small lie can snowball all the way to perjury, as we find a way to justify each next step of deception. Consider the following sequence of events:

- We begin with an innocent white lie—a minor untruth so as not to hurt another's feelings.
- This can lead to a fib—a small lie to avoid trouble or take advantage.
- Before long, we justify an exaggeration—stretching the truth about what happened.
- If stretching the truth is okay, then why not omission—withholding important information?
- This naturally leads to telling half-truths—or partial truths.
- If we're okay with telling partial truths, then why not state only those half-truths that help us mislead and discredit—or what we call *misrepresentation*?
- From here, it is an easy next step to falsification—distorting or inventing information.
- This leads us to discover how easy it is to step into the world of deceit—intentionally lying so as to trick others into thinking what is not true.
- And if we're okay with deception, what then will keep us from committing perjury—lying under oath in a court of law?

Do you see why Ephesians 4:27 warns, "Do not give the devil a foothold" (NIV)? There is no such thing as a "little white lie." This supposed tiny lie—even for a so-called noble reason like helping a coworker with her relationship problems so she doesn't get in trouble for missing work—is just the kind of "foothold" the devil is looking for.

Bottom line, the best friendships and alliances are built on truthfulness. People who commit to telling the truth can almost always find a legal and moral way to protect the interests of another. For example, Lisa could say to Kelli, "Why don't you take a vacation day, and I'll cover for you by working late for you tonight at work. The boss has signed off on this." It may be inconvenient and costly, but it is an honest plan of action. Cover-ups may feel noble as a way of protecting another, but at the end of the day, they are just lying, and lying is not the best policy.

SPEAK YOUR MIND TRUTHFULLY:

Emerson's Checklist for Morally Grounded Communication

- ☐ Do I live by a moral code like the expression "I will not lie, cheat, or steal"?
- ☐ Do I have a line morally and legally that I will not cross when caring for another, such as not providing false information to help this person?
- ☐ Do I recognize the pressure one can feel to provide misleading information to advance worthy interests, such as lying about someone's past failed relationship to their new boyfriend or girlfriend so as to not scare them off?
- ☐ Do I discern the negative consequences of deceitful protection when I lie to help someone's well-being in the short haul, since it doesn't help their well-being, or mine, in the long haul?
- ☐ Do I have the resolve to remain bound to my moral code even if someone begs me ("If you cared, you'd help me") or bullies me ("If you don't help me, you will suffer!") to deceive on their behalf?
- ☐ Do I humbly say no to someone who asks me to go along with their lie to keep what they took or to take what they want?
- ☐ Given my limited resources, do I hear God's call for me to entrust this person to His care and protection?

CHAPTER 2

TRANSFORMED BY THE TRUTH

At times we might be less than truthful because of our unresolved emotional or psychological issues. We may be aware of some of these issues but don't see them as a problem. Maybe other issues have not been dealt with because we never noticed them about ourselves. A godly, wise counselor may be necessary to help us realize and overcome these deep, unresolved issues.

Is it time to turn the corner on emotional or psychological issues that may have led to dishonesty in the past? Are you ready to commit to prioritizing honesty to improve your well-being and relationships?

In this chapter, we'll consider the struggle you can have with the truth because of deeper issues that have largely been left unaddressed. If you desire to speak your mind truthfully, you need not only to be aware of these weaknesses and temptations but be committed to living a transformed life as a person of integrity.

SELF-DELUDING VERSUS SELF-AWARE

Self-Deluding: Some claim I lie to myself. But that's a lie. I'm 100 percent honest with myself.

Self-Aware: I wish to be more cognizant of my shortcomings that hinder the best version of me as a truthful communicator, so I examine myself to reduce my bias and blind spots that work against my good reputation and healthy relationships.

It's not uncommon to hear about an alcoholic who runs afoul of the law with DUIs and has lost several jobs because of his drinking binges. But when he is asked, "Are you an alcoholic?" he'll sincerely deny it. He has suppressed the truth about the amount of liquor he consumes week after week (Rom. 1:18). He has convinced himself he has no problem. He can quit anytime, he tells himself.

In *The Brothers Karamazov*, Fyodor Dostoevsky wrote, "Above all, don't lie to yourself. The man who lies to himself and listens to his own lie comes to a point that he cannot distinguish the truth within him, or around him, and so loses all respect for himself and for others. And having no respect he ceases to love."[1]

How many of us lie to ourselves? Recently, I talked with a man who finally recognized two major character flaws in himself. In discussing why it took him twenty years to see these, he said, "I didn't see them as wrong because I convinced myself they were okay. I lied to myself." Of course, these two lies nearly destroyed his family. We can lull ourselves into thinking we have done no wrong. We are like the adulterer who insists, "I have done no wrong" (Prov. 30:20). Or like the son who declares, "It is not a transgression" (Prov. 28:24). Self-delusion is real.

How does this relate to speaking our minds truthfully? Maybe the deepest clue into why we lie to others in our communication is that we first lie to ourselves. We create *rational lies*, and from these we *rationalize* that what we communicate to others is justified. This is why William Shakespeare penned, "This above all: to thine own self be true / And it must follow, as the night the day / Thou canst not then be false to any man."[2]

SPEAK YOUR MIND TRUTHFULLY:

Emerson's Checklist for Self-Aware Communication

- ☐ Do I recognize that my default tendency is to deny my shortcomings and defend myself when my shortcomings are highlighted?

- ☐ Do I discern that others probably figure if I lie to myself as a self-deluded person, I will lie to them, so they back away?
- ☐ Do I try to be self-aware of my biases and blind spots that work against the best version of me, knowing these do me no favors when wishing to be an effective communicator?
- ☐ Do I realize the greatest of professionals undergo self-evaluation to improve themselves to become the best version of themselves?
- ☐ Do I overcome my fear of self-examination in order to be the best version of myself as a truthful communicator?
- ☐ Do I have a wise person in my life to talk through ways of being the best version of myself?
- ☐ Do I share with others both my strengths and weaknesses, rather than hiding or denying my flaws and pretending to have abilities I don't possess?
- ☐ Do I display an openness in receiving input from others to increase my self-awareness and be truthful in communication?
- ☐ Do I give myself grace after seeing things in myself I don't like, or do I turn inward with self-loathing and want to give up?

CHRONIC VERSUS RESISTANT

Chronic: I've always lied even when the truth was better. Something comes over me.

Resistant: While I used to battle chronic lying and the allure to deceive to gain something or get away with something, now I resist these tendencies and choose honesty, recognizing that it is the best and most empowering policy.

Most of us can recall an early point in our lives when we made a decision to lie or not lie as a way of dealing with problems. My observation is that chronic lying begins in preschool.

Unfortunately, that's the decision Joe made when he was young.

Today, Joe lies all the time. He texts a family member to say he's running late due to traffic and because his neighbor dropped in to ask his opinion on an electrical problem, which also put him behind. Neither of these is true, but lies fuel Joe's lifestyle. At work, when writing an e-mail about some issue, he tells another lie: "Hey, I didn't see that e-mail about the Clifford account. Sorry, I will need another day on this." Of course, that's a lie. He saw the e-mail. When receiving a voice message at home from his boss about showing up for work on Saturday morning, he later tells the boss he never received that call. He thinks one of his kids hit "delete all" on his phone's voicemails. Joe always thinks about how to lie since, to Joe, other things he is doing are more important. This is ingrained from childhood as a default reaction. It seems second nature.

Some argue that a chronic liar like Joe will never change. However, I am more hopeful for such a person. As is the case with any addictive behavior, a person can bring it under control. Certainly the Bible gives us that hope. Peter wrote, "Therefore, putting aside . . . all deceit . . ." (1 Peter 2:1). Making the decision to resist lying, even when doing so has been par for the course for most of your life, is both possible and expected. The incentive for Joe to change his chronic lying is that it is unlikely he will succeed in life when those who promote and reward say, "Joe isn't truthful or trustworthy." The following questions address chronic lying. While this might not have been an area of struggle for you, it's wise to take inventory to the degree that you have ever been prone to stretch the truth.

SPEAK YOUR MIND TRUTHFULLY:

Emerson's Checklist for Resistant Communication

- ☐ Do I confess that my chronic lying has been a serious issue for me and has not benefited me?
- ☐ Do I confess that chronic lying has hindered my developing and deepening relationships with people?
- ☐ Do I detect that much of my chronic lying stemmed from insecurities as a person who foolishly thought I could advance my self-interests with untruths?
- ☐ Do I see now that my lying surfaced from a strategy to prevent punishment or rejection but only compounded these?

- ☐ Do I now subscribe to the wisdom of this statement: Honesty is the best policy?
- ☐ Do I find satisfaction when I resist the impulse to lie and instead walk the path of honesty?
- ☐ Do I feel good about my commitment to be a truth-teller because of my clear conscience, positive reputation, and influence?
- ☐ Do I commit to making amends to those I lied to?
- ☐ Do I feel uncomfortable coming clean about the truth, but that discomfort pales compared to always looking over my back?
- ☐ Do I forgive myself and seek another's forgiveness when I slip back into a lie and then start again with honesty as the best policy?
- ☐ Do I have accountability with a trusted friend or counselor who keeps me on the straight and narrow path of truthfulness?

ASHAMED VERSUS CONFESSING

Ashamed: Out of embarrassment for the bad stuff I have done, I lie to appear good.

Confessing: I value the renewal I feel when being truthful and transparent, since this is the right thing to do. Nothing compares with a clear conscience and the inner peace that results from choosing confession over shame.

Lies about ourselves are usually related to something we have done wrong ethically, legally, or morally. We lie to hide wrongdoings from our past. We lie to cover up something immoral we plan to do in the future. We lie about unethical decisions we are currently caught up in.

For most of us, when we violate what is legal or moral, we feel shame. At that point we are at a crossroads. Will we confess, or will we conceal?

Several years ago my wife, Sarah, was caught speeding. As the officer approached the car, Sarah exclaimed, "I am guilty. Please give me a ticket. I was going like thirty miles over." Stunned, the officer said, "In all my years as a policeman, no one has ever said, 'Give me a ticket.' Ma'am, go on your way. Have a good day." Sarah then argued with him because she deserved a ticket and wasn't afraid of the truth or the cost. Why did Sarah respond this way? She doesn't lie when she has done something wrong. In the face of shame, she tells the truth to come clean.

"But, Emerson, what if telling the truth is costly, far more than a speeding ticket?" Telling the truth may cost us everything, as it does with an embezzler confessing his crime and going to prison. Or a husband confessing his adultery and his wife divorcing him and taking the kids to another state. However, it isn't the truth that is costing us everything; it is our wrongdoing. Truth is not the enemy.

I wish I could say something softer to those who have committed serious crimes, but I cannot. I can say that believers in Christ who come clean experience a supernatural peace, a clear conscience, meaningful meditations in Scripture, renewed power in prayer, joy in worship at church, and a fruitful ministry. None of these things was happening earlier due to the hidden sin and shame. Many have told me, "It is a trade-off but well worth it." I have observed husbands confess their adultery and be happier at that moment than they have been for months, even though their world is falling apart. Coming out from under shame is a very good thing.

Have you lied to your boss, coworkers, or clients about a product or service? Have you lied to your friends, school administrator, roommate, or even your spouse about something you are ashamed of in your past? Wherever you have lied, you cannot remove shame by lying about the lie. Only the truth removes the shame. Yes, the truth reveals the guilt, but the honest confession removes the shame.

When you choose to be honest about your dishonesty, the shame lifts. You are now doing what is right and good.

SPEAK YOUR MIND TRUTHFULLY:

Emerson's Checklist for Confessing Communication

- ☐ Do I walk and talk with integrity because of the satisfaction I derive from a clear and clean conscience?

- ☐ Do I prize honesty and transparency because of the personal freedom I feel from communicating truthfully?
- ☐ Do I own up to my past errors and no longer cover these up with half-truths, misrepresentations, falsifications, or deceit?
- ☐ Do I apologize for my transgressions and seek forgiveness from those I wronged to repair relationships and keep my life up-to-date before God?
- ☐ Do I take the time and make an effort to humbly resolve conflicts by having hard but honest conversations instead of lying and moving on quickly?
- ☐ Do I accept that I will never be perfect in what I say, but when I misspeak, I quickly confess and correct the mistake because of the peace I enjoy from such rectitude?
- ☐ Do I renounce returning to the days of feeling guilt and shame even when I can get away with a lie?

CHAPTER 3

FORTHRIGHT WITH THE TRUTH

For some people, the ability to deceive and manipulate others comes easily and naturally. Their lies are not due to ignorance, fear, or a desire to impress others. Instead, they lie simply because they're good at it, and more specifically, they're good at getting away with it. These are the crafty communicators.

Crafty communicators are expedient, brainy, and wordsmithing. They lie because it is quick and easy; they're smart enough to remember the lies and stay out in front of them; and they can twist the truth and meaning of words cunningly.

In contrast, forthright communicators are up-front, wise, and well-spoken. Though truth telling may be inconvenient, they address problems without hiding things; they use their intelligence to say only what is wise and true; and they use their God-given ability to craft words without being crafty.

I am certain that those reading this book, even those who admit they can lie to others fairly easily, do not defend this as an acceptable way to live. We are called to a higher level of integrity than this, of which I know you believe as well. But it requires a daily intentionality to keep us from falling into this trap our Enemy has set for us. We must choose to be candid about potential problems that others may try to cover up with lies. We must refuse to manipulate the facts with our shrewd abilities because we know that long-term truthfulness is always in our best interest, as well as the interests of others. We must decide—every day—to be honest, genuine, and forthright with everyone, even when the truth may not be pleasant to hear.

The challenge is to turn away from being crafty and turn to being forthright.

In this chapter, let's address those whose struggle is due to how simple and convenient it is to get away with lying. Because even if our lies go unnoticed by others, God sees all, and He holds us to a higher, holier standard than the world does.

EXPEDIENT VERSUS UP-FRONT

Expedient: I lie, since it is quicker and easier for me at the moment.

Up-Front: Though lying about something that might go wrong can be practical, I now sincerely reveal a potential problem ahead of time; speaking half-truths and falsehoods about a possible inconvenient truth is no longer an enticement—especially since most people want to hear the truth, no matter how difficult it may be.

The truth can be time-consuming and tough. The truth is a hassle, but a lie gets us out of the jam. The truth slows things down, but lying is expedient. Why not twist the truth when we have a demanding timeline?

If I lied on FundMe.com about a business start-up to build water wells in Africa, knowing that most of the money would go in my pocket, why come clean on this later when doing so would cause me nothing but time and trouble? It is easier to stay silent and get on with life. But what seems to be the expedient thing to do up front—to lie—usually proves to be the costliest later in life.

Ask seven-time Tour de France winner Lance Armstrong about the heavy costs later in his life after it was revealed that he had taken illegal performance-enhancing drugs. He could not undo what he had done. Early on, his lying to the press seemed so easy and natural. I wonder if he ever thought, *It is so easy to make people believe a lie.*

By the way, why is it often easier and quicker to lie to people? The listener tends to trust the speaker and doesn't detect the lie. The liar takes advantage of the other's trust. The liar says to himself, *They are bound by their moral code of being a trusting person, but I have no moral code about being trustworthy and truthful. They must give me the benefit of the doubt, since I am deemed innocent until proven guilty.*

But do you really want to live a lie even when lying is so expedient? Do you want to manipulate people's trust?

SPEAK YOUR MIND TRUTHFULLY:

Emerson's Checklist for Up-Front Communication

- ☐ Do I recognize that most people prefer hearing an inconvenient truth about a potential problem?
- ☐ Do I believe withholding information about a potential problem is unjustified even if the problem does not occur and giving the report proves to be a false alarm?
- ☐ Do I step back and take the time to communicate what I know about the facts of a potential problem?
- ☐ Do I communicate the whole truth, not half-truths, about an inconvenient truth that may or may not happen?
- ☐ Do I provide as precise, accurate, and complete a report as possible even though the information causes others to feel uncomfortable?
- ☐ Do I convey a complete picture, since withholding information will undermine my reputation and upset people, given the worst happens and my lie is exposed?
- ☐ Do I believe that over a lifetime, being up-front and complete on potential problems builds trust with others because they see me as honest?

BRAINY VERSUS WISE

Brainy: I'm smart, retaining both the lies and the truth. It's easy to get away with lying.

Wise: I stopped lying, though I am good at it, and am honest and plainspoken because I realized that it's foolish and arrogant to think I could outsmart and outrun God with my human expertise in deception.

Though today you may get by with a lie, next month you must recall the lies and the truth as you spoke them. This is hard and time-consuming work. *What did I say in September about why I couldn't get the report done by January 15? Where is that doggone e-mail that reminds me of what I said?* To lie effectively, we must remember both narratives.

Each of us must weigh our own intelligence. Are you smart enough to recall all lies and all truths, or do you know you'll likely end up forgetting what you said? It may not be the most noble of reasons, but some of us say, "I refuse to lie because I am not that smart." On the other hand, some of us stupidly give way to lies because we observe politicians and business leaders lying and getting away with it and say, "If they can, I can." Of course, I happen to believe that no one ever gets away with a lie. It is only a matter of time on earth or in heaven. We read in 1 Timothy 5:24, "The sins of some people are obvious, going ahead of them to judgment. The sins of others follow them there" (GW).

Most of us would agree with Ralph Waldo Emerson: "Character is higher than intellect."[1] Whether or not we are brainy, we can be wise enough not to lie. In the end, it isn't worth it, and the smart people figure this out!

SPEAK YOUR MIND TRUTHFULLY:

Emerson's Checklist for Wise Communication

- ☐ Do I remember stuff well that in the past enabled me to lie or tell the truth, whichever was to my advantage, and rarely did I get the stories mixed?
- ☐ Do I have very few instances where others caught me in a lie, which is why I must work hard at walking with integrity?
- ☐ Did I have a wake-up call spiritually that caused me to realize God is a God of truth and lying makes me an enemy of a core virtue of my heavenly Father?

- ☐ Do I take seriously that to lie is to be like the Father of Lies, Satan, who is my enemy, but to tell the truth is to be like my heavenly Father?
- ☐ Do I regularly remind myself that it is arrogant to think I have enough intelligence to outsmart God, as though I can fool Him with my lies?
- ☐ Do I soberly believe that lying to others is lying to God, and I remind myself of that daily as I pray and read the Bible?
- ☐ Do I use my ability to recall information to serve others to their advantage instead of to my advantage?
- ☐ Do I hang out with others who are equally committed to truth-telling and keeping me accountable?

WORDSMITHING VERSUS WELL-SPOKEN

Wordsmithing: I find it easy and fun to twist words, using double meanings that mislead.

Well-Spoken: In the past, I used my ability to be an effective communicator to twist the truth cunningly, but now I use that ability to be persuasive, eloquent, direct, and clear so my speaking and writing can be a positive influence.

I heard of a pastor who left his first pastorate after only a year, but he then spent more than forty years at his next church. When asked about the extreme opposites in tenure, he said it was due to the bullfrog illustration.

He explained, "Bullfrogs in a pond have the ability to echo, which gives the impression that scores of bullfrogs reside in the pond when actually there may be just one or two. In my first pastorate, a person said to me, 'Everybody is saying they don't like what you do as a pastor.' At the time, I didn't know he was a bullfrog. He gave me the impression that the majority of the congregation disliked me. I left the church. His comments empowered him, and it worked.

"In the second church a person told me the bullfrog story, so when complaints arose, I would ask, 'Who feels this way?' They wouldn't name anybody, so I decided to disbelieve them. I did not want to discount their concerns, but I refused to make a major decision based on their individual croakings. When they claimed 'everyone,' they were making a misleading comment. Maybe 'everyone' in their clique felt as they felt, but not 'everyone' in the church."

I once heard that a report was given about a battle in Vietnam. The American military told the press that our casualties were light. What they meant was that the soldiers were all under 160 pounds. Maybe that example of wordsmithing is a bit more extreme than what we are guilty of, but do you sometimes twist words in ways that are ambiguous at best and intentionally misleading at worst? Have you ever said any of the following? If so, what would have been your answer had you been asked the follow-up questions?

- "Everybody feels this way."
  Who?
- "Experience has proven . . ."
  The experience of whom?
- "There is a growing body of evidence . . ."
  Please show it to me.
- "This is award winning."
  Who gave the award and why?
- "Our product is regarded as the best."
  Based on what test(s) and criteria?
- "Research reveals . . ."
  Who did the study, and were there opposing studies?[2]

The intent behind wordsmithing is not always bad. People can have compassion and goodwill. Don't we soften a little when we learn the company didn't "fire" people but rather "downsized"? Don't we prefer the government's use of the term "job seekers" rather than "unemployed"? And don't the police say "physical persuasion," not "violence"?

None of these expressions is inherently bad, but they remind us that we can cross a line into misleading statements. Using discretion is one thing, deception another.

SPEAK YOUR MIND TRUTHFULLY:

Emerson's Checklist for Well-Spoken Communication

- ☐ Am I bound by a moral code, and do I operate within this boundary, like walking in integrity?
- ☐ Am I committed to being authentic, transparent, and effective in my verbal and written communication?
- ☐ Do I strive to create understanding skillfully and artfully?
- ☐ Do I avoid crafting language with double meanings or other wordsmithing tricks that mislead or deceive?
- ☐ Do I use my gift with words to be precise, clear, and persuasive about the truth?
- ☐ Do I use my ability to communicate directly and clearly to be a positive influence?
- ☐ Am I mindful of being winsome in tone while still conveying the truth?
- ☐ Am I disciplined in using my words to inform and inspire people with what helps them?

CHAPTER 4

MORAL WITH THE TRUTH

At times, others might try pressuring us to lie for them. We can be tempted to give in because we feel compelled to maintain a certain image. Sometimes our previous lies give us reason to lie again, and we see no way out other than to keep avoiding the truth. Whether it's out of "peer pressure" or because "everybody else lies" or just because we feel we no longer have any other choice, if we later admit to lying, we pass on the blame. "It's not my fault," we try telling ourselves, as well as anyone who catches us in our web of lies.

Obligated communicators are entrapped, copycatting, and perpetuating. They feel sworn to secrecy about a lie; they feel pressured to go along with the crowd; or, once telling a lie, they believe they must keep going with the lie.

On the other hand, moral communicators are integrous, individualistic, and self-correcting. They abide by the moral compass of integrity, they stand on their principles even if it means standing alone, and they change course, realizing lies only beget lies.

Will you commit to being the real deal and telling the truth no matter what? Even when others lie, will you refuse? Even if you have lied in the past, you can still repent from those past mistakes and begin the process of healing any relationships hurt by your past lies. It's never too late to become the person of integrity you know you are called to be.

Next, let's consider those who struggle with lying because they feel they "have to." But we never have to lie; we always have a choice. Will you choose to remain true to yourself, to others, and most of all to God?

ENTRAPPED VERSUS INTEGROUS

Entrapped: It's not my fault. I was lured into swearing secrecy and facilitated a lie.

Integrous: Though lured by others into swearing secrecy to facilitate a lie, I refuse to be entrapped, since I have a moral compass about walking in integrity, and will not compromise even when others claim I do not care about them and try to guilt-trip me to do what they want.

Some of us can be lured into making a promise to guard another's lie. Other people tell us of their wrongdoings and then say, "You must not tell anyone else what I just told you about what I did wrong and my cover-up." If we swear to secrecy about their lies, that information puts us in a position to withhold truth from others who have a right to know. We are facilitating a lie.

Not only are we complicit, but we are entrapped. We feel bound by an oath to stay silent about their wrongdoings. How ironic that we let our integrity cause us to keep secret another person's lack of integrity! They use our virtue to hide their vices. They expect us to be true to our word while they are untrue to theirs.

We must resist being subjected to this kind of coercion. People have no right to coerce us to swear to secrecy regarding their deceptions. For this reason, we must guard against succumbing to their attempts to guilt-trip us when we refuse to keep their lies a secret. They may quickly blame us as the bad person in all of this!

As a clergyman, if a church member confessed to me, for example, "I'm committing adultery with my secretary, but I don't want you to tell my wife when you meet with the two of us about our marriage," I would reply, "No, I won't agree to those terms. I would be participating in your pretense, and I don't have the liberty in my heart to do that. I won't keep from your wife what she has a right to know. Instead, I expect you to tell her." If the person acted offended and tried to guilt-trip me, I would reply, "The problem here is your adultery and deception. I am not the cause of your problem but am here to help you solve this problem. I care about you, your marriage, and your family. I am for you. But I cannot knowingly mislead your wife."

Each of us must tread wisely and avoid keeping secret a lie that someone else intends to keep telling. We must not join in with his trickery. A false narrative is a false narrative, and although we did not create the lie but only echoed what another claimed, that does not mean we get a free pass in the eyes of others.

SPEAK YOUR MIND TRUTHFULLY:

Emerson's Checklist for Integrous Communication

- ☐ Do I hold to a standard of personal integrity that does not allow me to facilitate another's lie?
- ☐ Do I refuse to be entrapped into facilitating a lie when others attempt to guilt-trip me into doing so "if I care about them"?
- ☐ Do I withstand the guilt-tripping and shaming tactics of others who try to get me to go against my values and beliefs?
- ☐ Do I recognize that enabling others to be irresponsible for their wrong choices by covering up for them as a "responsible" person is a silly contradiction?
- ☐ Do I empathize with another's painful plight, even validating their needs, but recognize that my relationship with the truth is more important than my relationship with them?
- ☐ Do I humbly but clearly explain why I will not lie for them while reassuring them of my deep love for them, which is why I will not lie for them?
- ☐ Do I prepare myself emotionally for another's rejection and resentment for not going along with their request that I lie?
- ☐ Do I hold steadfast to my integrity, since the negative consequences to me and others, given that I lie for them, do not achieve anything noble and good long-term, and do I tell them that?

COPYCATTING VERSUS INDIVIDUALISTIC

Copycatting: I'm not really interested in lying, but everybody else lies, so I do too.

Individualistic: I stand alone on my values and principles, strong and independent in telling the truth, even when those around me have a mindset to lie and expect me to copy them and shrewdly deceive others for personal gain.

Parents often tell their kids, "Just because others take drugs doesn't mean you can take drugs. Because others drive recklessly doesn't mean you can. We are not copycats in this family. We don't go along with the crowd."

Just because almost everybody lies at one time or another does not make lying an acceptable thing to do. We must not proclaim this as an inevitable law of nature (though it is part of sinful human nature).

When family and friends lie, we must resist the idea that we have no choice but to go along with it. We have a choice, albeit a tough one. We must say no to lying; otherwise, our family and friends can pull us into that swamp. That is why the Bible warns, "Do not be deceived: 'Bad company corrupts good morals'" (1 Cor. 15:33).

When your adult sibling posts on social media a lie about supposed horrible treatment by a local business, will you like or share the post for no other reason than he's your brother? Will you let him corrupt your morals? Or, when your work associate lies to a customer, will you support her lie lest you be excluded from the office in-crowd that meets daily for lunch? Each of us can be truth-tellers who stand strong and stay true to our convictions and conscience. We need not throw away our moral compass, even if we are never again invited to lunch.

We are not helpless or hopeless. Copycatting is a decision we make. We are spiritual beings made in the image of God who control our own moral destinies.

SPEAK YOUR MIND TRUTHFULLY:

Emerson's Checklist for Individualistic Communication

- ☐ Do I have a moral code prohibiting me from going along with the crowd who sees lying as street-smart and beneficial?

- ☐ Am I aware of the negative influence my social network can have on me, leading me to lie because they lie?
- ☐ Am I willing to confront, because I care, those who are less than truthful among my network of friends, doing so humbly and respectfully?
- ☐ Do I stay strong and independent as a person of honesty even when I must stand alone and swim upstream?
- ☐ Are my integrity and clear conscience priorities over fitting in or getting high fives for lying?
- ☐ Do I accept that people who lie will not favor my commitment to being a truth-teller and typically will shun me?
- ☐ Do I let go of relationships that demand I lie to be included in the group?
- ☐ Do I hope that people in my network of friends will eventually come around to what I believe as they see the benefits of truth-telling and the consequences of lying?
- ☐ Do I seek out people who live and love the same moral code that I do of integrity, honesty, and truth, forming a new community with like-minded people?

PERPETUATING VERSUS SELF-CORRECTING

Perpetuating: I lie to stay ahead of other lies I have told, not concerned that lies beget lies.

Self-Correcting: My previous strategy of lying to stay ahead of exposure—having to lie about lies—not only was exhausting but impeded healthy relationships, so I amended my ways and changed course by prioritizing the moral value of honesty, and I am much happier.

I read once about a guy who had to perpetually lie in order to juggle three girlfriends at the same time, none of whom knew of the others. Whenever he went out with one of them, he had to come up with reasons why he could not be with the other two. He then had to remember which excuse he'd made to which girl, and then try to come up with stories that happened at any fake events he invented as part of his lie.

It was relentlessly hard work, he admitted. Stories like these prove how stupid and unloving it is to lie.

One lie feeds on another lie like a food chain. The first small lie becomes food for a slightly larger lie, which in turn feeds a bigger lie. We lie about the lie, and then we lie about the lie about the lie. It is endless and expansive! Lies can grow exponentially. Truly, it is a web of lies. It is demanding and draining to stay out in front of all these lies. Many have finally said, "I am done with lying. It isn't worth it. I am exhausted." We who are perpetuating lies need to stop.

Some of us need to confess the lie that started it all. We cannot outrun an avalanche. It will catch up to us. When caught in all our lies and forced to confess, who will believe we are authentic? But taking the initiative on our own sends the message of sincerity and remorse. Most people forgive those who want to stop perpetuating falsehoods. And when we come clean, we feel clean!

SPEAK YOUR MIND TRUTHFULLY:

Emerson's Checklist for Self-Correcting Communication

- ☐ Do I 100 percent agree that lies beget lies, and a chain reaction of dishonesty is never worth it, as I will know on my deathbed?
- ☐ Am I all-in on telling the truth from the get-go?
- ☐ Am I all-in on walking in integrity so that telling the truth does not entail confession of not telling the truth?
- ☐ Have I stopped lying to myself, since chronic liars who perpetually lie are good at lying because they convince themselves the lie is true?
- ☐ Do I now own up to my past untruths?
- ☐ Do I set the record straight with the truth, even if it means admitting my mistakes?
- ☐ Do I make amends for the hurt I have caused by misleading people?
- ☐ Do I remind myself of the consequences of lying and let that provide an incentive to stay on the straight, narrow path of truth-telling?

CHAPTER 5

INFORMED OF THE TRUTH

I truly believe in the goodwill of the vast majority of people, especially those concerned enough about something to read my books or attend one of my conferences. But even goodwilled people committed to the truth can wrongly assume they were right about something and make unfounded assertions. They didn't intend to lie, but unfortunately, they did not investigate fully whether something they said was entirely true. Now the deed is done, and though they had not meant to deceive anyone, they're tempted now to excuse themselves, saying, "It's not really a lie if you don't know you're lying."

To learn how to speak our minds truthfully, we must move from wrongly assuming and jumping to conclusions to ensuring we have all the facts before we say something.

Presumptuous communicators are emotional and inattentive. If it feels true, some blurt out information emotionally, even if they have not validated their assertion. Others state things they think are accurate, but later discover they were careless in sharing what turned out to be untrue.

On the other hand, informed communicators are factual and observant. They confirm their feelings with the facts before making a claim. They guard against being inattentive or unobservant to the facts—and if they mistakenly share an untruth, they quickly correct their oversight.

Each of us has a responsibility to research to make certain any reports we give are accurate. It comes back to the courtroom oath of reporting "nothing but the truth" so others can rest assured that every word we communicate, to the best of what we have been able to determine, is true.

We are charged with holding the truth—all truth—in the highest regard. Do you respect the truth enough to verify the accuracy of everything you claim? And if you unintentionally lie, even though you thought you had researched all you needed, can you humble yourself enough to admit your mistake and correct your error with the truth?

EMOTIONAL VERSUS FACTUAL

Emotional: If it feels true, I say it; I don't need all the facts when I feel I'm right.

Factual: When I feel something is true or right, I fight against saying it or acting on it until I have all the facts; otherwise, I can jump to wrong conclusions based on my emotions or impulse.

Emotions are wonderful, but not when feelings aren't consistent with the facts.

I have frequently written pieces on our Love and Respect Facebook page about God's command for a wife to put on a respectful demeanor toward her husband, based on Ephesians 5:33 and 1 Peter 3:1–2. As counterintuitive as this can feel to a wife, showing her husband respect motivates him to be loving. However, on reading my post, certain women new to our Facebook page inevitably blast away in the comment section, claiming that my position is to always blame the woman. They do not check out earlier posts in which I challenge the husbands to love their wives unconditionally based on Ephesians 5:33 and Hosea 3:2. In most everything I write, I have a teeter-totter approach, going back and forth. Had these women looked through the earlier posts, they would have whistled a different tune. Instead, they judged me as unfair. They let their feelings, probably based on their negative experiences with men, govern their words. They are not being irrational, yet they are clearly emotional. As a result, they wrongly presume my stance.

I feel bad for those who let their feelings dictate their scathing rebukes. They jump the gun before they do their homework. Benjamin Franklin stated, "Presumption first blinds a Man, then sets him a running."[1] And the Bible offers the wisest of insights. Proverbs 18:13 states,

"He who gives an answer before he hears, it is folly and shame to him."

Just because someone feels something is true does not make it true in fact. That's why when we make assertions without facts to back our claims, we face the prospect of looking foolish and feeling ashamed. Every effective communicator must ask: Is it true in fact? When we speak based on facts, not on our feelings alone, we restrict our comments before speaking. I'm not saying feelings are always wrong, just that good communicators confirm their feelings with facts. The presumption can be accurate, but the feelings first need validation.

SPEAK YOUR MIND TRUTHFULLY:

Emerson's Checklist for Factual Communication

- ☐ Do I agree that feelings are not always reliable predictors of truth, and intuition is not the final determinant of truth?
- ☐ Do I admit to myself that my bias can cause me to act on my hunches rather than the evidence?
- ☐ Do I know my anger or fear can trigger an irrational reaction, so I avoid that pitfall?
- ☐ Even though I have intuitions and strong feelings, which can be right, do I live by evidence-based thinking before coming to conclusions?
- ☐ Though my initial instinct can be correct, do I let these sentiments drive me to verify with facts?
- ☐ Do I take the time to gather all the relevant information before drawing a conclusion or making a decision?
- ☐ Am I willing to acknowledge when I don't have all the necessary information and seek out all the facts?
- ☐ Have I established a healthy pattern of trying to avoid reacting based on my gut instincts and impulses contrary to the proven facts?

INATTENTIVE VERSUS OBSERVANT

Inattentive: I didn't know that what I said was inaccurate; everyone makes mistakes.

Observant: When I am inaccurate in what I say, I try to be attentive and set the record straight when I learn the facts. Previous ignorance is no excuse nor self-justification for perpetuating an untruth.

When you believe a statement to be true though the statement is false, are you a liar? No, but it is still a lie. An untruthful statement doesn't become true because you believe it to be true.

Perhaps you didn't know it was untrue when you communicated it but found out after the fact. *No harm, no foul*, you tell yourself. However, an honest error in judgment does not make it okay, especially if you repeatedly make such mistakes.

Some lazy and neglectful individuals keep making mistakes and claim they did not know the truth. For example, in submitting financial reports as part of his quarterly responsibility, Steve made an error because, in his hurriedness, he added incorrectly. After the supervisor caught the error, which was a loss to the company of several thousand dollars, Steve pleaded that it was an honest mistake. However, over the last twelve quarters, Steve had made four similar mistakes. He was not guilty of knowingly making this mistake, but he was guilty of carelessness and inattentiveness, which caused the error. We must aggressively get our facts straight to avoid a routine of "honest" mistakes.

Inattentiveness can create severe consequences. A medical doctor can misdiagnose a condition that ends up costing a person thousands of dollars on medication or his very life. Proverbs 14:12 states, "There is a way which seems right to a man, but its end is the way of death."

Our hearts can be in the right place as we clearly communicate what we feel to be true. But that doesn't make it right any more than hitting and killing a pedestrian is to be overlooked because there was no malice. A person still died. Being inattentive is no excuse just because we had no premeditation. Manslaughter is still manslaughter.

The good news is that most inattentive communicators can move forward by correcting the mistake. I have a friend whose teenage son plays competitive golf. In a recent state tournament he played in, he discovered that because of some scoring confusion, he had unknowingly reported a lower score than his actual tally. Like many golf competitions at this level, the winners are determined by self-reporting scores.

Because of this, he could have gotten away with his honest mistake, none the worse for wear. But because he knew that to remain silent would be the same as lying, he and his coach confessed the mistake to the tournament director and risked the consequences. Unfortunately, his scores from the first two days of the tournament were disqualified, and he lost any chance he had to place near the top of the tournament.

However, this young man could still rejoice, not because of any trophies or cash prizes he may have won but because of the imperishable reward Scripture says awaits us when we do what we do unto the Lord. "Whatever you do," the apostle Paul wrote, "work at it with all your heart, as working for the Lord, not for human masters, since you know that you will receive an inheritance from the Lord as a reward. It is the Lord Christ you are serving" (Col. 3:23–24 NIV). And it is the Lord Christ you are confessing the truth to when correcting a previous mistake.

SPEAK YOUR MIND TRUTHFULLY:

Emerson's Checklist for Observant Communication

- ☐ Do I pride myself on being a person who chases after accuracy and is known for my attentiveness to the facts?
- ☐ Do I see the danger of having my mind made up and latching on to any bit of information to reinforce that bias even though it is not the truth, the whole truth, and nothing but the truth?
- ☐ Do I detect a desire within me to be willfully ignorant so as to advance my narrative for self-serving aims?
- ☐ Do I refuse to double down on my assertions to save face under the political strategy of never admitting wrong?
- ☐ Do I humbly agree that I do not always get everything right, and so I am attentive to miscommunications on my part?
- ☐ Do I do my homework to figure out why I got it wrong in the first place?
- ☐ Do I readily learn from my mistakes and resolve to prevent a repeat of such miscommunication?
- ☐ Am I answerable for my incorrect communications by apologizing and setting the record straight?

CHAPTER 6

ALTRUISTIC ABOUT THE TRUTH

It is human nature to be tempted to make a selfish decision that would benefit us in that moment. Unfortunately, some people selfishly prioritize their interests above others' and are willing to mislead to advance their own agenda. To avoid looking less than admirable in others' eyes, they share only what they feel others need to hear so as to keep up appearances. Their priority is looking good and making others like them, so they're less concerned with what is true than they are with what they think others want to hear.

To speak our minds truthfully, we must seek to be as concerned about the well-being of others as we are of ourselves. That means we decide not to lie to get what we want or to prevent others from getting what they need. We refuse to be so self-absorbed that we manipulate every conversation to be about the fulfillment of our wishes instead of the concerns of others.

As we have highlighted, some people are untruthful because they are self-obsessed. Their communication is selfish, prideful, flattering, oath-making, and self-amusing. They lie for various reasons: to advance their selfish interests; to create a more favorable image of themselves; to manipulate others by telling them what they want to hear to gain something in return, even invoking God when necessary to appear credible to others; and sometimes simply for their own amusement.

On the other hand, truthful communicators are altruistic. Their communication is unselfish, humble, genuine, reverent, and mindfully humorous. They prioritize win-win solutions over a win-lose agenda, maintain transparency about themselves and the truth without arrogance, affirm the truth about others without resorting to false praise, demonstrate reverence toward God (never saying "I swear to God"), and use their wit to enable people to laugh without demeaning others.

Admittedly, we all struggle in these selfish ways from time to time. However, though we will not ever handle every moment perfectly, we can make the decision every day to prioritize the well-being of others above our own interests. We can choose to go against the grain of our human nature and be unwilling to mislead, even if it means sacrificing our own agenda. Of course, we want to please others, as everyone should, but ultimately we serve the truth and God above all. If the truth conflicts with whatever answer may help us in the short-term, the truth should win out. Above all, we are to be people of integrity, even when we feel the alternative decision would benefit us more.

In this last chapter about speaking your mind truthfully, we will discuss how to remain committed to the truth, even when being honest does not benefit us in the moment.

SELFISH VERSUS UNSELFISH

Selfish: What can I say? Lying works to my advantage, advancing my agenda.

Unselfish: All people are made in God's image and have equal value, which requires fairness and win-win solutions. Therefore, I consider the just interests of others and not solely what benefits me at their expense, even if lying may work to my advantage.

A peer at work is up for the same promotion that you seek, and only one of you will get it. The CEO asks if you are able to provide information to this peer on a certain project. If you provide the information, you would enable this peer to succeed and mar your chances for the advancement, so instead you lie: "Sorry, I don't have that information."

Or perhaps you're a wife who, seeking empathy from the friends you value, tells only part of the story about the fight you had with your husband. You describe in detail what he did wrong but say nothing about what you did to prompt his negative reaction.

We are all capable of manipulating information for self-serving purposes, telling others incorrect information to advance our interests, and suppressing information that might block our progress. When we want something badly enough, we are tempted to lie to gain it if we see an opportunity to get away with it.

Each of us must decide if forgoing the truth to get what we want is the course we should take. Lance Armstrong denied doping charges for years, and the public believed him. He rebutted the allegations in interviews and through every social media outlet. He would defend himself with, "I never tested positive or was ever caught for anything."[1] Eventually, a fellow rider, Floyd Landis, confessed to the drugging on the US Postal Service team, and the rest is history. So why did Lance lie? He wanted to be number one at any price and convinced himself that because others drugged themselves too, this leveled the playing field. Yet he validated a Russian proverb: "With lies you may get ahead in the world—but you can never go back."

In saying that we need to think before we speak, we should actually say, "*What* will we think before we speak?" Some of us think, *I need to lie to get what I want*, and we move forward with our communication.

SPEAK YOUR MIND TRUTHFULLY:

Emerson's Checklist for Unselfish Communication

- ☐ Do I see all people as made in God's image and having an equal value with me?
- ☐ Do I consider the just interests of others and not solely what benefits me at their expense?
- ☐ Because people are made in God's image and have an equal value to me, do I treat them as I would want to be treated (i.e., the Golden Rule), with fairness and win-win solutions?
- ☐ Do I recognize what selfishness and lying do to undermine healthy relationships?

- ☐ Do I take responsibility for any hurt or deprivation I have caused others and seek to repair those moments when I acted selfishly at the expense of someone else's needs?
- ☐ Do I find win-win solutions in the sense that I explore creative alternatives or third options that satisfy both of our core self-interests on the matter?
- ☐ Do I aim for an altruistic approach to people and conflicts because this keeps my conscience clear as it aligns with my faith and values?
- ☐ Do I sometimes realize the other person's concerns far outweigh my own and thus defer to their needs?

PRIDEFUL VERSUS HUMBLE

Prideful: I need to look better than I am so others will feel good about me and like me.

Humble: Striving for authenticity and sincere, respectful relationships, I resist the temptation to lie about being better than I am to feel good about myself and to gain approval. As I will not lie about my inadequacies to prevent rejection, I have ceased projecting a false image at the expense of the truth about who I am.

One of the most common reasons people lie is to impress others. If we succeed at dazzling them, we think they will feel good about us and we will feel good about ourselves. What better reason to hedge on the truth? Everybody feels good! So we decide to embellish our achievements to enhance our image.

But this need not be overt. A woman told me, "My dad came over one day, and my daughter was being crazy disobedient. He asked me, 'So are you putting that on Facebook?' Of course I wasn't! I have an image to project that I'm perfect, I have this great job, and I have this great daughter. I don't put the unfavorable truth out there." I refer to this tendency as *Fake*book.

I recently read that millennials are changing the face of travel.

One article said, "If there's one thing millennials love more than traveling, it's bragging about the places they've traveled . . . They go for the bragging rights of being the first in their circle . . . More than 50 percent of millennials post vacation photos on social media to make friends and family jealous."[2] What a way to live.

We must ask ourselves, *When I communicate what I know is untrue but favorable about myself, am I so hollow and insecure that I let my hubris compel me to lie?*

SPEAK YOUR MIND TRUTHFULLY:

Emerson's Checklist for Humble Communication

- ☐ Do I find my worth solely in my accomplishments or possessions?
- ☐ When hearing constructive criticism, do I get defensive and even deny the truth?
- ☐ Am I so insecure that I boast or exaggerate my strengths while denying my weaknesses?
- ☐ To gain acceptance and approval from others, do I mislead them about my importance and competencies?
- ☐ Do I believe that walking in humility and truthfulness is foundational to cultivating meaningful relationships and self-esteem?
- ☐ When I don't know something, am I comfortable communicating, "I don't know"?
- ☐ Though uncomfortable when mistakes or flaws arise, do I admit to them?
- ☐ Do I gladly receive the insight others have and enjoy engaging them in mutual learning?
- ☐ Do I predict that on my deathbed, I will reflect on my life as an honest person who helped others and be content with that?

FLATTERING VERSUS GENUINE

Flattering: I want to be truthful and tactful, but insincere praise works better for me.

Genuine: Though flattery or false praise may work in the moment, people eventually see through the insincerity, so I have committed to affirming what is true about others without exaggeration.

Being a person who communicates what is true frequently demands tact, and at times it can feel like sidestepping land mines. It takes work to be both truthful and tactful. Some say, "I *want* to be discreet, but truth demands sincere thoughtfulness, and I'm not interested in developing that skill. Telling the other person what they want to hear instead of what they need to hear is the route I prefer to take with people looking for my affirmation."

This is clever lying, not tact. It is insincere. It is tickling another's ears. In many organizations some workers learn to tell the boss what he wants to hear. He feels good, and they experience job security. But withholding bad news, which the boss needs to hear, doesn't make that bad news any better.

Setting aside flattery—being truthful, tactful, and sincere—is tough.

For example, a culturally recognized question from a wife to her husband—"How does this dress make me look?"—has been quoted countless times in Western societies. Some women advise husbands to respond with "Honey, you are beautiful to me no matter your dress," which is a great and true answer for many. However, we must consider two realities.

Reality #1: Body Image Issues. If a wife is concerned about her figure, this topic will likely emerge years into the marriage. When it does, a husband finds himself in a difficult place. Many wives can freely discuss weight loss strategies with friends, but husbands are often expected to remain silent or provide only positive affirmations. This can make the husband's genuine concerns or supportive advice seem insensitive, though he may echo the sentiments of his wife's mother, sister, or friends.

Reality #2: Double Standard in Communication. Ironically, a wife can critique her husband's clothing selections and appearance, doing so with very negative opinions about his choices and image, yet often without him personalizing her words. On the other hand, if a husband gently expresses a preference for one dress over another, his wife might interpret it as a comment on her looks and accuse him, with disgust in her tone, of not loving her unconditionally. This double standard requires a nuanced approach of the husband.

To navigate these sensitive conversations, husbands can truthfully and wisely respond. Here are some suggested replies.

1. "You look beautiful to me, no matter your dress."
2. "You look beautiful to me no matter what you wear. If you feel unsure about this dress, try the blue one—it always looks great."
3. "You look beautiful to me no matter what you wear. If you're feeling uncertain about this dress, I think the blue one complements your eyes and fits the occasion. But if you have concerns more broadly about your health, I'm here to support you in any goals you set for yourself. Let's find what makes you feel most confident and comfortable."

Men, when communicating with your wife, especially if she feels distressed by comments about her appearance, it's crucial to approach the conversation with empathy, understanding, and careful communication. Start by acknowledging her feelings and expressing genuine concern: "I understand that comments about appearance can feel sensitive. It's important to me that you feel heard and respected. I realize societal pressures can be overwhelming. I want you to know that I recognize these challenges and am here to support you however I can. If there are ways I can be more supportive or if certain comments are unhelpful, please let me know. I want to learn how to communicate in a way that reveals that I understand and value you."

He should focus on overall health and well-being, providing a balanced perspective that avoids reinforcing negative body image perceptions while promoting a healthy lifestyle.

Some lying only appears sincere and tactful. Telling a person what he or she wants to hear may feel like tact, but it is not if it is a lie. One wonders about the parents of some untalented adult children who audition for television talent shows like *The Voice*. In many cases, a parent should have humbly spoken the truth: "Son, God has given you talent but not as a singer."

At the same time, it is tactless and tasteless to blurt out what is true if it is received as cruel and coldhearted. For example, imagine a medical doctor reviewing a patient's chart and saying matter-of-factly, "Unfortunately, there is no cure. You have six months to live. Any questions before I leave?" Such truth without tact is heartless, though sincere.

The consolation is that when we work hard at being sincere, honest, and compassionate, most people will receive our communication, even if it doesn't come out perfectly. They may not like what we say, but they will trust our humble, loving hearts.

SPEAK YOUR MIND TRUTHFULLY:

Emerson's Checklist for Genuine Communication

- ☐ Even if it may seem easier to flatter someone to get something out of them, do I have a distaste for manipulating people?
- ☐ Do I believe that my disingenuous flattery usually backfires, since most people see through it?
- ☐ Have I concluded that flattery harms relationships, since people see me as deceptive and controlling?
- ☐ Do I guard myself against using inappropriate, dishonest, or insincere labels?
- ☐ Do I praise someone for their hard work by showing them my appreciation and respect?
- ☐ Do I affirm what is positive and true about another's character without exaggeration?
- ☐ Do I encourage another's character, since that best motivates them to endure adversity and resist temptation?
- ☐ Do I exercise tact in being truthful about another's deserved praise while ensuring I do not step over a line into false assertions for my selfish benefit?

OATH-MAKING VERSUS REVERENT

Oath-Making: I admit that when hedging, I sometimes swear to God so others believe what I'm saying.

Reverent: In my communication, others need me to be trustworthy and competent; they do not need me to coerce them into believing I am credible and truthful because I say, "Honest to God" or "I swear to God."

We have all been around people who exclaim, "Honest to God, I'm telling the truth. I swear to God." In effect, they are taking the Lord's name in vain.

They aren't "honest to God." They are *dis*honest to God and others. They are lying under their own oath, doing so to manipulate others into believing their lie. Such people lack confidence in the truth of their own words (because they aren't telling the truth), so they use God as a persuasive trump card. They want the other person to conclude "Anyone who swears to God must be honest. I will buy what they're selling."

Do liars make oaths and swear to God? Perhaps more than most! "A liar," wrote Pierre Corneille, "is always lavish of oaths."[3]

Jesus said, "Make no oath . . . by heaven, for it is the throne of God" (Matt. 5:34). He continued, "But let your statement be, 'Yes, yes' or 'No, no'; anything beyond these is of evil" (v. 37).

Before communicating, let's think: *Am I about to make an oath by swearing to God about something I know isn't true? Is that what I should do? Would Jesus say to me, "What you are about to communicate is wrong. Though it is easy enough for you to swear by bringing God into the conversation, this is evil in My eyes"?*

SPEAK YOUR MIND TRUTHFULLY:

Emerson's Checklist for Reverent Communication

- ☐ Do I realize that most see as insincere and untrue a person who habitually says, "Honest to God" or "I swear to God," which undermines trust and healthy relationships?

- ☐ Do I have confidence about how I live so I don't need to say "Honest to God" or "I swear to God" when I communicate?
- ☐ Do I make myself credible by my trustworthiness and competency so that people receive what I say when I communicate?
- ☐ When necessary, do I validate my communication using reliable resources, logical reasoning, or eyewitness accounts?
- ☐ Do I live with a God-consciousness in that I realize I live before an audience of One and therefore resist irreverently blurting out, "Honest to God" or "I swear to God"?
- ☐ Do I refuse to say "Honest to God" to intimidate people into thinking they must believe me, falsely asserting that disagreeing with me is the same as disagreeing with God?
- ☐ Do I oppose saying "I swear to God," since I should be able to convince another of my sincerity and truthfulness without employing an oath before God, which makes me suspect, since when I swear, I must be unpersuasive?
- ☐ As a Christ follower, do I take it seriously when Jesus instructs me not to be one who "swears" by God who dwells in the holy temple or by God who sits on the heavenly throne (Matt. 23:21–22)?
- ☐ Do I say "Yes, I will do this" or "No, I won't do that" without invoking God's name, since Jesus told me to let my yes be yes and my no, no without bringing God into the equation disrespectfully?
- ☐ Do I apologize after slipping up by swearing to God, and do I seek God's forgiveness?

SELF-AMUSING VERSUS MINDFULLY HUMOROUS

Self-Amusing: Frankly, I view tricking others as an exciting and entertaining game.

Mindfully Humorous: In the past, I might have used inappropriate, disrespectful, and offensive humor to amuse myself, but that hurt others, so I decided to get serious and sincere to help others with problems by using my quick thinking to assess the truth and creatively find innovative solutions. I now try to use only good humor for comedic relief.

"On the whole, lying is a cheerful affair," wrote Isabel Fonseca. "Embellishments are intended to give pleasure. People long to tell you what they imagine you want to hear. They want to amuse you; they want to amuse themselves; they want to show you a good time. This is beyond hospitality. This is art."[4] Some people exaggerate out of a desire to entertain. In many social settings, we give grace to a storyteller who embellishes the funny episode.

However, there is someone other than the entertainer. There are those who find delight in misleading others. Some people enter politics because they derive personal fulfillment from the political chess game. The key is to put a better spin on an issue than the other candidate and to put the opposition in checkmate. They like the polemical game they are caught up in. It amuses and invigorates them. Furthermore, in this environment they do not suffer liability for slander and lies. They get a pass in politics. They can pull a statement their opponent said in passing and broadcast that but remove the follow-up comment that said, "Having said that, let me explain why that might not be true." Rightly representing is not the name of the game. Winning is the name of the game. Thus, after a televised interview, they high-five with their party peers when their spin of misleading comments proves persuasive.

We often hear, "You can fool some of the people all the time, and all the people some of the time, but you cannot fool all the people all the time." Some people are involved in trying to trick the masses, though ultimately they cannot pull it off. Oddly, a few do it for the challenge and fun of it. They derive a sense of delight in trying to fool large numbers of people on a regular basis. There are any number of reasons people create fake news, but some do it as a game to see if they can get away with it.

Before we communicate something, we need to ask: *Is this about what I can get away with for self-amusing purposes?*

SPEAK YOUR MIND TRUTHFULLY:

Emerson's Checklist for Mindfully Humorous Communication

- ☐ Do I use good humor for comedic relief?

- □ Do I think a witty person displays that talent by getting people to laugh at how they insult and belittle others?
- □ Does my caring and empathetic nature put a check in my spirit when I am about to say something that, though funny, is also derogatory?
- □ Do I see that when I am quick-witted and funny at the expense of another, I reveal not only my insecurity and boredom as a person but also my lack of empathy and respect for others?
- □ Do I recognize that a laugh for me pales compared to the damage I cause by making others the laughingstock?
- □ Do I grasp the destructive force on relationships when I subject others to mocking laughter that ridicules them as stupid?
- □ Do I see myself as a talented and creative person who uses humor that is wholesome and fun-loving, not humiliating and misleading?
- □ Do I value people as equal in worth to me in the eyes of God and therefore avoid using them as objects of entertainment to amuse me?
- □ Do I say no to using inappropriate, disrespectful, and offensive humor to amuse myself, but which hurts others?
- □ Have I decided to get serious and sincere to help others with problems by using my quick thinking to assess the truth and creatively find innovative solutions?

PART 2

SPEAK YOUR MIND WITH KINDNESS

People hear your words of truth, but they feel your words of kindness. In other words, they feel your love and respect. I am defining *kindness* as being a loving and respectful person.

Thumper the rabbit said, "If you can't say something nice, don't say nothing at all."[1] I would add, if you do not appear as a caring and honorable person when you speak, don't say anything at all, at least not yet. Words that sound unloving and disrespectful stomp on people's hearts and discredit you.

Some believe kindness is optional, like table manners where one uses the smaller fork with a salad and the larger fork with the main course. I disagree. Kindness is not a nice add-on. You may tell the truth all day long; but if you do so while being unkind, hateful, and contemptuous, you are making more enemies than friends. I once heard a person say, "When I know you hate me, I cannot hear you." Our hostility and disdain close off the spirits of others to the truth we wish them to hear.

Some feel that kindness compromises the truth. They equate kindness with giving others license to indulge in wrongdoing. However, kindness is not about acquiescing or agreeing with others' positions.

Kindness has to do with who we are. We are caring and honorable people who deliver the uncompromising truth in a loving and respectful manner. Absolute truth is nonnegotiable. But truth is not advanced by being mean-spirited, hateful, and rude.

In any interaction, we must work diligently to speak in loving and respectful ways. In Ephesians 5:33, God commands a husband and wife to show love and respect in their marriage. That's why we need to learn from couples who succeed in marriage. One husband wrote, "Our arguments would escalate because I would come across as unloving and she would come across as disrespectful. Now, we take a step back and try to understand where the other is coming from and why we are angry at each other. We have found that most of our fights are because we act in unloving or disrespectful ways, not over the little thing that triggered the fight."

Labor unions and management oftentimes fail to come to an agreement not because the proposals are unreasonable but because during the process unions felt management didn't care and management felt the unions did not respect them. The same can be said about our elected officials debating laws in Washington, DC. Why is it so often said that "nothing gets done in Washington"? Just listen to the way so many of them speak of their colleagues across the aisle—with an undercurrent of mean-spiritedness. When this undercurrent is present, it subverts the trust and thus the deliberations.

A question for us to ask before communicating is, *Am I addressing the issue or attacking the person?* If the person feels attacked, the negotiations will be difficult. When attacked, we put up walls. We may be present, but we're so guarded that we don't really listen.

How about you? During a conflict, do you approach another as a friend, not a foe? Do you assume he or she has goodwill and is trustworthy unless presented with facts otherwise? Do you seek to remain positive and affirming while addressing concerns?

When seeking to persuade others, we need to keep asking: *How can I speak what is true and necessary and clear without others feeling I am unkind? How can I differ with people without them feeling unloved and disrespected?*

THE HEART OF COMMUNICATING WHAT IS KIND

I once heard a story about a Frenchman who was a Christian. He lived under the Nazi regime during World War II and harbored Jews until the Germans caught him. He was brought before a German officer known as the Torturer. As this godly Frenchman entered the presence of this Nazi officer, the peace of Christ flooded his soul—a peace that transcends all understanding, as Philippians 4:7 reveals. This officer observed his tranquil expression and interpreted it as snideness. He screamed, "Get that snide look off your face! Don't you know who I am?" There was a brief pause, and the Frenchman humbly replied, "Yes, sir. I know who you are. You are known as the Torturer, and you have the power to torture me and kill me." Then he kindly added, "But sir, you do not have the power to get me to hate you."

In a similar way, another person cannot get my heart to be unkind, unloving, or disrespectful. Instead, I decide who I will be, independent of the other person. I won't blame my unkindness on someone else.

If I am feeling provoked by another's behavior and react like a madman, I will be seen as a madman along with the other person. Even though the other person came at me first, my rude and mean-spirited reaction reveals me as a rude and mean-spirited person.

We may not intend to be unkind, but it makes little difference when others interpret our communication as unloving and disrespectful. When we communicate in ways that sound unloving and disrespectful, will we blame others and circumstances for our unkind remarks? For example, as the family of six drives away from McDonald's, Dad notices that two of the orders are missing, so he turns the car around and heads back. As he enters the restaurant and goes to the counter, he exclaims to the manager, "I can't believe your incompetency! You failed to put in the two Big Macs we ordered. Everyone here is one french fry short of a Happy Meal." After the manager gives him what he wants, this dad walks out in a huff. He will give himself plausible excuses for his behavior, since he feels inconvenienced. Being an honorable man who speaks respectfully doesn't enter his mind. To him, the extent to which he communicates "kindly" is the extent he loses power and influence. His anger and autonomy assuage his guilt. But we all know he could have achieved the same objective by walking in and saying, "A mistake was made. Can you help me here?"

Here's a critical question: Did their carelessness *cause* him to be angry and disrespectful or *reveal* him to be an angry and disrespectful person? I remind myself that the sun hardens the clay but melts the butter. By that I mean the sun doesn't cause the clay to harden and butter to melt; the sun reveals the inner properties of each. When things heat up, we reveal our true colors.

Truth be told, our unkindness comes from within. Jesus said in Mark 7:21–22, "For from within, out of the heart of men, proceed . . . slander . . ." Other people don't cause us to be the way we are; they reveal our predisposition to express disgust and disparagement.

THE GOLDEN RULE OF KIND COMMUNICATION

Are people unkind in today's social media? Some are. One problem area is trolling, which is "posting inflammatory or provocative remarks on a social network or forum to trigger an emotional response, deliberately provoking other users or readers into arguing back."[2]

But we don't like when people are unfriendly and mean-spirited toward us, whether online or in the real world. We know kindness is fundamental for relationships to work well in the family, neighborhood, legislature, workplace, or wherever. We tend to avoid unsympathetic, inconsiderate, and nasty people. For instance, we take our business elsewhere when a store owner talks to us in an uncaring way.

But when we're pushed to the edge and feel kindness is getting us nowhere, do we turn unpleasant, disagreeable, and uncivil? Do we compromise kindness to get what we want or to prevent losing what we have? Do we appear hostile and contemptuous? Do we intimidate? Do we bully? Do we use abusive speech? Or are we committed to speaking lovingly and respectfully no matter what because we have resolved to be a loving and respectful human being?

This raises an important question: Do we intend to do toward others what we expect them to do toward us? Will we be kind communicators because we expect others to be kind communicators with us?

Ryan Anderson, an intellectual who promotes traditional values on college campuses, encountered something sobering on this topic of civility. This exchange between Anderson and a *New York Times* reporter moved me to tears:

> [While] Anderson repeatedly made the case for civility and respect for opposing perspectives, the reporter responded with, 'Why shouldn't I call you names?,' and 'Civility is not always a virtue,' and 'Some people are deserving of incivility,' and 'Obviously some policy views render people unworthy of respect.' Anderson explained, 'People are always worthy of respect, even if their policy views are misguided. Nothing renders people 'unworthy of respect.' He continued: 'I think even when we vehemently disagree with someone the person still has innate human dignity, still worthy of respect.'[3]

Is this *New York Times* reporter the new secular Pharisee who is self-righteous, angry, judgmental, and damning? Does he envision himself as having divine rights and someone like Ryan Anderson as deserving of stoning? This boggles the mind.

However, when the roles are reversed, the victimizer turned victim begs for mercy and justice. The formerly uncivil soul treated with incivility protests the hatred and contempt. "Unfair!" come the shouts. Why can't the *Times* reporter recognize this while he's spewing his contempt? He wants others to abide by the Golden Rule when communicating with him but refuses that right to Ryan Anderson.

I have observed this avoidance of the Golden Rule spilling over into marriages, workplaces, and other daily communication as well.

One woman carried around a book in front of her husband with the title, in effect, *How to Live with an Evil Man*. She was mad at him and wanted him to change, so she used uncivil treatment to motivate him to love her! When he fumed in anger, it defeated her because it confirmed her deepest fears: "He doesn't love me." However, what would she feel if her husband carried around a book titled *How to Live with an Evil Woman*?

Though the end can be worthy (to be loved and respected), when each spouse uses unholy means (unloving and disrespectful words and actions), it will not achieve those ends. We must treat others as we would want them to treat us. To deny this makes us arrogant, or fools, or both.

BACK TO THE ASSESSMENT

For the remainder of part 2, I invite you to consider more fully the twenty descriptors of those who speak unkindly that you read about in the self-assessment. Did any of these remind you of the inner script you speak to yourself and others about why you can be unkind at times when communicating?

As I studied more closely the twenty descriptors for those who speak unkindly at times, I noticed connections between many—what I call clusters:

- If you want to speak your mind with kindness, you must focus on being *caring with your words* (chapter 7).
- To steer away from being cold, distant, and unfeeling, you must work on being *sensitive with your words* (chapter 8).
- Though your natural instinct may be to blame others, if you are to speak your mind with kindness, you must learn to become *responsible with your words* (chapter 9).
- Finally, you must fight against the urge to bemoan every little adversity that comes your way, tempting you to speak unkindly toward others, but be *resilient with your words* to exhibit grace and kindness despite your circumstances (chapter 10).

As part 2 unfolds, we will consider each of these clusters of communication as we learn how to speak our minds with kindness.

CHAPTER 7

CARING WITH YOUR WORDS

None of us will escape life without experiencing bad days or even a bad moment within a perfectly fine day when, having become irritated, we snap at someone. Thankfully, a weak moment does not make for an unkind person. However, this does not mean one has the right to speak unkindly to others for no other reason than they are mean-spirited and uncharitable. Unfortunately, speaking this way sometimes appears to work out well for some people. Their view is that, if you get your way in the end, is that not proof that it pays to be unkind to others?

However, to speak our minds kindly, as God intends, we must move from speaking with cruelty to choosing words that sound kind. I believe, in the long run, a person who speaks the truth kindly will have significant influence.

Cruel communication is bullying, retaliating, vanquishing, intolerant, and abusive. People who are cruel communicators employ intimidation to get their way (might makes right), subscribe to an "eye for an eye" perspective when feeling wronged, seek to defeat the opposition by meanly attacking who they are as a person, cannot stomach the other person or their position and convey this disgust, and angrily threaten abuse to achieve their own ends.

How interesting that many believe such communication empowers them.

On the other hand, caring communication is gentle, benevolent, affirming, tolerant, and peaceable. Caring communicators tell the truth uncompromisingly yet politely and courteously, try to express a blessing on the heels of being cursed, acknowledge valid perspectives graciously, patiently understand that others will hold contrary beliefs, and strive to be conciliatory in resolving differences. Caring communicators never compromise the truth; during the dialogue, they set forth their contention with conviction. But they see no reason for being cruel about it.

Ultimately, the real winners in life are those who commit to being compassionate, kindhearted, and generous as they live in this world of conflict and competition. Every day, in every situation, we get to choose how we want to live; and the goodwilled person chooses to be kind. That doesn't mean we are to become pushovers who run from confrontation, for we should believe soundly in Scripture's call to speak the truth in love (Eph. 4:15). Though occasionally we will miss the mark, we should strive every day to speak kindly to everyone and at all times.

In this first chapter on speaking your mind with kindness, let's consider opposite ends of the spectrum that most of us glide back and forth on throughout our lives: the kind and the unkind. The fierce and the loving. The cruel and the caring. Though it may not be your intent to communicate unkindly, is there a specific area in which you struggle more than others? Where is God challenging you to speak in a more caring and kind way?

BULLYING VERSUS GENTLE

Bullying: When I am mean-spirited, it works. When I intimidate, I get my way.

Gentle: My gentle demeanor and kind words can break down others' walls, encourage teamwork, prove winsome, and maintain my good reputation. Therefore, I do not use bullying and intimidating tactics.

It is difficult to argue against the short-term results of bullying. Bullying "works." Telling your classmate to give you money or you'll give him a bloody nose can put cash in your pocket. Getting ugly with a waiter about your overcooked steak can get you a free meal. You raise your voice at a retailer, demanding a refund, and presto, it works. You threaten to leave the relationship, and your partner changes their behavior. You tell the landlord you intend to sue because of the broken pipes, and he not only replaces the pipes but also paints your apartment.

We are unkind because bullying proves time after time to have better short-term results than being gentle.

But we need to ask ourselves, *Can I get what I want only by intimidation? Can I not use my good heart to motivate others?*

Quality people believe that our own character and appealing to the good character in others best motivates people. We believe civility and gentleness most effectively protect and advance our interests in the long-term.

When people feel that we are loving and respectful, they move in our direction and seek to help us. Over time, people who choose to be gentle, loving, and respectful influence others because others prefer to be influenced that way.

Before we communicate we need to ask, *Will this correspondence, voice message, or discussion sound mean-spirited or courteous?*

SPEAK YOUR MIND WITH KINDNESS:

Emerson's Checklist for Gentle Communication

- ☐ Do I believe that a gentle demeanor and kind words have the power to break down walls where barriers have been erected?
- ☐ Do I agree that being gentle in my communication may take more strength than bullying or demanding people do as I say?
- ☐ Do I agree with Proverbs 15:1 that a gentle answer turns away wrath?
- ☐ Do I value being winsome and maintaining a good reputation, best resulting from speaking the truth in love when necessary?
- ☐ Do I seek to empathize with others and kindly listen to their concerns even though I feel they have neglected to treat me this way?
- ☐ Do I maintain a gentle demeanor during a conflict because I strive to focus on the solution rather than taking up an offense and attacking?
- ☐ Do I refrain from tactics in communication that seek to intimidate people to comply and conform?
- ☐ Do I have self-awareness when I am hurt, frustrated, or angry, and acknowledge that these three act as culprits against a gentle response?

- ☐ Do I discern that I can misinterpret a conflict with another and then react in an unkind way because of my misread?
- ☐ Do I rebound by seeking forgiveness when I fall prey to an unkind response?

RETALIATING VERSUS BENEVOLENT

Retaliating: I'm mean only when others are unkind to me; it's an eye for an eye.

Benevolent: I choose to be a kind person who returns good for bad, which allows me to speak the truth about another's lack of kindness rather than stooping to their level with tit-for-tat vindictiveness.

Retaliation is comparable to the sting of a honeybee. After a bee stings its victim, its barbed stinger cannot be pulled out. If the bee does try to pull it out, it instead rips out its abdomen and digestive tract and dies from the rupture. Retaliation is our attempt to sting another. Even if we succeed at inflicting a mortal wound on the other, it ends in double graves.

Imagine how you would feel if an associate at work, in front of others, made an unkind remark about the outfit you're wearing and then added, "But that's nothing compared to losing the Houston account." Humiliated, you would feel hurt and then angry. You would want to hit back to even the score. After all, you have your dignity, and responding with hostility and contempt would send the message "Don't you dare treat me as you did the other day, or there will be a price to pay."

But this "eye for eye, tooth for tooth" retaliation reduces you to your associate's level (Ex. 21:24). To convict the other, you need to act on the wisdom of the ages: "If your enemy is hungry, feed him; if he is thirsty, give him something to drink. In doing this, you will heap burning coals on his head" (Rom. 12:20 NIV).

Before responding to someone's unkindness, ask yourself if what you are about to say is rooted in retaliation. Evening the score will only keep the retaliation going. Another approach is to show a desire to empathize with the other person's needs. Doing so can hopefully bring about mutual understanding concerning the issue rather than escalating attacks on each other.

SPEAK YOUR MIND WITH KINDNESS:

Emerson's Checklist for Benevolent Communication

- ☐ Do I accept, albeit sadly, that some people have issues and their toxic tendencies spill over onto others, including me?
- ☐ Do I refuse to bite back when bitten, since that feeds a cycle of negativity, so I seek to take the high road and return good for bad?
- ☐ Do I refuse to sacrifice my peace of mind and moral compass to retaliate against someone who wronged me?
- ☐ Do I kindly speak the truth about how another's adverse treatment of me hurts me by saying, "What happened here hurts me"?
- ☐ Do I exercise a forgiving spirit toward those who wrong me, even though that differs from absolving them of all wrongdoing?
- ☐ Do I let go of anger and bitterness, since that ruins my well-being?
- ☐ Do I see the wisdom in responding to unkindness with kindness and then truthfulness about their unkindness?
- ☐ Do I recognize that "hurting people hurt people" like me, so I seek to understand what is underneath their negative, unkind remarks, and I do so while maintaining a kind and respectful demeanor?
- ☐ Do I look for opportunities to do random acts of kindness for the person who does not treat me kindly?
- ☐ Do I ask God to help me be kind and benevolent and guard against the desire to plot revenge?

VANQUISHING VERSUS AFFIRMING

Vanquishing: To win, I'll lie and dishonor my competition. My end justifies my means.

Affirming: As a secure and value-driven person, I kindly compliment others' achievements, even when they outshine mine, and though this praise could contribute to their advantage over me, I am comfortable being truthful and validating about their character and diligence.

Baseball manager Leo Durocher was reportedly the first to say, "Nice guys finish last."[1] Winning demands toughness, but some add ruthlessness. Some adhere to the idea that in order to win, one may need to be cruel, mean and demeaning, mad and mouthy.

However, nice guys *do* win. Just ask former NFL quarterbacks Peyton and Eli Manning, who each won two Super Bowls. If we are decent, friendly, and agreeable, we can still win. We can vanquish fairly by our superior play.

What is interesting is that when people cannot win on the merits of their performance, products, or positions, they are tempted to cross a line and speak horribly of the opponent, perhaps even lying. Former presidential candidate Dr. Ben Carson said, "Intelligent people tend to talk about the facts. They don't sit around and call each other names. That's what you can find on a third-grade playground."[2] But mudslinging often brings victory. So it comes down to the type of person you will choose to be.

We all must ask ourselves, *Will I compromise my character and the truth to win? Will I succeed no matter the cost?* For those of us who know what is right and good, *Will I live by the light I possess? Will I remain true to who I am, or will I go over to the dark side?* That doesn't mean every decision will be easy. There are gray areas. But we will not falsely call people evil and do evil so we can cross the line first. That's not a victory; that's a vice.

SPEAK YOUR MIND WITH KINDNESS:

Emerson's Checklist for Affirming Communication

- ☐ Do I refuse to win by lying and dishonoring my competition so I can vanquish them by any means possible?
- ☐ Do I recognize my limited view that produces envy and unkind remarks toward another's success because it only sees their blessings and not the sacrifice and suffering they endured to get there?

- ☐ Do I refuse to belittle another who is a quality person and works diligently with success so I can feel good about myself after this act of unkindness?
- ☐ Do I have it in me to kindly validate others for their character, competency, and credibility without flattery and in honesty?
- ☐ Am I sufficiently secure in my skin about who I am as a person that I freely and kindly affirm another's strengths?
- ☐ Do I see myself as a quality person who considerately affirms others, and in providing honest compliments, I develop more as a quality person?
- ☐ Do I see a connection between my gratefulness and my affirmation of others in that my thankfulness for others results in validation and encouragement?
- ☐ Do I affirm another not because it is expected but because doing so is an opportunity to exemplify who I am as a person?
- ☐ Do I believe that my affirmation, kindly offered, has the potential to start healthy relationships, deepen trust, foster cooperation, and motivate greater productivity?

INTOLERANT VERSUS TOLERANT

Intolerant: I detest and cannot stomach those who hold to beliefs at odds with mine.

Tolerant: I recognize that differing opinions are a reality, and though I might hold contrary convictions and will not compromise them, I treat those who reject my beliefs kindly, with a spirit of tolerance.

We are free to reject the beliefs we deem false. But civil people do not hate those who adhere to systems of belief they find abhorrent. Civility does not mean we sanction their "truth claims." However, to bring them out of their false persuasion, we must show them love and respect. If we don't, we won't win their hearts. Furthermore, we sour them to what we believe.

When we post vile comments about those who differ and wish to silence them, we subscribe to the philosophy that says, "When I deem you wrong, you lose all rights." That only shows the weakness of our own position. I have said over the years, "Let any religion or philosophy be preached alongside me as I preach Jesus Christ. I do not fear their position. I have confidence in the message of Jesus Christ."

Those who are kind and show respect evidence a contentment and confidence in what they believe. Those who silence others show how fearful they are that they are wrong in their supposed truth claims. This doesn't mean we let others control our individual faith communities, only that in the public square we do not show hate, contempt, or violence. Truth carries its own weight, and we should feel confident about this. When we yield to "might makes right," something is inherently wrong in what we believe, and we know it.

All of us must adhere to the idea that we can debate the views of others while defending their right to hold these views.

SPEAK YOUR MIND WITH KINDNESS:

Emerson's Checklist for Tolerant Communication

- ☐ Do I recognize that there will be honest differences of opinion in matters such as economics or social issues, which are not necessarily unbiblical, immoral, or illegal, and I must approach a discussion with kindness and understanding?
- ☐ Do I show a spirit of tolerance toward those who reject my beliefs because I am a person who acts with civility, respect, and kindness regardless?
- ☐ Do I understand that being tolerant of others does not mean I must agree with, endorse, or support their position?
- ☐ Do I know how to live in the tension that when in conflict, both parties can have valid reasons for their position, since in the gray areas, neither is wrong, just different?
- ☐ Do I accept that I can strongly disagree with others and even separate while displaying tolerance and respect for their choices?
- ☐ Do I hold firmly to the assertion that if I am to persuade others to think and believe as I do, I must treat them kindly to engage them in discussions?

- ☐ Do I describe other peoples' positions so well that they feel I understand them, even though they know I do not agree with them?
- ☐ Do I look for common ground and express our similarities as a way of motivating mutual tolerance and kindness?
- ☐ Even though I believe I am right and hold my convictions firmly, do I actively listen—as an open-minded person—to what others believe and invite them to explain the journey that brought them to that place?
- ☐ Do I acknowledge where I have been wrong or limited in my understanding about what I formerly thought when that has been pointed out to me?

ABUSIVE VERSUS PEACEABLE

Abusive: I'm not abusive, and whatever idiot says that better watch their backs.

Peaceable: I used to react with aggression, combativeness, and threats when mad, but this damaged relationships, caused shame, and pushed God away, so I strive to be conciliatory by actively listening, speaking calmly, acknowledging goodwill, and finding common ground—and this works!

The verbal and emotional abuser often is blind to their abuse, mostly because the abuse they are guilty of isn't physical. One strikes not with fists but with words that leave emotional wounds and scars. But verbal abuse shows how empty and unconvincing one feels about the merits of the concern. The abuser doesn't believe that loving and respectful words will carry the message, so they turn toxic to disparage and defame.

Often the abuser feels insecure, inadequate, or rejected. Verbal abuse empowers. The abuser, though, has lost touch with the root issue, which often is the feeling of being unloved and disrespected.

For example, the bagger at the grocery store accidentally drops one of your bags, and all four wine bottles smash on the ground. Enraged, you curse at him. You then seek out the manager and scream, "The service here is always terrible! Every bagger drops bags, every self-checkout is broken, and every aisle has empty shelves. Where did you go to management training—the circus?" Fixated on mistakes, you globalize to "every" and "always." From there you conclude that the staff doesn't care about you. So you spew venom. Your harsh rhetoric evens the score and ensures change.

If the above scenario sounds like your communication, my conjecture is that at the root you feel unloved and disrespected—probably erroneously—and speak abusive words of hate and contempt. Do you see this in yourself? George MacDonald penned, "A beast does not know that he is a beast, and the nearer a man gets to being a beast the less he knows it."[3]

SPEAK YOUR MIND WITH KINDNESS:

Emerson's Checklist for Peaceable Communication

- ☐ Do I recognize that reacting with aggression, combativeness, and threats when angry not only is abusive but precipitates the same in return?
- ☐ Do I see that abusive anger never works in maintaining healthy relationships or advancing God's purposes?
- ☐ Do I see it as fruitless to invalidate, castigate, humiliate, intimidate, and manipulate others?
- ☐ Do I seek forgiveness and reconciliation after being unkind and offensive?
- ☐ Do I prize being conciliatory with people I interface with regularly, since contentiousness leads to misunderstandings, lack of teamwork, and unhappiness?
- ☐ Do I see being a peacemaker as being one who finds a win-win solution, meaning my healthy self-interest matters as much as the other person's?
- ☐ As a peacemaker, do I actively listen, speak calmly, acknowledge goodwill, and find common ground?
- ☐ Do I act on the simple truth that to be a peacemaker, I must have a peaceful demeanor?

- ☐ Do I realize that a peacemaker first articulates others' positions to let them know I fully understand their concerns?
- ☐ Do I turn to a third party, if necessary, for counsel and support to bring about a solution that both parties find mutually satisfying?

CHAPTER 8

SENSITIVE WITH YOUR WORDS

Sometimes we struggle with communicating kindly because we're insensitive to our surroundings or unaware of our unkind tendencies. Our brazenness may not be intentional, or at the very least it isn't our first choice to come across as so brash, but nevertheless people are hurt by our harsh words and reactions.

To learn how to speak our minds kindly, we must avoid speaking necessary truth without considering another's feelings. This is not about withholding the truth but about choosing sensitive words that enable the other person to hear the truth. It is as simple as saying, "Is this the best time to talk?"

An unfeeling communicator is unempathetic, impatient, unmindful, unintentional, and oblivious. They either have no real understanding of another's feelings or don't really care, are in a hurry to convey the truth without considering emotions, don't recognize the heartfelt concerns of the other person, justify their insensitivities by claiming they meant no unkindness, and do not learn from their past unkindness but blame others for being hypersensitive.

On the other side of the equation, sensitive communicators are empathetic, polite, aware, amending, and reflective. They speak kindly because they understand the other's concerns, they are unhurried and warm when communicating an important and necessary truth, they revisit the conversation when realizing they overlooked certain concerns, they repair the damage from earlier insensitive comments, and they keep on assessing their communication to limit unkindness.

For some more so than others, a daily effort is required to be aware of the needs and wants of others so they may respond wisely even when the circumstances may be unfair to them. Though selfless consideration like this may not be part of our natural makeup, none of us is excused from making an effort to be considerate, polite, and sensitive to the need to show kindness to those around us.

Let's consider struggling communicators who, perhaps unknowingly, come across as more unkind than they actually are. How can they become more aware of and concerned about their need to be sensitive regarding how they communicate?

UNEMPATHETIC VERSUS EMPATHETIC

Unempathetic: I'm no teary-eyed hand holder. The feeble need to toughen up.

Empathetic: I understand others' struggles and approach them with consideration and kindness, not dismissive judgmentalism, when addressing the burdens and shortcomings that they are navigating.

I know of one leader who expressed this unempathetic communication: "I am not going to spoon-feed them like children!" This comment became the straw that broke the camel's back, and he lost a half dozen of his loyal staff, who felt defeated by his condescending posture.

Such a view overstates the case as a way of excusing the call to be empathetic. When we can create a straw man of what an empathetic person ought to be, we can blow it over quite easily. We claim that if we must bawl when others weep, then we must reject the expectation of comforting those in pain. After all, we don't bawl.

What it does reveal is that we have chosen to be insensitive and unaware. We characterize people in need as feeble, not us as unfeeling; we profile them as pathetic, not us as unempathetic. We interpret their true vulnerability as false victimhood. We contend that they pretend.

The truth is, when someone turns to you at a vulnerable time, this is a great compliment to you. The person isn't asking you to cry your eyes out. Instead, they wish for you to see through their eyes. That's what empathy is. Why profile this person as pitiful and weak when they turn to you and your strengths for understanding?

Most people don't want us to be responsible for them. Most aren't looking for us to heal them but to understand their wounds. They are not asking for us to be kin but kind.

SPEAK YOUR MIND WITH KINDNESS:

Emerson's Checklist for Empathetic Communication

- ☐ Do I first listen to understand others' feelings and thoughts—as an expression of kindness—when they share their concerns or burdens with me?
- ☐ After listening, do I repeat what they expressed to know if I heard them correctly?
- ☐ Do I readily see others' heavyheartedness and respond to them with language that sounds kind and caring to them?
- ☐ Do I express, "I am honored that you took me into your confidence"?
- ☐ Do I look for stresses and sorrows I have encountered, and if parallel with others' circumstances, do I share this to let them know I identify with them?
- ☐ Do I distinguish empathy from endorsement, which means I can feel another's pain without agreeing with and approving of why they feel that way or how they are coping?
- ☐ Though at times I cannot imagine struggling where another struggles, do I avoid being dismissive and judgmental, the opposite of kindness and empathy?
- ☐ Do I steer clear of rudely and crudely saying, "Look, I don't have time to hear you complain; toughen up and quit being such a wimp"?
- ☐ Do I realize that the best way to support this person with my kindness is to think through a plan on how they can rebound and be resilient?
- ☐ Do I maintain involvement, since empathy is not a one-and-done cry session?

IMPATIENT VERSUS POLITE

Impatient: I don't have time for polite greetings but need to get to my point.

Polite: I am patient and warm when communicating a difficult but necessary truth with another, and I refrain from hurrying the conversation, interrupting, and making it too brief.

Jumping right in on our urgent point is okay when the relationship is solid. However, if the other person does not have a relationship with us, they will most likely interpret our to-the-point remarks as abrupt and then seek to decipher the tone. Most people interpret abruptness as the communicator feeling negative or indifferent.

We shouldn't forget the old saying, "You can catch more flies with honey than with vinegar." Sour, impolite demands will not achieve our ends better than politeness will, not long-term, when we live in community. For example, what does the customer service worker for Peterson's Oil Company think when a customer calls, complaining, "You overcharged me by $175. You got it wrong. Here is my account number. Get it right and make it right"?

This customer has a justifiable concern and isn't evil for calling, but the worker will most likely then be in a defensive posture. While the customer might get what they want, could they have gotten the same results with a different communication approach?

When we blurt out what we feel is unfair, the hearer assumes we are ticked. Why not instead address the concern with "It might just be an honest oversight, but I believe I was overcharged $175. Could you let me know what happened? And if it is an honest mistake, I'm fine with you crediting my next month's bill, if that's easier for you"?

Do we actually think the first approach achieves our ends better than the second approach? This returns to the Golden Rule. If the roles were reversed, we would appreciate the second approach and likely respond differently. Yes, it would demand that the person not jump to the conclusion that we were trying to pull one over on them and instead allow us to research and explain our side; but the "honey" method would catch our attention, and this patient demeanor would free us to admit and correct our mistake.

SPEAK YOUR MIND WITH KINDNESS:

Emerson's Checklist for Polite Communication

- ☐ Do I care enough for others that I am willing to communicate a tough truth they need to hear?
- ☐ Do I have a reputation for being patient and warm when communicating a difficult truth?
- ☐ Do I select a time that is best not only for other people so they can be most available to listen but also for me so that I do not hurry the conversation in a way that feels unkind?
- ☐ Do I prepare for the tough conversation by making sure my facts are correct and that I will speak kindly and clearly about what is necessary?
- ☐ Do I communicate clearly and kindly without withholding necessary information or adding unnecessary information?
- ☐ Do I maintain empathy and humility, even though the other has fallen short and needs to hear the truth, doing so because "there but for the grace of God go I"?
- ☐ Do I ready myself emotionally for another's defensive reaction, since that is a normal response when hearing a hard truth?
- ☐ Do I speak calmly and respectfully if the conversation turns back at me negatively and chaotically?
- ☐ Do I remain open-minded to new information that could change my opinion about the hard truth I thought I needed to deliver?
- ☐ Do I commit to moving forward by serving others in any way I can, which may mean enlisting the support of others?

UNMINDFUL VERSUS AWARE

Unmindful: Truthfully, I am preoccupied and don't have time to think about how others might be inadvertently hurt by my neglect.

Aware: I am sensitive to the needs of others and am attentive to showing kindness by immediately responding or rebounding when I innocently overlook their concerns.

The husband forgets their anniversary, as his wife waits for him to express his love in a text. The teen forgets to call home, leaving the parents fearful for a short period. The manager forgets to cancel the meeting, and several people show up.

Preoccupation makes us unmindful of very practical things.

Few who are preoccupied intend to be unloving and disrespectful. We can be absorbed in other important matters. The husband who forgets his anniversary can be engrossed in solving a client's insurance problem, doing so with a compassionate concern to help. The manager can be working on a health package for his employees, doing so with such obsession he forgets they are waiting in the conference room for him. The teen is a teen out having fun, that's all. As one thing takes up our attention, it distracts us from something else. We've all been there.

It isn't what we say that is unkind but what we don't say that proves unkind. The enemy of the good is not always the bad but our failure to do what is the best. When others have a need for our kind communication and we neglect them, we hurt them. A parent never saying "I love you" to their child is more painful than the child shouting "I hate you" to the parent.

A man said to me once, "My wife complains to me about our marriage. But I'm home every evening. I don't go out drinking, and there are no other women." His argument reminds me of the husband who declares, "I don't beat my wife." That's great, but do you love her, and does she feel that love?

Some of us are horrible communicators, and it has nothing to do with what we say. It has everything to do with what we don't say.

SPEAK YOUR MIND WITH KINDNESS:

Emerson's Checklist for Aware Communication

- ☐ Do I see myself as sensitive to and even empathetic of the true needs of others in my sphere of influence and respond when I can?

- ☐ Do I think about the potential needs of others and plan ahead of time to meet those needs?
- ☐ Do I have the wisdom not to promise to help more than possible so I do not ignite unrealistic expectations?
- ☐ Do I rebound by kindly serving others' needs when I discover I had overlooked their distress?
- ☐ Do I accept that sometimes the actual needs of those in my sphere of influence exceed the resources of time, counsel, and money I can provide, and I must collaborate with others?
- ☐ Do I understand that, like the Good Samaritan, I may not directly care for the needy soul but invite an "innkeeper" to bring help and healing?
- ☐ Do I recognize that I am not the savior of the world who can do everything for everybody every day?
- ☐ Do I agree that I do no one any good when I neglect my own needs and burn out in meeting the needs of others?
- ☐ Do I not let myself be overwhelmed by the excessive true needs around me but plod at doing what I can with small acts of kindness?
- ☐ Do I follow up with individuals I have helped, asking how they are doing?
- ☐ Do I periodically step back and do an inventory on how well I am responding to the true needs of people?

UNINTENTIONAL VERSUS AMENDING

Unintentional: I didn't mean to be insensitive or coldhearted; I was just upset.

Amending: I humbly acknowledge that I meant no ill will, though I reacted unkindly, and I will change my ways and make things right.

Most of us do not intend to hurt other people. But because our unkind words slip out without ill will does not mean other people should let the verbal bullets bounce off them like marshmallows. When I accidentally spill hot water on the person sitting next to me, they still get scalded.

A common situation I've seen as I counsel couples is where one partner tells a friend something private about the relationship, and that information gets back to the other partner. The first partner wasn't intending to be unkind; they wanted to vent or find emotional support from a friend. But when that information gets back to their partner, they can be wounded or feel betrayed.

Or consider a person who is overlooked for a promotion for the second time in a year. One day in the boardroom he lets loose and lambastes the company for advancing employees who are less competent. After finally "speaking his truth," he realizes his lack of maturity in how he expressed what he still believed to be unfair. He can either amend the situation by taking ownership for his immature way of speaking the truth and humbly asking for an opportunity to show himself a loyal employee, or he can try to justify what he did, saying, "I was just really upset in that moment. Sorry if I offended anybody."

Unkind words scald. Whether accidental or intentional, the effects are pretty much the same.

But here's the real challenge. When the hot water gets spilled repeatedly, those around us no longer believe in the innocence of the claim that it was an accident every time, and our reputation is undermined.

If we are regularly apologizing for unkind speaking, we need to step back and consider if we need better self-understanding. Just because we did not intend to be mean doesn't mean we are not mean—if you know what I mean.

SPEAK YOUR MIND WITH KINDNESS:

Emerson's Checklist for Amending Communication

- ☐ Do I fully realize my tendency to make excuses for what happened and naturally default to justifying myself and even blaming the other person?
- ☐ Do I hold back on saying, "You ought not to be upset by something I never meant to do; you are too easily offended and immature"?
- ☐ Do I acknowledge how difficult it is to confess that I was unkind when there was no intention of being unkind and I think the other person is hypersensitive?

- ☐ On the heels of an unintentional mistake that hurt another, which I now see as an unkind action, do I humbly acknowledge I had no ill will?
- ☐ Do I avoid blaming the other person for my appearance of being unkind but take responsibility in better representing myself?
- ☐ Do I humbly express regret for my appearance of unkindness?
- ☐ Do I not only apologize to people who feel I treated them unkindly but also ask for their forgiveness?
- ☐ In making amends, do I repair what needs repairing fairly and unbegrudgingly?
- ☐ Do I change my ways and make things right with the other person when I see how my words or actions appear unkind?
- ☐ Do I commit to a plan of action that helps me guard against doing things that appear unkind, even though I was never motivated to be unkind?

OBLIVIOUS VERSUS REFLECTIVE

Oblivious: I think others are hearing things; I don't hear unkindness in my voice at all.

Reflective: I strive to be a self-examining individual who is not only conscious of the impact of my unkind words on others but open to feedback on how I may not always hear what another is trying to say so I can improve my interactive communication.

Do people often ask you, "Are you angry about something?" Do family members ask, "What did you mean in that e-mail? Is there a problem between us?" Has a coworker asked you, "I got the feeling from your voicemail that you're peeved. Are you?"

These questions may provide a clue that we are oblivious to our tone even if we mean no unkindness. If we are constantly replying to others, "I didn't mean it the way it sounded to you," then we have a problem in what we voice and what we write.

When it comes to your face-to-face interactions, a great question to ask yourself is this: *Would a blind person be attracted to me?* Blind people hear the tone of your voice and your word choices, and they feel the gentle touch of your hands. They have no idea what you look like. A drop-dead gorgeous movie star might get away with sounding unkind and disrespectful to others, but a blind person would be turned off to her. What's a pretty face to a blind person?

Some of us are good-hearted, caring individuals, but we are oblivious to our tone of unkindness. It could be our deep voices and matter-of-fact way of communicating that make others feel we are mad, our high-pitched voice that makes others feel attacked and on edge, or our blunt writing style that makes others feel we lack compassion. There is a discrepancy between who we want to be and see ourselves to be and how we actually sound in voice and writing. But with honest self-reflection, we can improve our communication. We need only evaluate what we are about to communicate. *Will this be heard or read as loving and respectful, or will the other person incorrectly read between the lines that I am peeved?*

The words we say are only half of our communication. The other half is what others hear. Will we hear what they hear? Or will we obstinately claim, "They are hearing things"?

SPEAK YOUR MIND WITH KINDNESS:

Emerson's Checklist for Reflective Communication

- ☐ Do I hear what others say about my unkind reactions, since I do not intend to discredit myself as oblivious and callous?
- ☐ Do I resist a dogmatism that declares, "I think others are hearing things; I don't hear unkindness in my voice at all"?
- ☐ Do I try to humbly consider others' feedback on my unkind expressions or what they deem as insensitive?
- ☐ Do I remain humble in that everyone has blind spots, and one of mine can be putting my foot in my mouth when I say something inappropriate and offensive?
- ☐ Do I apologize for those moments I seem heedless and heartless in such things as my sour looks, condescending words, and disrespectful reactions?

- ☐ Do I adjust how I communicate instead of dismissing another's comment about appearing harsh and disdainful?
- ☐ Do I recognize that specific individuals can be hypersensitive? But given several others have confronted me on my unthinking unkindness, do I own up to this as my issue and come up with a plan to address this appropriately?
- ☐ Do I agree that hearing about my unkind behavior from others can be challenging, but to be the best version of myself, I accept constructive feedback as a necessary step for growth in overcoming shortcomings?
- ☐ When others make me more aware, which helps me be more credible and fruitful, do I thank them?
- ☐ Do I engage with others for accountability purposes as we reflect on my communication style? Is self-awareness about how I communicate what I think and feel one of the items I want my feet held to the fire for?

CHAPTER 9

RESPONSIBLE WITH YOUR WORDS

"It's their fault, not mine!" Too often, that's the excuse we give when others are hurt by our careless words. People misinterpret us and are hurt, and we have the audacity to blame them. We say they're too sensitive. Or we tell them to chill out—this is just how we talk, so stop taking offense. In our eyes, this is more their problem than it is ours. If they don't like the way we communicate, then they're the ones who need to make an adjustment, or so we believe.

To learn how to speak our minds kindly, we come to a crossroad between being responsible for our words no matter the conversation or blaming others for our rudeness, malice, and coldness.

As mentioned earlier, an unkind communicator is blaming. They are not responsible, but others are; and if anyone deserves any blame, it's not them. Their words are blunt, resentful, conditional, trendy, and family-bred. By these I mean such unkind communicators are brutally harsh, are infuriated when feeling dishonored, are of the mindset that the other person must earn their kindness, are going to talk as the culture talks (and in this culture kindness is a sign of weakness), and are talking as their family talks, so others must live with it.

Juxtaposed, a kind communicator is a responsible communicator. Their words are thoughtful, gracious, unconditional, time-tested, and accountable. They think about landing the inconvenient truth kindly, control their righteous indignation while kindly addressing the provocation and remedies, seek to be verbally respectful and kind even when another dishonors them, resist using the "everybody talks this way" line, and do not use upbringing as an excuse to say, "This is the way my family talked, so get over it."

Yes, people can misinterpret our honest, goodwilled communications when our styles or upbringings are different from theirs. Certainly some people struggle with being overly sensitive, but that doesn't excuse us from taking ownership for speaking and acting with kindness, even when others don't take ownership of their own communication struggles. We can't control how others act or react, but we can control ourselves. We are held responsible for our words, as well as for doing all we can to clarify any misunderstandings when we offend people unintentionally.

Let's look at those who may not be mature enough to consider that sometimes the problem might just be found in the mirror. How can those struggling in this way learn to consider how they can be a kinder and more thoughtful communicator, when everything inside them wants to place the blame on the one misinterpreting them?

BLUNT VERSUS THOUGHTFUL

Blunt: I'm not harsh but brutally honest in telling others what they don't want to hear.

Thoughtful: Being brutally honest can come across harshly, so I responsibly think about the time, place, and way to kindly and tactfully share my opinions on an inconvenient but necessary truth.

One woman wrote to me, saying, "The truth is the truth . . . it really doesn't matter how you communicate it. How the other person receives the truth lies in their ability or emotional frame of mind to receive it."

On the one hand, I see her point. Some are sitting on unresolved issues from childhood, and that spills over onto us. We can communicate the truth in the best of manners, but the person can only react and attack like a wounded bear.

On the other hand, sometimes we unlovingly dump the truth on people and blame them for not receiving it. We claim we're brutally honest, but we are just brutal.

Though some who hear us are unteachable, some of us do not have a loving and respectful demeanor when writing or speaking. People shut down on us because we are blunt and rude, but we blind ourselves to how we communicate.

When others do not respond to our communication, we need to look at our communication style. Is the other person incapable of hearing what we have to say? Or are we abrupt, brusque, and curt?

Do we see ourselves as some kind of honorable prosecutor who upholds the truth but is impolite? Do people feel we are putting them on trial? Are people on the defensive because we are offensive? Does this have little to do with truth and everything to do with our lack of love?

SPEAK YOUR MIND WITH KINDNESS:

Emerson's Checklist for Thoughtful Communication

- ☐ Do I detect that when someone closes off to what I communicate, it may not be their lack of humility or teachability but rather my tendency to be rash, tactless, condescending, and demanding?
- ☐ Do I avoid unkind bluntness, since it shuts a person down, ignites unnecessary conflict, and damages relationships?
- ☐ Do I take steps to steer clear of rudeness, since it impedes communication and thwarts reasonable solutions?
- ☐ Do I see others as equal in value to me before God and therefore take seriously their thoughts about the situation I wish to address?
- ☐ Do I consider the best time and place for my listener?
- ☐ Do I recognize that thoughtfulness does not mean withholding the truth but exploring the wisest ways to communicate the truth?
- ☐ Do I acknowledge that I have biases and blind spots, so I may not see the whole picture as I prepare to communicate what I deem best for the other person and me?
- ☐ Do I think about what is true, necessary, and clear before I communicate, and then about how to say it kindly?

- ☐ In sharing an inconvenient truth, am I sensitive in tone and word choice while conveying the whole truth, so as to soften the hearts of my listeners and energize them to be receptive to my thoughts?
- ☐ Do I have goodwill and a pure motive when sharing an inconvenient truth, and do I convey this to my listener?

RESENTFUL VERSUS GRACIOUS

Resentful: I have been dishonored and treated unfairly. I'm infuriated and gruff.

Gracious: I am composed when dishonored, responsibly controlling my anger, and then as best I can, I kindly assert that I have boundaries against such mistreatment as I seek a peaceful solution, going more than halfway in extending unmerited favor.

I'm amazed at the evil some people have been subjected to. I once met a gentleman who had been tortured for years by a Communist regime. And several women have reported to me the sexual abuse they endured as children.

What strikes me about these particular people is that they did not become bitter but better. The injustice of life didn't cause them to become resentful and unkind. This is why I find it peculiar when others in lesser situations turn resentful toward any and all. God didn't allow them to be born into a wealthy family, so they blame Him for every financial strain the rest of their lives. Or their parents could not fund their education, so they have to take two years off from college to work and are bitter because of it.

In all these circumstances, nothing evil happened. Instead, they didn't get what they wanted and turned bitter. They turned cynical and see everyone as intending to mistreat them, unless given proof to the contrary. Most often they dish it out first before anybody has a chance to mistreat them. E-mails manifest a chip on the shoulder. Texts have an unkind edge. Phone calls are unpleasant. All of this is out of self-protection, but it only causes people to profile them as resentful and gruff.

Might this describe you? Are you infuriated by past injustices, but you have turned bitter and take it out on people who have never wronged you? Do you tend to be unkind in your communication with the people around you because others hurt you years ago? Is this who you want to be? Sometimes the most sensitive people turn insensitive and do toward others what was done to them—which is an amazing irony. Those who were dishonored earlier in life turn unloving and gruff to prevent further hurts. But dishonoring others does not lead to honor.

Returning to those I mentioned previously who maintained graciousness despite the evils and injustices committed against them, how were they able to pull off this supernatural feat? You may be familiar with the often-quoted scripture "I can do all things through [Christ] who strengthens me" (Phil. 4:13). But are you aware that the apostle Paul was writing this verse from prison? "Not that I speak from need," the gracious prisoner wrote, "for I have learned to be content in whatever circumstances I am. I know how to get along with little, and I also know how to live in prosperity; in any and every circumstance I have learned the secret of being filled and going hungry, both of having abundance and suffering need. I can do all things through Him who strengthens me" (vv. 11–13).

Even when one's dismal and depressing circumstances do not show signs of improving, a resentful communicator can still become gracious through the strength and power of Jesus.

SPEAK YOUR MIND WITH KINDNESS:

Emerson's Checklist for Gracious Communication

- ☐ Do I recognize that there are good people who act bad (and evil people who act bad), and I can be the victim of their hostilities?
- ☐ Do I know that anger, resentment, and bitterness can be rooted in righteous indignation over unjust treatment?
- ☐ As much as I could let myself resent and retaliate, do I face others' dishonor and mistreatment of me without igniting negative emotions and actions?

- ☐ Do I have the wisdom to know that some people are unwilling to express genuine sorrow and seek my forgiveness, but that does not mean I am destined to be hurt and bitter?
- ☐ Do I accept that the person who mistreated me must confess their transgression and show genuine repentance by their actions in order to potentially restore the relationship, but I cannot coerce that, since that must come from their heart?
- ☐ Though I may not have initially responded with grace and composure when dishonored and mistreated, am I determined to truthfully confront others in such a way that they feel my unmerited favor and inner peace?
- ☐ Do I invite the person who mistreated me to tell me their perspective on what happened, why it happened, and how to move forward? Will I seek to understand as best I can and look to affirm what I can?
- ☐ As much pain as I might be in, do I approach the situation with an open mind and a determination to see things from the other's perspective without compromising what I need to happen going forward?
- ☐ Do I engage the other person with the hope that my forgiving spirit, graciousness, composure, and fair boundaries for discussion will bring a workable resolution?
- ☐ Do I see this conflict and hopeful resolution as an opportunity to model how to be gracious yet truthful and firm before family and friends?
- ☐ Do I know that as far as it depends on me, I am to live at peace with people but some do not intend to resolve or reconcile?

CONDITIONAL VERSUS UNCONDITIONAL

Conditional: People who don't earn my respect don't deserve it. Period.

Unconditional: I refuse to treat others with contempt because I feel they haven't earned my respect; instead, I am a kind and respectful person regardless of the conditions.

When we deem another person as not having earned our respect, does this give us license to show him or her disrespect? A person wrote to me once, saying, "Respect was not something I learned in my childhood. My parents have a very verbally destructive marriage, so I learned well how to be ugly with my voice and words. I learned that respect is earned. Either you work hard to earn it or you don't."

When we have the attitude that we are justified in showing others disrespect because they have failed to meet our standard, what makes us think they will keep responding to us in the long-term? Disrespect doesn't influence hearts.

In today's world, we need to keep two groups with whom we communicate in mind. Group one consists of people in our lives. Group two consists of people "out there," like those on the internet. Some of us are uncivil toward people "out there," but this attitude also spills over onto our everyday interactions with people in our personal world. We can't think we can treat those "out there" with contempt without it affecting our daily interactions. The truth is, we are who we are. This disrespectful demeanor inevitably shows up at work, when dating, in our families, and among neighbors.

This isn't about others being worthy of respect; this is about us communicating our message respectfully even if the other doesn't deserve it. This is unconditional respect, which seems like a contradiction but simply means being a respectful person regardless of another's actions. Does this mean we give others license to do whatever they selfishly demand? No. Unconditional respect means we confront their wrongdoings respectfully. We do not become uncivil because they are. Who they fail to be does not determine who we will be.

SPEAK YOUR MIND WITH KINDNESS:

Emerson's Checklist for Unconditional Communication

- ☐ Do I agree that hostility and contempt undermine effective communication and positive cooperation, put others on the defensive, and ignite their counteraggression, creating a cycle of negativity?
- ☐ Do I perceive the error in thinking that says, "If I show respect to this person who has acted in unrespectable ways, that means I must respect bad behavior, and I won't respect what is unrespectable"?

- ☐ Do I reject the false belief commonly held that proudly pronounces, "Because they have not earned my respect, they don't deserve respect, and I don't have to show them respect"?
- ☐ Do I acknowledge that by claiming someone doesn't deserve my respect, I may rationalize and erroneously excuse my lack of respect toward them?
- ☐ Do I understand that showing unconditional respect doesn't demand that I feel admiration for someone who behaved disrespectfully; rather it's based on my character and not governed by negative feelings toward the other person?
- ☐ Do I believe that showing unconditional respect and love means I will act independently of who the other person fails to be, even when they fall short of meeting my appropriate expectations?
- ☐ Do I understand that unconditional respect and love involve showing positive regard for the other person's spirit regardless of circumstances, while confronting unrespectful and unloving behavior?
- ☐ Do I approach people with unconditional positive regard not only because this is who I choose to be but because this person is created in God's image, and I distinguish the sinner from the sin?
- ☐ Do I understand that showing unconditional respect during conflicts requires confronting unrespectable behavior respectfully, without giving in to bitterness and contempt, as it is not conditioned by the external situation but by who I choose to be as a person?
- ☐ Do I recognize that an approach of having unconditional respect is the most powerful influence on the hearts of others over time, since people feel valued rather than demeaned and invalidated by my hostility and contempt?

TRENDY VERSUS TIME-TESTED

Trendy: People need to get over it and get with it. This is how we talk and text now.

Time-Tested: Not everything from the past merits continuation if it is outdated; even so, I am committed to conserving proven and universal virtues like kindness, responsibly accepting these as immutable truths.

Some find it ridiculous to try to communicate with awareness of and sensitivity to the feelings of others. At one level this is understandable. Some are triggered emotionally by the smallest of offenses. However, many communicators today speak abusively of those they deem wrong on any number of issues. Instead of seeing their poor verbal manners as a mirror of the kind of people they are, they think they are better than this other person, who as a lesser human being deserves their coarse comments. "This is who I am, and this is the way my generation talks."

There is also a syrupy politeness that can cover over a subversive agenda. I'm not recommending false and superficial manners but true and sincere manners. I'm recommending the cessation of coarse talking and texting and, instead, always communicating in ways that sound loving and respectful. Ultimately, this is the most effective way of persuading and affecting hearts.

I appeal to you to be the type of person who you would turn to if in a predicament. The type of people who are always dropping the f-bomb not only show their limited vocabulary but also appear angry. Do folks turn to such people in crisis? Do you? Vocabulary reveals the heart, according to Jesus (Matt. 12:34).

Much of this over-the-top language is popular today, but it will be short-lived. By way of analogy, I envision people with tattoos all over their wrinkled bodies at age ninety-two. What seems normal now will appear quite abnormal then.

Unkind, rude, ill-mannered language may be avant-garde for a season but not for a lifetime. What is profanely popular to utter will soon be seen as nothing but the gutter. When we have children who follow our example of profanity and drop the f-bomb in church, we change our word choices. Language matters, and we know it.

Old-fashioned manners may be old, but they are still in fashion. Traditional ways of speaking with respect, politeness, and consideration can be defined as timeless and universal. They are proven in fostering the most positive of relationships. The trendy way of expression is not worth offending, undermining credibility, evidencing a limited vocabulary, appearing unprofessional, and inspiring a child's imitation.

SPEAK YOUR MIND WITH KINDNESS:

Emerson's Checklist for Time-Tested Communication

- ☐ Do I believe there are immutable truths that have stood the test of time—such as speaking what is accurate and necessary in a kind and clear way?
- ☐ Am I committed to conserving proven and universal virtues as foundational and permanent, like speaking truthfully with kindness and clarity?
- ☐ Do I resist the temptation to go along with the crowd that pressures their group to be liars and rude, given it advances their cause, and all the more when observing the utter hypocrisy of this group screaming in reaction to those who rudely lie to them?
- ☐ Do I realize how easy it is to go along mindlessly with what is trendy, like cancel culture, which means silencing others with whom I seriously differ rather than openly dialoguing and respectfully debating as an act of kindness?
- ☐ Do I hold to traditional values like communicating truthfully and kindly because I believe these are vital values necessary for healthy relationships and reflect who I am as a virtuous person, someone who is kind and true?
- ☐ Do I have a conviction about embodying what I espouse and what I expect others to emulate when it comes to true, kind, necessary, and clear communication?
- ☐ In holding to traditional values that I wish to conserve, do I avoid discrediting myself by giving in to an angry and unkind reaction in defending the preservation of kind and true communication?
- ☐ Do I accept that I will never be perfect in my communication, but I am committed to rebounding by expressing sorrow for unkind and untrue comments and seeking forgiveness?

FAMILY-BRED VERSUS ACCOUNTABLE

Family-Bred: People need to chill out. This is how my family of origin reacts in conflict.

Accountable: My upbringing might have instilled in me unacceptable patterns of talking, like yelling, pouting, and stonewalling, but I take responsibility for correcting these negative communication patterns—even meeting in an accountability group—and refuse to blame others for being thin-skinned when I am answerable to God for my unkind and ugly discourse.

Some families deal with their issues by yelling at one another, and then they feel better for a while until the next altercation. Or some shut down in anger until it works out of their system, but they avoid talking about the conflict.

Whether we're talking about outbursts of anger or a total shutdown, this is not a kind, loving, and respectful way of resolving serious tensions. Unfortunately, as adults, this way of dealing with conflicts and stresses in our families of origin often spills over into our daily lives.

Sadly, we make excuses: "This is how I am. This is how my family deals with conflict. You need to chill out. I'm angry now, but I'll get over it soon. Don't take it so personally even though, at the moment, I'm taking it out on you. Give me some time, and I'll be good to go."

I could've used that excuse myself. I saw my dad attempt to strangle my mom. Years later, there were moments that I could feel anger rise in me, the anger I saw in my dad. But I was determined to be different. I consciously said, "I will not be like Dad."

A man wrote to me, "My mother used anger to control me as I was growing up. Therefore, I would interpret any raised and loud voice as someone expressing anger toward me. . . . I would respond by either shutting down or I would retaliate with anger."

I do not minimize the predispositions we have from our families of origin. That is inescapable at one level. However, predispositions must never be interpreted as predestinations. We are not destined to explode or implode because our parents did, and we do not have to treat others the way our parents treated us. We must not buy into that lie. We are free to take a new course, and we must.

Furthermore, to tell others to chill out puts the onus on them to change. No, we need to change. Our default reaction from childhood is a defect from childhood. Our family-of-origin reactions serve not as an explanation but as an excuse. The sooner we own up to this, the sooner we will be more effective communicators.

SPEAK YOUR MIND WITH KINDNESS:

Emerson's Checklist for Accountable Communication

- ☐ Do I reflect on how my upbringing affected my communication style, good and bad?
- ☐ Do I discern what triggers my childish reactions, given I have observed these thin-skinned behaviors in myself?
- ☐ Do I accept the idea that I may have a predisposition toward a negative communication style due to my family of origin, but I reject the notion that this is a predestination to raise my voice, name-call, sulk, and give the silent treatment?
- ☐ Despite what I feel is a negative communication style ingrained in me from my parents, do I take responsibility for how I talk, since I have the inner freedom to change for the better, making an effort to speak what is true, kind, and necessary?
- ☐ If people nag me or neglect me, do I refuse to blame them for my tendency to lash out, since such people do not cause me to be the way I am but reveal the way I am?
- ☐ Do I seek forgiveness when I default to my childhood ways of communicating, which include raising my voice, name-calling, sulking, and silent treatment?
- ☐ To grow as a truthful and kind communicator, do I have a keenness for self-improvement, seeking feedback, and making necessary changes?
- ☐ Do I view myself as a person on a journey developing the best version of myself as a kind and truthful communicator?
- ☐ Do I seek feedback from others I trust and respect as wise and who can affirm my strengths as a communicator but also have

my permission to offer constructive criticism where I am proving ineffective?

- ☐ Do I believe I must give an account to God for every careless word I communicate?

CHAPTER 10

RESILIENT WITH YOUR WORDS

Some people can be unkind for no other reason than because they are immature and self-pitying. They are aware of the need to speak with kindness and love, and they also know that doing so is not a strength of theirs, but they're not interested in going along with the Golden Rule. They will be however they want to be, regardless of how others perceive them.

A crucial aspect to speaking our minds kindly lies within our hearts. Instead of dwelling on injustices, we have the freedom to cultivate resilience. Our communication serves as a mirror reflecting our steady character. As we have seen, Jesus stated, "The mouth speaks out of that which fills the heart" (Matt. 12:34). Our speech is a witness to our beliefs and attitudes. While certain painful and unfair circumstances touch us deeply, we've all encountered individuals who possess the capacity to rebound from hardship without resorting to excessive complaints about life's perceived unfairness. In a hard time, they are not unkind.

Some folks cease speaking kindly because it doesn't work for them due to some woeful fault of their own, so they think; because life is horribly unfair, since others have it so much better; because they refuse to conform to the demanding norms about kind speech when others deserve a piece of their mind; because unkind speech successfully pushes annoying people away; and because when they cannot stand themselves (i.e., self-loathing over their inadequacies), they have little interest in saying kind things.

Conversely, kind communication is resilient. Resilient communication is empowered, grateful, cooperative, friendly, and self-accepting. Instead of bemoaning their plight during tough times, resilient communicators maintain self-control and thus are in control of their words; they regularly seek to give thanks to God and others despite their hardship; they conform to kind speech without feeling this is a convention that undermines autonomy and influence; they have a pattern of communicating in neighborly ways to even bothersome people, since they choose to be amiable while still maintaining boundaries; and they have firmly appropriated God's loving view of them, which prevents self-loathing and unkind remarks.

The goodwilled person is well aware that they have been called to a higher standard of communication. Even in the face of adversity, we should attempt to exhibit grit, optimism, and kindness as we resist self-condemnation, social resentments, and doubt about God's love. Even on a bad day, we should know who we are in God's eyes and remain filled with Christ's love in our hearts. Because of this, we strive to be compassionate, loving, and thankful for all we've been given.

Let's consider those who live as though they report only to themselves. What might it look like if they lived instead knowing that they serve an audience of One?

DEFEATED VERSUS EMPOWERED

Defeated: Showing kindness doesn't return kindness. It backfires. It must be me. I must be to blame.

Empowered: I will not let others' unkindness toward me define who I am, as though I have no worth; instead, I will be confident in God's love for me as His beloved child and act on this. I will be kindhearted even toward the unkind and will not change my course of action or belief that this best enables me to influence people.

When others don't respond to our kindness, some of us move into self-deprecation. We think, *There must be something inherently wrong with me. I'll stop trying to be so kind. It doesn't work.*

Charlie Brown famously said in *Peanuts*, "Nothing takes the taste out of peanut butter quite like unrequited love."[1] Anytime we are genuinely kind, loving, and respectful and are ignored, we feel kicked in the gut. Some of us blame ourselves. We did something wrong—again. However, we have to exercise discernment. If everything we did was truly loving and respectful, we cannot conclude that something is wrong with us simply because the love was not returned.

Sarah, my wife, and I have often asked, on the heels of being mistreated by someone, "Is this our issue or their issue?" We have to be honest. Sometimes it is the other person's problem, not our failure to be a positive influence, so we are not going to despise ourselves because he or she gives off the air that we are the ones with the problem. I say this because some kind people take the blame inappropriately and conclude kindness weakens them.

When your kindness goes unrewarded, you must not feel defeated. There are irregular people out there, and this is their problem, not yours. At another time, with another person—a receptive and appreciative soul—your kindness will deeply affect them.

SPEAK YOUR MIND WITH KINDNESS:

Emerson's Checklist for Empowered Communication

- ☐ Do I actively resist the feeling that because showing kindness isn't returned kindness, but backfires, then it must be my fault for acting wrongly?
- ☐ Do I strive against letting others' unkindness toward me define who I am and my worth, since when I give in to this, I act way too defeated?
- ☐ Do I recognize the power of defeat and that I can let particular defeats lead me to spiral down into a feeling of powerlessness?
- ☐ Instead of personalizing another's unkind expressions and retaliating, do I seek to take the higher road and empathize with folks who struggle with their own battles within themselves?

- ☐ Do I refuse to let another's unkindness embitter me, instead maintaining a forgiving spirit, since this is their issue, they cannot control me, and God is at work in and through me independently of them?
- ☐ Do I realistically accept, without condescending judgment, that some people in my world have unresolved issues that erupt in unkind ways toward me, but they cannot coerce me into reacting with unkind expressions?
- ☐ Do I act and speak with kindness because I am confident in God's love for me as a beloved child, which means He is for me, not against me, and therefore provides a positive, grateful, and persistent mindset?
- ☐ Do I, as a growing person, set goals of being a resilient communicator who continues to speak the truth kindly in the face of the unresponsive and unappreciative?
- ☐ Do I accept that to be empowered as a truthful and kind communicator around those who de-energize me, I must be devoted to these two timeless virtues and seek the support of others who motivate me to stay the course of my devotion?

ENVIOUS VERSUS GRATEFUL

Envious: Life is unfair to me. I don't have what others do.

Grateful: Even though I have less than others, I have more than most; therefore, I will not begrudge those better off but will give thanks from a heart filled with gratitude for all my gifts received and treat with kindness those who have more.

Envy is desiring what another has and being discontent with what we have. You say to your husband, "I wish you made more money so we could have a house like the Andersons have." Or your colleague receives a pay raise, and you have to hold back from giving your boss a piece of your mind.

Such envy is selective in what it sees when another possesses more.

If all the offices are without windows, we do not envy other workers. Let a skylight come to a peer, and now we feel envy. Also, we envy others' rewards, not their risks; the pleasure, not their pain; their successes, not their sacrifices. We are selective.

I heard a person say, "You want what they now have, but you didn't want to go through what they went through to get what they now have." Sure, the medical doctor living next door may have a new Mercedes, but do not forget his twelve years in medical school and residency or his four hours of sleep every night for a decade.

In addition, why would we envy others when our condition is the result of the good choices we made? For instance, we married who we did for love, not for money. We could have chased after someone with wealth, but that's not what we wanted then, and we really don't want it now. We must remind ourselves of our choices. To conquer envy, we must revisit why we are where we are.

We must also recognize that people have their struggles. Ironically, the woman in the luxury home envies the love of her friend's husband and four children. A Danish proverb says, "If envy were a fever, all the world would be ill."

"But, Emerson, what if another gets what he doesn't deserve and I don't get what I do deserve?" For example, what if the wife down the street has the love of a husband and plenty of money in the bank, and you lost all of your money in an embezzlement scheme and your husband has stopped loving you? Martin Luther King Jr. understood this injustice: "I have a dream that my four little children will one day live in a nation where they will not be judged by the color of their skin but by the content of their character."[2] What did Dr. King suggest we do? "Darkness cannot drive out darkness; only light can do that. Hate cannot drive out hate; only love can do that."[3] When life is unfair, the person of character moves forward as Dr. King modeled on this front.

Letting our envy create nasty and complaining communications will not lead others to rescue us. Instead, they'll tune us out when we speak, delete our e-mails, and avoid us when they see us on the street.

SPEAK YOUR MIND WITH KINDNESS:
Emerson's Checklist for Grateful Communication

- ☐ Do I look at what I don't have, which others do have, and feel envy; or do I look at what I do have, which others do not have, and feel grateful?
- ☐ Do I work at not begrudging those better off than me because envy poisons my heart with self-pity and relationships with resentment?
- ☐ To neutralize envy, do I cultivate inward contentment, appreciation of others, and thanksgiving to God?
- ☐ Do I see my life as unique and being about my God-given purpose, personal development, and service to others, deriving deep satisfaction from these, so why be envious and unkind?
- ☐ Do I work at being content by examining why I am discontent, like journaling my thoughts to get in tune with my dissatisfaction?
- ☐ Do I treat those who have more and those who have less with the same love and respect, neither coveting the plenty of one nor patronizing the lesser of the other?
- ☐ Do I develop appreciation by actively rejoicing with what others have received, like writing a note to the person?
- ☐ Do I foster thanksgiving to God by verbally and regularly giving thanks to Him for specific blessings in my life?
- ☐ Do I understand some short-term envy will arise, and it is not bad, given I channel those feelings into a challenge to improve, excel, and be resilient where I am planted?
- ☐ Do I see the emotional, psychological, and physical benefits of gratefulness in that it reduces stress, sparks a measure of happiness, makes relationships more positive, and sustains resilience?

REBELLIOUS VERSUS COOPERATIVE

Rebellious: I can't stand rules like being told to be kind. I'll be any way I wish to be.

Cooperative: I affirm healthy autonomy and strongly resist blindly adhering to convention, but bemoaning and rebelling against social virtues like kindness just because others urge mutiny against it is not productive in achieving long-term cooperation, which requires a steadfast commitment to working with people, not against them.

Some of us declare, "It's my life. I make the rules." At one level such independence is commendable. No one wants your codependency. But what occurs when you say to another, "If I wish to communicate unkindly to you, I will, and it's none of your business"? Soon enough it becomes my business. When you speak rudely to me, you cross a line; you violate a basic rule. Hayden Fry, the former football coach at Iowa, said, "In football, like in life, you must learn to play within the rules of the game."[4]

Unkindness is outside the rules of engagement.

When a wife rebels against the Love and Respect message we teach, based on Ephesians 5:33, and the power of showing unconditional respect toward the spirit of her husband, it is oftentimes because she does not want to hear what she might be doing to contribute to their marital conflicts. She can only focus on what her husband is doing wrong, and as a result she becomes disdainful toward who he is.

Instead of believing that her husband has any measure of goodwill, she kicks into a mantra of rebellion: "I don't feel respect and won't be a hypocrite in showing respect when I don't feel it. Respect is earned, not given." Instead of seeing respect as meeting a husband's deepest need, she arches her back in fearful rebellion as though she will lose her identity and power as a woman if she confronts her husband respectfully. She rebels against the rules of engagement that unconditional respect will get her off of what we call "the crazy cycle" because this approach in her mind makes her a doormat, not a welcome mat.

Perhaps it is the word *rule* that ignites your ire. What if we quoted Franklin D. Roosevelt, who said, "Rules are not necessarily sacred; principles are"?[5]

The same applies to a rebel husband when he hears God's call in Ephesians 5:33 to love his wife as he loves himself and as Christ loves the church. This man defaults to the script of his old man, who often yelled in the home, "If you don't like the way things are done by me in this home, don't let the door hit you on the way out!" To his two sons, this man would sometimes say when mad at their mother, "When you get married, don't let the woman wear the pants." This type of man avoids church when the pastor preaches on marriage. Or when his wife asks him to attend a marriage conference, he says he has a hunting trip planned. His calloused, unkind heart rationalizes his responses as being "manly" and proving he is in charge rather than following God's rule to love his wife unconditionally regardless of her shortcomings.

When we consider the commitment to be kind, loving, and respectful, we are operating on a sacred principle. Doesn't it make sense to speak the necessary truth kindly and clearly to others? This is about being a person of principle. How can that be an oppressive and totalitarian idea? The rebel needs to be honest with themselves. This is far less about being controlled by others and more about being stubborn, insubordinate, and defiant.

SPEAK YOUR MIND WITH KINDNESS:

Emerson's Checklist for Cooperative Communication

- ☐ Do I refuse to bemoan and rebel against social virtues, as in the case of kindness, even though others urge mutiny against kindness?
- ☐ Am I alarmed by this thought: *I can be so fixated on what I believe is right for a society that I view any opposition as dangerous and, therefore, will use any means necessary, including total censorship and physical violence, to achieve what I believe is right for society*?
- ☐ Do I know that opposing goodwilled people who strongly differ from me rarely achieves anything mutually beneficial, can trigger ongoing combativeness and division, and sparks and fuels hatred and contempt?
- ☐ Do I see that being productive in achieving long-term cooperation requires a steadfast commitment to working with people of goodwill, not against such people?
- ☐ Am I open-minded toward people with differing ideas, as it is necessary to find common ground and win-win solutions among people of goodwill?
- ☐ Though it requires time, thought, and effort, do I prize cooperation and collaboration with the belief that though two parties differ,

a negotiated peace can be found that allows both sides to advance their self-interests and enjoy their relationship?

- ☐ Am I unafraid of engaging in open discourse with opposing arguments (instead of censoring my opponents), since I have confidence in my proposals to persuade others, which fosters collaboration?
- ☐ Because I believe people have dignity and worth equal to my own, even those whose positions trouble me, do I speak in ways that sound respectful and loving and reveal me to be a kind and empathetic person?
- ☐ Do I acknowledge to myself and others that I do not have a corner on the truth and, though I have strong convictions, I wish to resolve conflicts in a humble manner?

ANTISOCIAL VERSUS FRIENDLY

Antisocial: I want to be left alone, so I push people away. I don't want to be bothered.

Friendly: Though people may fall short, I recognize the value of every person created in God's image and strive to be approachable and kind like Jesus, an enduring friend of sinners, while still maintaining healthy boundaries and alone time.

A work associate invites us to a social gathering at her home. Do we ignore her e-mail instead of graciously declining? When we tire of another socially, do we unfriend him by removing him from our social network instead of just leaving well enough alone? Do we ignore our parents' invitations to come for a visit as a way of declaring they are harassing us when the truth is we don't want to maturely engage them on making arrangements for Thanksgiving and Christmas at Grandma's house?

Is not wanting to spend time socially with others always a horrible thing? Some of us who are introverts need to get away from the crowd. We feel suffocated and de-energized. Audrey Hepburn said, "I have to be alone very often. . . . That's how I refuel."[6] Refueling to reengage with people is most understandable and acceptable.

But that differs from getting time alone by being unkind to people, pushing them away. In a bizarre way, some use rudeness as a method to ensure solitude and avoid the social demand to be friendly.

Being true to one's shy temperament does not demand hate and contempt toward others to ensure breathing room. Why de-energize others who are more social by pushing them away in order to gain energy for ourselves? We can find win-win, not win-lose solutions. What right do we have to serve ourselves by depriving others of their right to receive something from us?

For example, we notice a neighbor at a restaurant on Saturday morning, so we seek seating on the opposite side in a booth out of sight. That might be appropriate, but we need to prepare ourselves to be a bit more social in a public setting. Entering a public place increases the chances of seeing someone or being seen, and it takes too much energy to always be jumping behind bushes. In seeing someone you know, you need to be prepared to say hi and ask how the other person is doing, while standing there, and then move to your seat. If the person asks you to join him or her, there is no need to blurt out, "No, I can't sit with you. I have other things to do." With this response, the neighbor is made to feel as though he or she is out of line for asking. Instead, you can—without guilt—decline graciously with "Thanks for the invitation, but I'm going to grab a quiet booth and collect my thoughts. But thank you; you are kind to ask." The two messages are the same, but the first is self-focused and ignores honoring the person. With the second, though we are saying no, we are seeking to be courteous while being truthful. Most people will respect our kindly and graciously given reasons, since they themselves have been in a similar situation.

SPEAK YOUR MIND WITH KINDNESS:

Emerson's Checklist for Friendly Communication

☐ As much as I sometimes feel bothered by others and wish to push people away and be left alone, do I realize such antisocial posturing only results in isolation, loneliness, and superficial relationships?

- ☐ Do I know how to be alone for rest, restoration, and reflection so I have far more stored that can be drawn upon to be a giving, friendly person who encourages and helps?
- ☐ Though I need my alone time and healthy boundaries, do I avoid remaining cloistered, since God has a role for me to play in the lives of people created in His image?
- ☐ Do I accept that people are imperfect and will fail me, but that is no reason to become antisocial to prevent disappointments?
- ☐ Though people can be irregular personalities due to their unpleasant attitudes and actions, do I look beyond some of this to the deeper person created in God's image and their inherent worth to Him, which enables me to be more accepting and engaging?
- ☐ In being a friendly person who is not antisocial, do I include the vital reality of forgiveness, both seeking forgiveness when I fail to be kind and a resilient friend who is always there and seeking to forgive those who disappoint me?
- ☐ Despite my limitations in resources, ability, and time, do I seek to be attentive, kind, and giving to those in my immediate world, since this not only is the right thing to do but makes for genuine relationships?
- ☐ Do I seek to emulate the example of Jesus (albeit very imperfectly), who was known as the friend of sinners, providing these folks the freedom to approach Him from the recognition that He loved them as He spoke truth to them?
- ☐ Am I known for my friendly demeanor, which means not only that I am glad to see people when we meet up, but that I listen to understand, empathize with their struggles and sorrows, affirm their good pursuits, and serve their needs where I can?
- ☐ Do I respect the healthy boundaries of others and maintain the same for myself, since we can become too enmeshed and codependent and find our identities in other people and not in God and His purpose?

SELF-HATING VERSUS SELF-ACCEPTING

Self-Hating: Stressed out, underexercised, and overeating, I react. I don't like myself.

Self-Accepting: When overwhelmed with life's responsibilities, I do not let myself edge into self-loathing, since hatred of self makes me appear unkind and hateful toward those around me. Therefore, I call a time-out and revisit God's love for me and meet with someone for guidance and inspiration to be resilient spiritually, emotionally, and physically.

I have received thousands of e-mails from people sharing the struggles of their souls, many much like the one from this woman: "I was depressed. I hated myself both for how I looked and for letting myself get that way. . . . But this didn't inspire me to start cutting back on snacks or start jogging. No, I just ate more snacks while I felt sorry for myself."

All of this undermined her relationships with others. Hating herself prevented her from loving and honoring others. She became self-focused.

My heart goes out to her because I can relate. As a young boy, I experienced a lot of family tension and conflict. Food apparently comforted me because from third grade through my freshman year of high school, I was overweight.

One day in the fifth grade, I stood at a table with two classmates working on an art project. One classmate was the cutest girl in the class, Debbie, and the other was Danny. From the other side of the table, Danny blurted out at me, "You're fat!" Of course, I had heard that before from others, but this scene remains clear to me all these many decades later because Debbie turned on him and rebuked him. "He is not fat!" That made my day, and her kindness is a story I still tell fondly sixty years later. Even so, as powerful as that moment was, Debbie did not rescue me or change me. Because the truth is, I was a big kid back then. I even wore Husky pants at this time. (Husky pants first came on the scene in the 1950s to cater to boys who did not fit into the standard sizing for children's clothing.)

Despite Debbie's heroic defense of me that day, walking around in Husky pants made me self-conscious, not other-conscious. I don't recall thinking, *How can I serve others and do something for them?* As I had not been raised in a Christian home, that challenge did not come to me, and my weight kept me up against the ropes. I was on the defensive, guarding myself against people like Danny.

Eventually God used these types of sorrows and challenges to create empathy in me for others. At age sixteen, I came to a turning point when I accepted Christ, which resulted not only in the hope of eternal life, but in forgiveness, peace, and purpose.

Let's think about Danny and Debbie as communicators. Danny was truthful but unkind. Debbie was kind but untruthful. (As kind as she was, she knew she was lying through her teeth.) What I needed was both: truth *with* kindness, kindness *with* truth.

I had a major struggle in my developmental years from ages eight to thirteen. I know in my case that self-loathing can make it tough to love other people. I find it fascinating that when Paul wrote to husbands in Ephesians 5:28–29, he said, "He who loves his own wife loves himself; for no one ever hated his own flesh." In other words, when we do not appropriately love ourselves but hate ourselves, we will not love others as they ought to be loved. I needed to hear that message, though it was difficult to hear. I was not free within myself to serve others as Jesus calls us to serve.

One wonders if the many who lash out on social media may actually hate themselves. Yes, they are upset about some issue, but it goes deeper. Having no self-respect, they show no respect. Having no self-love, they communicate no love. They hurt others by their unkind words because they are hurting.

When the circumstances in our lives cause us to hate and disrespect ourselves, we will react to others in unkind ways. We expect others, including those we appear to despise, to recognize this and maybe rescue us. That, of course, doesn't work out. We cannot motivate others to love us when we act hatefully toward them.

The challenge for people who tend to use self-hating language is to learn to see themselves as God sees them. How does God, our all-powerful Creator and Designer, see us? Again, I had to work through this when I was sixteen and heard the gospel for the first time. According to God,

- I am precious in His eyes (Isa. 43:4).

- He takes delight in me (Zeph. 3:17).
- I have been fearfully and wonderfully made (Ps. 139:13–14).
- He considers me His workmanship (Eph. 2:10).

And this is to only name a few! The One who made me, and you, knows us better than anyone, and He declares that He loves us, values us, and intends to use us for His purposes. Imagine how knowing and believing such truths could affect your communication toward others.

SPEAK YOUR MIND WITH KINDNESS:

Emerson's Checklist for Self-Accepting Communication

- ☐ When overwhelmed with responsibilities and feeling like I am dropping the ball, do I guard against letting myself edge into self-loathing?
- ☐ Do I recognize that self-loathing can spill onto others with hateful and unkind expressions?
- ☐ Do I see the probability that my negative feelings about myself will not translate into the most positive treatment of others, since I will be less attentive to their concerns, even when I try to compartmentalize my self-disgust?
- ☐ When I am edging toward self-loathing, do I call a time-out and revisit God's love for me and my wholesome purpose in life?
- ☐ Do I act in faith on the biblical promise that God is for me because He loves me, and this is so because He does not lie and is good, loving, faithful, and sovereign?
- ☐ Do I revisit what it means to have realistic and doable goals so I do not expect performance levels to require perfection?
- ☐ Do I exercise, rest, and eat well to be physically healthy and prevent burnout?
- ☐ Do I refuse to give in to misleading comparisons with others who appear perfect, but instead learn how they rebounded after they fell short?
- ☐ Do I have people I meet with who can guide and inspire me to be resilient spiritually, emotionally, and physically when I feel myself giving into self-loathing?

- ☐ Do I seek God's forgiveness when failing to do all the right things and accept His forgiveness?
- ☐ To offset inappropriate self-loathing, do I allow myself the right to acknowledge my strengths and successes in most areas of my life instead of obsessing over where I dropped the ball?
- ☐ Do I enter the discipline of thanking God that He works all things together for good and appropriating the truth that where there is sin, grace abounds?

PART 3

SPEAK YOUR MIND ONLY WHEN NECESSARY

After asking ourselves if a communication we are about to make is both true and kind, we next need to consider if it is even necessary to share, at least at that specific moment. Should we actually say that which we are about to communicate, or would it be wiser to refrain at this time? Ecclesiastes 3:7 reminds us there is "a time to be silent and a time to speak." In other words, we must determine if this is a moment to stay quiet or speak what is on our hearts and minds.

The apostle Paul gave us a clue when he wrote, "Let no unwholesome word proceed from your mouth, but only such a word as is good for edification *according to the need of the moment*, so that it will give grace to those who hear" (Eph. 4:29). When the other person needs to hear something in that moment, and we can convey it in a wholesome and uplifting way (or in other words, kindly and clearly), then it is necessary to communicate.

Before we get into the heart of communicating what is necessary, let's begin with a quick checklist to help us answer if something we are about to communicate is necessary:

- If untrue, unkind, or unclear, then *no*, I will not communicate it. When is it ever necessary to say something that is a lie, mean, or confusing?
- If the other person needs to hear the truth, and I can communicate it kindly and clearly, then *yes*, I will communicate it. Because I care about the truth and because I care for the other person, I will courageously and kindly speak up in a way he or she understands. When we conclude the other person needs the light of the truth, and we can speak it lovingly, respectfully, and coherently, then we ought to communicate it. We must speak our minds for the sake of the truth and for the sake of the other person.
- If, based on the second checklist item, the answer is *yes*, it is necessary to communicate that which I desire to do, but it is not the right time, I will *wait*. For instance, we may need to wait because the other person is not ready to hear from us today because he or she has been up all night and needs to rest. Or we need to wait until we can communicate face-to-face instead of over the phone. A basic rule is: When in doubt, wait twenty-four hours. If the communication that is necessary to share must be done over e-mail or text, but you are upset and not feeling like your normal self, wait at least a day before writing anything. A new sunrise can do wonders on your attitude and approach when communicating an uncomfortable but necessary-to-say truth.

THE HEART OF COMMUNICATING WHAT IS NECESSARY

As we have quoted, Jesus said in Matthew 12:34, "The mouth speaks out of that which fills the heart." He went on to say in verses 36–37, "But I tell you that every careless word that people speak, they shall give an accounting for it in the day of judgment. For by your words you will be justified, and by your words you will be condemned." Careless words come out of an uncaring heart.

My mom was a wonderful model of someone who would think before she spoke so as to better refrain from saying what was unnecessary.

My parents divorced when I was one, remarried each other, then separated again for five years. Even though Mom could've thrown Dad under the bus while raising me on her own, I appreciate that she refrained from doing so. She expressed later in her life that it was unnecessary for me to hear such things. Mom was other-focused. Because of her heart of love for me, she sought to serve my needs with her words. She was not careless in her words because she cared. She pulled back from communicating information that I didn't need to hear, even though she may have felt better after sharing it.

As I have reflected on my mom, who is in heaven now, I do not recall her doing any of the following. She had a sense about what was necessary and what was not. She wasn't perfect, but she was mature.

Toward me, she did not

- provide too much information that overwhelmed me and caused me to tune her out;
- explode in anger and spew out hollow threats;
- make truthful comments at the wrong time that caught me off guard or cornered me;
- keep asking questions about things she knew would invade my privacy;
- keep rehashing something that upset her;
- feel sorry for herself and look to me or others to hear her complaints;
- think she could say anything at any time because she cared, and caring excused imprudence;
- dislike silence to the extent that she filled the room with empty chatter to hear herself;
- overstate and exaggerate;
- interrupt because what she had to say trumped anything I had to say;
- grumble about unmet pleasures; or
- keep thinking of one more criticism to pile on.

I thank God that my mom worked at saying only what was necessary. She did this because she had a good and discerning heart.

THE GOLDEN RULE OF NECESSARY COMMUNICATION

How does the Golden Rule apply to unnecessary words?

Since we do not enjoy people who exhaustingly talk on and on, tell things about us to others who have no right to know, rehash the same episode about us without ever forgiving and forgetting, feel a compulsive obsession to fill in the silence with the sound of their voices, and keep dumping judgmental information on us that floods us emotionally, then why would we dare speak this way to others?

Since we do not enjoy people who explode with anger to make themselves feel better, never express gratitude for all the good in their lives, grab the attention in conversations because they are disinterested in others, and spew out their inflated woes to anyone lending half an ear, then why would we communicate this way?

Since we do not enjoy people who constantly police our activities to catch us, confront us, and control our mistakes; ask too many questions that invade our privacy and feed their selfish curiosity to know; sidestep our honest questions to evade addressing the essential issue; and bring up subjects that are unfitting and distasteful, then why would we do such things?

Since we do not enjoy people who have an uncanny ability to habitually say the right thing at the wrong time, start talking before they have grasped the real concern on our hearts, mouth motherly platitudes that make us feel like toddlers, interrupt us when we are thoughtfully engaged with another person, and feel a divine call to lecture us like a bald-headed man selling hair-restoration oil, then why would we express ourselves this way?

BACK TO THE ASSESSMENT

It is now time to consider more fully the twenty descriptors for those who speak when it is unnecessary, as introduced in the self-assessment. Perhaps some of these rang true for you. Some of the inner scripts might be regular parts of your reasoning for speaking much of what you do. Had you even realized you were speaking unnecessarily in these times?

As with the descriptors for true and kind communication, there are many connections (clusters) in the twenty descriptors of necessary communicators. We will discuss more thoroughly each of these twenty descriptors by looking at their clusters.

- If we want to learn how to speak our minds wisely, we need to focus on being *prudent when necessary* (chapter 11).
- If we struggle with being flustered, causing us to say what we shouldn't, we must become more *composed when necessary* in order to improve as communicators (chapter 12).
- To work on cutting out our improper communication styles, we must seek to be *honorable when necessary* in everything we communicate (chapter 13).
- Those who are more verbose than they should be must learn the discipline to be *restrained when necessary* instead of communicating everything that comes to their minds (chapter 14).
- Finally, because our egos are the cause of many of our unnecessary communications, we must intentionally strive to be *other-centered when necessary* with our communication about and toward others (chapter 15).

CHAPTER 11

PRUDENT WHEN NECESSARY

Do you struggle with speaking only that which is necessary because you tend to be insensitive and intrusive at times? With good intentions, you feel strongly about an urgent communication that must be shared, and in your mind there is no time like the present. "Say it now and say it loud" is your mantra. If others have a problem with it, the onus is on them, not you—or at least that's what you tell yourself.

To learn how to determine when it is necessary to speak your mind, you must move from being imprudent about what you communicate toward being a prudent communicator.

When assessing unnecessary communication, I created the cluster called *imprudent*. Imprudent communication is untimely, nonlistening, mothering, and unprayerful. In other words, imprudence surfaces when a person says things at the wrong time and in the wrong place, listens only to speak and not understand, is meddlesome and overbearing while thinking they caringly say things, and doesn't wait on God in prayer but blurts out their thoughts.

Conversely, the cluster called *prudent* consists of communication I label as pertinent, contemplative, diplomatic, and kneeling. In other words, prudence appears when a person says what is germane at the right time, listens first to fully understand so they can say the wise and necessary thing, makes sure their concern is tactfully expressed, and allows God to speak His wisdom into their own heart before they speak to another's heart.

If we are to speak our minds only when necessary, we must become more thoughtful, prayerful, and timely. Only then will we recognize when something we are about to communicate is, in fact, unwarranted. We must be "slow to speak" (James 1:19), not just for the sake of speaking less but so as to become more discreet, intentional, and prudent with our speech—*all* our speech.

In this first chapter on speaking your mind only when necessary, let's consider those who—though they may be goodwilled—far too often speak quickly, rashly, and without much consideration. It is here where we should keep Ephesians 4:29 in the forefront of our minds and try to speak only "according to the need of the moment," even when that means saying nothing at all.

UNTIMELY VERSUS PERTINENT

Untimely: What I said was true; it doesn't matter that it was the wrong time and place.

Pertinent: I appropriately communicate thoughtful, applicable, and germane information and avoid unnecessary intrusions.

When something is true but unnecessary to say at a given moment, it means that while the information may be accurate and valid, it is not the appropriate time to talk about it. If a son is facing academic challenges and failing grades, parents will need to come alongside him and address a positive way forward. However, the parents should refrain from addressing this issue in front of his siblings. One of the siblings may make unkind comments like "See, I told you that you are stupid." The parents aim to protect their son from such harm. The metaphor of those words being etched on the soul emphasizes the lasting impact words can have on a person's self-image. It underscores the idea that sensitive information should be communicated thoughtfully and in a timely manner.

A husband who typically spends his days in an office recently took a day off to assist a friend with a demanding twelve-hour move. The strenuous labor left him utterly fatigued, and at 10 p.m. he intended to crawl into bed. Earlier that day, his wife had a heated argument with their teenage daughter, leaving her frustrated and questioning her parental effectiveness. Burdened about their daughter, she looked forward to her husband coming home so she could recount the altercation. When he arrived, she began informing him of the earlier conflict; but a few minutes into her report, the husband, his eyes heavy with exhaustion, interjected, "I am sorry, honey. Can we talk about this in the morning?" Taken aback, she said, "No, I need to talk now. This is weighing heavily on me, and we need to say something to her about her consequences in the morning."

In marriage, such moments arise when both spouses have valid needs and emotions, but their timing and circumstances clash. The husband's exhaustion from working manual labor and the wife's pain over her altercation with their teen leave both with reasonable appeals based on their concerns but in direct conflict. She feels a need to talk, and he feels a need to rest. Neither is unreasonable, but who makes the decision?

The interplay of timing and communication within the context of marriage often presents challenges. The scenarios of "untimely" and "pertinent" highlight the significance of considering when and how we share information. Saying something true but unnecessary at a given moment can have lasting consequences. It's a reminder that while information may be valid, its timing and context matter.

Are you about to communicate something but are unsure if now is the right time to do so? Though it may be both true and kind, will it arrive at such a bad time that the truth and kindness will feel to the other person as though you have forced your message on them? As many of us have heard, timing is everything. If you are uncertain if this is the best time, press pause for the moment. Wait until after the next sunrise to discuss it. Perhaps a night of rest will give you a better mindset on the matter. If it's an e-mail you are itching to send, put it in your drafts and come back to it when you have certainty about the timing. Right words at the wrong time don't feel right to the other person.

SPEAK YOUR MIND ONLY WHEN NECESSARY:

Emerson's Checklist for Pertinent Communication

- ☐ Do I think before I communicate by asking: *Is it necessary to say at this time?*

- ☐ Do I realize that though something true can be said kindly and clearly, it simply isn't necessary to say at this time or at all, sometimes because it has already been said?
- ☐ Do I listen to understand what the other person needs to hear so I don't jump to a conclusion about what they need to hear when they don't need to hear this?
- ☐ Do I consider the timing in that I can say what is true, kind, and clear but the other person has had a long day and can't stay awake long enough to hear me?
- ☐ Do I recognize that I can unnecessarily intrude into another's privacy, for instance, while they are playing at a park with their kids or having dinner with a spouse, though the information is necessary for them to know at some point?
- ☐ Do I recognize that though another must hear what I have to say, that does not mean I must say it unkindly and cause them undue stress?
- ☐ Do I work hard to ensure that what I communicate is relevant and applicable; that is, it pertains to the subject at hand and helps advance the discussion in a truthful and fruitful way?
- ☐ Do I ensure that the information necessary to solve a problem is provided?

NONLISTENING VERSUS CONTEMPLATIVE

Nonlistening: My style is to listen until I know what I want to say and then I say it.

Contemplative: I listen first to understand the need, then contribute to the conversation what is wise and edifying for the moment's need in the way Christ would.

Six-year-old Johnny asked his mother, "Where did I come from?" She had prepared for this moment and went into a full explanation of human sexuality and the birth of a child. After she finished, she asked him if she had answered the question. Johnny said, "Maybe. Jason down the street just moved here, and he told me that he came from New York. I wanted to know where I came from."

We can miss what is being said. The other day I was talking to a husband who listened to his adult son share his heart with his mother. For whatever reason, she was extremely defensive. She was so defensive that she went off on topics that were tangential to the issue being addressed by her son. At one point, the husband said, "Honey, I don't think you're hearing what he is trying to say. Here is what he's feeling in his heart," to which his son totally agreed. The dad said to me, "I was amazed that she had no idea the extent to which she was missing his heart. I think she felt accused, since the conversation got off on the wrong foot with him yelling at her, and she felt he intended to condemn her as a bad mother. She filtered everything through that grid. She sat there fearful of what she might hear and thus didn't hear."

Proverbs 18:13 says, "He who gives an answer before he hears, it is folly and shame to him." Any one of us can end up missing the deeper issue, and every father can confess the same failure to really hear the heart of a child. We respond with a nasty comment only to realize we misunderstood, and now we have to apologize.

I am stunned when people make comments on social media platforms in response to some point that a person has supposedly made; but when I read what the first person wrote, it becomes clear that the one replying completely missed what was being communicated. Then others jump in and give their opinions too. Before long, a thread of replies has piled up that has nothing to do with the original point or questions. All of the commentary is unnecessary. Finally, a wise woman chimes in: "Everyone is missing the point here." She then recaptures the original comment and pulls everyone back to the main concern.

We should make it our goal to echo the person who says, "I used to listen in order to speak, but now I find myself listening to understand."

Have you ever noticed that the letters in the word *listen* are the same as in the word *silent*? Before communicating, try asking yourself, *Have I remained silent long enough so as to listen carefully and understand the exact issue on the table?*

SPEAK YOUR MIND ONLY WHEN NECESSARY:

Emerson's Checklist for Contemplative Communication

- ☐ Do I avoid listening with half an ear and only long enough to formulate what I want to say, since this risks devaluing the other person, creating a new problem, and not solving the problem at hand?
- ☐ Do I seek to listen first to understand fully so I do not speak prematurely and unnecessarily, which makes the other feel unheard?
- ☐ Do I sometimes realize as a result of listening and reflecting that I don't need to say anything, since they need my presence, not my words?
- ☐ Do I recognize that I can be biased and have blind spots on what I think is necessary for the other person?
- ☐ When I become aware that I misheard or misspoke, do I apologize and correct my misunderstanding or miscommunication?
- ☐ Do I provide feedback by repeating what I heard them say and then asking, "Did I hear and understand correctly?"
- ☐ Even after listening, do I ask myself, *Is what I am about to say true, kind, necessary, and clear?*
- ☐ Though some people in conversations get hurt, frustrated, and angry, and either shut down or verbally react, all of which can be their problem, is my first course of action to consider if I said something untrue, unkind, unnecessary, or unclear?
- ☐ Do most people who share their thoughts and feelings comment that I understand their perspective and emotions?
- ☐ Is my aim to communicate what is true and uplifting so folks will say, "Thanks, that was hard to hear, but I am grateful that you thoughtfully spoke into my life and did so in such a way that I felt you were for me"?

MOTHERING VERSUS DIPLOMATIC

Mothering: When others aren't listening to me, I say it anyway because I care.

> **Diplomatic:** Though I care for others and would love to put in my two cents, I do not blurt out my opinion just because I care, since kindness without tactfully stating what is true is unnecessary and unhelpful.

It is one thing to be a mother who tells her son to be careful when he drives to school. Though she knows he isn't listening, she says it anyway. Perhaps she says it for fear something bad will happen to him and she does not wish to live in guilt for failing to give warning. Or perhaps she says "be careful" because she wants others to say that to her as a way of saying, "I am thinking about you because I have you on my heart."

However, there is another type of mothering that's inappropriate. At work, a female employee mothers a male peer by telling him to put on his jacket and comb his hair, or telling him he should reconsider his vacation to Chicago in light of the crime going on there. Though she isn't romantically interested in him, she has a special affection for him as a type of brother. (The roles can be reversed, and the man hovers over the woman.) However, she needs to discern if this is something he feels comfortable with. Unfortunately, she blinds herself to his unease with those maternal comments. Such a woman has so strong a longing to be needed that she ignores the man's visible discomfort. She does not ask herself, *Am I out of line? Are there boundaries here that I have no right or responsibility to cross? Am I seeking validation as a person?*

She must not let her need to care trump her need to be discerning and prudent, or eventually, this male peer will tell her, "Look, I don't need you to mother me, okay? I appreciate that you're concerned, but you are here to do the tasks assigned to you by management." In hearing this, she is crushed. However, she brought this on by "caring" where that type of care is not appropriate at work. She may have a caring personality, but, like the rest of us, she must operate according to the code of behavior at work. She must not let her care override protocol or cross the boundaries that others have for themselves.

Similar to acting like a mother, a husband can exhibit inappropriate paternalistic tendencies. For instance, consider this scenario when a husband tells his wife, "Tonight, as we attend my boss's retirement party, I'd appreciate it if you could be more sociable. At the last work event, you remained in the corner and didn't engage with anyone.

In fact, several people asked me if you were okay, and it was rather embarrassing." He admonishes her as though she were an antisocial teenager deserving of parental reprimand.

While he believes his words are true and necessary, attempting to change her introverted ways is not his role, which makes his comments unnecessary. Instead of wandering off to discuss work matters with his peers, he could stay next to his wife and include her in conversations relevant to her interests. It's no surprise that she chose to sit alone, not only because the subjects were work-related but because she is inclined toward introversion. Regrettably, over the past few years, such belittling comments have caused her to withdraw even more from him. She feels rejected and unloved. While he may believe he's demonstrating care, from her perspective, his actions appear quite the opposite.

Interestingly, caring mother figures can overstep their boundaries by declaring others do *not* care. The classic example is Martha, the sister of Mary (Luke 10:38–42). When Jesus visited Martha's home, Martha was doing all the work preparing for the meal while her sister sat at the feet of Jesus. Martha said to Jesus, "Lord, do You not care that my sister has left me to do all the serving alone? Then tell her to help me" (v. 40). Note two things: First, she accused the One who is perfect in love of being uncaring. Second, she commanded Him to get her sister to care. Caring people like Martha can be a bit self-righteous and bossy but not see it. May I suggest to you that she overreached with the Son of God?

Before communicating your goodwilled concerns in a parental way, ask, *Am I about to mother someone beyond appropriate rules of engagement or wrongly judge another as uncaring?*

SPEAK YOUR MIND ONLY WHEN NECESSARY:

Emerson's Checklist for Diplomatic Communication

- ☐ Do I avoid excusing my undiplomatic expressions by claiming that I cared and had good intentions, so the one offended should recognize that and not take everything so personally?

- ☐ Do I agree that good intentions do not prevent misunderstandings, hurt feelings, and unpleasant consequences, since what we say, how we say it, and how the other person hears it all enter the equation?
- ☐ Do I discern that my two cents' worth is sometimes best left unsaid because verbal blurting leads to verbal blundering?
- ☐ Do I recognize that caring for others, like a mother hen caring for her chicks, does not justify saying what is on my heart when it's untrue, unkind, unnecessary, or unclear?
- ☐ Though I believe my communication is true and kind, do I require tactful diplomacy from myself to ensure that I do not speak rashly and unthinkingly, which could lead to confusion and offense during the conversation?
- ☐ Do I approach tough conversations by asking myself, *First, what is necessary for me to hear and understand, and then, what is necessary for me to say?*
- ☐ When I realize my caring communication appeared undiplomatic and imprudent, sounding insensitive and offensive, do I seek forgiveness and word myself differently?
- ☐ Do I have a good handle on listening without interrupting when another tries to explain something to me, asking questions so I understand, and communicating what is necessary from what I understand?
- ☐ Do I avoid confrontation where possible, but when I cannot, do I seek to wisely understand another's view, use tact and maintain a calm demeanor, speak respectfully, and negotiate win-win solutions?
- ☐ To be a caring communicator who speaks what is true, necessary, and clear, do I regularly seek reliable guidance from books, podcasts, videos, communication experts, and other wise resources so as to enhance my prudence in accurately and appropriately conveying information?

UNPRAYERFUL VERSUS KNEELING

Unprayerful: Maybe I should wait quietly in prayer, but I feel they need to hear it now.

Kneeling: I want to make sure the words from my mouth reflect the heart of God, so I go to Him first and ask for His wisdom, and sometimes He tells me, *Not now.*

Within the church community we often hear people readily confess that they can get preachy with people in their world, whether in the home or at work. Though they do not stand on a street corner with a tambourine and a Bible, they relay their sense that they should be more prayerful and patient.

When we are too preachy, the listener tunes us out. A person confessed that he used preachy, pushy, nagging, and complaining words that turned the other person off. He recognized that his unnecessary communication triggered resentment in the other person.

Though Paul asked, "How are they to hear without a preacher?" (Rom. 10:14), Peter also instructed certain people to refrain from using words that are not getting through (1 Peter 3:1–2). Many of us have heard the statement errantly attributed to St. Francis of Assisi: "Preach the gospel at all times, and if necessary use words." While it is impossible to effectively spread the gospel of Jesus without words, there are still other times when it is more necessary to pray to our heavenly Father than to preach to our peers.

Take a look at what a few people wrote to me:

- "I have come to the conclusion that maybe this is one of those times that God is telling me to keep my mouth shut and just continue to pray."
- "I decided to keep my mouth shut (for the first time in a while), listen, read, and let God show me."
- "I continued to pray and kept my mouth shut! Guess what happened . . . I believe God provided us a miracle because I chose to control my tongue and my attitude."

We need to allow God to be God in the other person's life. A statement about God I once heard that grabbed my attention was this: "He's God; you're not." Before sharing something on our hearts, we should ask ourselves if this communication will feel to others as if we are hitting their sins. Do we need to reconsider this communication for the time being and instead pray for and serve them?

SPEAK YOUR MIND ONLY WHEN NECESSARY:
Emerson's Checklist for Kneeling Communication

- ☐ Do people characterize my communication as inwardly thoughtful, outwardly respectful, and upwardly reverential?
- ☐ Do I refrain from rushing at people who need to see areas to change but quietly and patiently pray for them first?
- ☐ Do I spend time in Bible reading and prayer to deepen my walk with God so my communication with others reflects His love and truth?
- ☐ Do I often pray, asking for wisdom from God (to be prudent) as to whether what I wish to say is true, kind, necessary, and clear?
- ☐ Do I wait in prayer for God to tell me, *Don't say this at all* or *Don't say that right now*?
- ☐ Do I wait on God in prayer and let Him act in the lives of the people I am concerned about, since He commands prayer, loves them, and has the power to provide the information they need?
- ☐ As a peacemaker, or wanting to be, do I engage conflict in the gray areas of life with the prayer to find mutual understanding and a win-win solution instead of declaring I am right and they are wrong?
- ☐ Am I a kneeler because at the end of the day, I wish to be His prudent conduit in speaking what is true, kind, necessary, and clear, especially at it relates to His love, forgiveness, and strength?
- ☐ Do I have godly, wise confidants whom I can bounce my ideas off of to ensure that my advice for another person is necessary and, if so, reflects the heart of God on the matter?
- ☐ When I jump ahead of God and say what I should not say, do I seek forgiveness from Him and others for my imprudence?
- ☐ Do I remind myself as the kneeler that He is God and I am not?

CHAPTER 12

COMPOSED WHEN NECESSARY

Do you struggle with being too emotional and overwrought in your communication? Though you are a goodwilled person who honestly believes in the good intentions behind your emotions, not everyone sees your passionate reactions the same way as you. Before you know it, misunderstandings have resulted in a negative cycle that has you confused and even flustered at how these "overly sensitive snowflakes" cannot see for themselves how much you truly care for them, which is why you react as you do.

To learn how to speak our minds necessarily, we must move from being a flustered communicator to a more composed communicator.

I describe some types of unnecessary speech as *flustered*. This cluster consists of communication that is volcanic, pity-partying, exaggerating, and grumbling. Flustered communicators say unnecessary words because they believe pent-up feelings are repressive, so verbal explosion is healthy; when feeling victimized (i.e., "woe is me") and desiring to tell their sob stories; when feeling no one will listen unless they dramatically amplify their plights; and when feeling life circumstances have given them a right to gripe and vent discontent.

By contrast, necessary speech in this cluster is *composed*. This communication I describe as processing, discriminate, matter-of-fact, and accepting. Composed communicators speak necessary words because they get in tune with their feelings and express them without emotional eruptions; they have boundaries and talk of personal matters only with those who have a right and need to know; they keep to the facts, since untruthful comments undermine what is necessary to convey; and they constructively engage normal life challenges without uncalled-for grumbling and griping.

To speak your mind only when necessary requires a disciplined and composed approach. You must learn how to cultivate a cool, calm, and collected speaking style so as to avoid letting your emotions trigger words that are excessive, unrequired, and irrelevant. This is no easy task, but it's not impossible. You can control how you react in a situation.

In this chapter, we will compare and contrast those who have learned how to take control of their emotions with those who too often allow their emotions to take control of them.

VOLCANIC VERSUS PROCESSING

Volcanic: I have to vent my pent-up feelings; it isn't healthy to repress my negativity.

Processing: I can sort through my feelings inwardly before speaking so that I don't erupt but instead express accurate and necessary things that serve the other person.

Volcanic eruptions can happen during a phone conversation with a family member who accuses us of not caring and even lying, when replying to an e-mail from someone who just did an end run around our authority, with a coworker who criticizes our work again, or when posting on social media about a candidate we can't stand. When upset, some of us let it fly like hot molten lava.

I have known people with serious anger problems who explode at those around them, but afterward they feel great and expect those burnt to a crisp to say, "Hey, no problem. We fully understand."

When you use volcanic communication, most people close off to you and may resent you. You may hear them saying, "I have to walk on eggshells around this person." They see you as unpredictable, emotional, and irrational when hurt, frustrated, confused, angry, fearful, or offended. If they employ you, eventually they unemploy you. On social media, people skip over your posts because the lava overrides the point.

Can a volcanic communicator change? Absolutely. One person wrote to me after recognizing her volcanic tendencies, "Now, I am aware enough to stop and think when I feel myself wanting to say things out of my frustration. I don't shoot my mouth off. I think about how I come across."

This mindset comes in handy before we blow our tops as though we were Mount Vesuvius!

SPEAK YOUR MIND ONLY WHEN NECESSARY:

Emerson's Checklist for Processing Communication

- ☐ Do I stay in tune with my negative emotions like apathy, boredom, disappointment, sadness, anxiety, anger, envy, guilt, loneliness, disgust, and hopelessness?
- ☐ Do I avoid the rationalization that says, "I must vent my pent-up feelings because it isn't healthy to repress my negativity"?
- ☐ If things escalate beyond my self-control, am I disciplined enough to disengage and take a time-out?
- ☐ Do I take the time to sort through my emotions and identify the root issue before communicating with the other person to avoid saying anything unnecessary?
- ☐ Because I care, do I take the time to process so I do not speak impulsively and rashly and end up damaging the relationship?
- ☐ Do I process the four questions about my future communication: Is it true, kind, necessary, and clear?
- ☐ Do I have composed ways of communicating my negative emotions to someone without lashing out as a flustered person would?
- ☐ Do I provide time for other people to process their thoughts and feelings so I do not push their vulnerability to erupt?
- ☐ When I communicate what isn't true or necessary from a place of negative, erupting emotion, do I seek forgiveness afterward?

☐ Do I have people in my life to whom I can turn for help in processing my emotions so I can figure out what I am feeling and say only what is necessary and true to others?

PITY-PARTYING VERSUS DISCRIMINATE

Pity-Partying: I have sorrows, okay? I look for anyone who will listen to my burdens.

Discriminate: As I navigate the obstacles I am facing, I share my burdens only with those who contribute to my emotional or spiritual growth and never to those who do not.

Over the years, I have noticed individuals who hop from counselor to counselor. These people have no intention of changing their attitudes and behaviors. They simply want to tell their stories of woe to gain empathy. They derive energy from people who feel sorry for them. However, when a counselor shifts focus to what the person could change, he or she usually finds another counselor. Some people have an addiction to therapy.

Counselor hoppers do the same at work. They corner someone at the drinking fountain, dumping out melancholy melodramas. The next day, they're at lunch with a different coworker, doing the same thing. They are not seeking help but feeling sorry for themselves and attempting to persuade the listener to feel sorry for them. They are having a pity-party and inviting anyone who will show up.

Many people post on Facebook for this very reason. They vent about some issue with the hope that half a dozen people will affirm what they are thinking. The fact that no one knows the backstory beyond what the post says is convenient. Facebook does not demand two or three witnesses to confirm the facts of what they report. However, Moses, Jesus, and Paul did make that kind of demand (Deut. 19:15; Matt. 18:16; 2 Cor. 13:1). This biblical requirement to confirm facts with witnesses, which should apply in principle in all communication, escapes the notice of some.

For several years, I unofficially tracked the number of people who e-mailed me to tell their stories of woe, but when I made several recommendations on what they could do, I never heard from them again. Before you share your sad story with someone—whether it be with a coworker, your BFF, or everyone on social media—ask yourself, *Why am I communicating this information? Am I having a pity-party and wanting others to feel sorry for me, or am I seeking wisdom on how to climb out of the pit?* If the latter, I encourage you to pray and ask God to direct you toward a godly, wise leader or counselor who will be qualified to lift you up and direct your steps.

SPEAK YOUR MIND ONLY WHEN NECESSARY:

Emerson's Checklist for Discriminate Communication

- ☐ Do I discern my tendency, when feeling I am a helpless victim who has been unfairly treated, to complain to anyone around me?
- ☐ Do I guard against those sad moments when I feel self-pity and am tempted to look for anyone who will listen to hear my tale of woe?
- ☐ Do I guard against such self-pitying moments because few have a right to know or need to know of my "woe is me" lament, especially when I cross the line and bad-mouth others I hold responsible?
- ☐ Do I approach my victimization and sorrow not as one who is helpless and hopeless but as one who can be resilient and composed in rebounding?
- ☐ Do I subscribe to the truth that my response is my responsibility, so though mistreated, I will grow through this and mature, since no one can control my inner person?
- ☐ Though all of us can feel ashamed of feeling unable to cope with the pain from circumstances and people, do I not give in to such shame but turn to those who understand my plight?
- ☐ When overwhelmed by stress and sorrows, do I accept that it is okay to receive counseling and support?
- ☐ Do I consider this situation an opportunity to develop greater control of my emotional ups and downs and turn to competent people who can aid me now?

EXAGGERATING VERSUS MATTER-OF-FACT

Exaggerating: Honestly, to ignite empathy and change, I jarringly overstate reality.

Matter-of-Fact: I refuse to exaggerate or jump to conclusions in an overly dramatic fashion to gain empathy but instead stick to the necessary facts in my speech, though not without feeling.

I received an e-mail from a woman who wrote, "Last week he blurted out he wanted a divorce, which he has said before but never acted upon."

Why does the guy say he wants a divorce? He seeks to convey the depth of his pain in the relationship with her. He makes an outlandish remark with the underlying desire that she will hear his cry and change. Of course, his exaggerating communication comes across as a threat or ultimatum for his self-serving purposes, attempting to coerce her into doing what he wants. Instead of meeting his wife's need for love, he speaks unnecessary words to frighten her into doing what he deems necessary.

Another woman admitted to me that in a moment of frustration over not being promoted, she, as a vice president in the company, exclaimed to her all-male management team, "I feel like all the men on this management team hate women. You give the impression to outsiders that there's no glass ceiling in this organization, but that's not true." In private, she told me that she didn't believe much of what she said, but she said it nonetheless. She expected her colleagues to decode the real meaning behind her words. However, when we say untrue, unkind, and unclear things—which, obviously, are unnecessary—there is a price to pay. After this woman was removed from the management team, she relayed to me that the company's response had less to do with her femininity and more to do with how she exaggerated in a dishonoring way how the company was being run. I counseled her to request a meeting with the management team so that she could name her exaggerations as dishonoring and wrong. I hoped that her humility would lead to a restoration of trust and allow for an opportunity to start over.

When you're feeling hurt, frustrated, angry, confused, fearful, or offended, do you burst out with unnecessary injections? You don't mean it like it sounds. You're trying to bring about some change in the situation or relationship. You hope those around you will decode the meaning behind your exaggerated outbursts and rescue you by apologizing and making things right. But that doesn't happen often. When you make inflammatory exclamations such as "Go ahead and divorce me!" or "I should have never taken this job!" you undermine the very aim you hold deep in your heart.

SPEAK YOUR MIND ONLY WHEN NECESSARY:

Emerson's Checklist for Matter-of-Fact Communication

- ☐ Do I grasp the seriousness of language that is not accurate, such as exaggeration, hyperbole, misinformation, misrepresentation, distortion, fabrication, deception, and falsification?
- ☐ In order to be accurate in my communication, do I hold off from speculation, assumption, conjecture, supposition, jumping to conclusions, hearsay, gossip, and unfounded accusations until I know the facts?
- ☐ Am I aware that my tendency to react melodramatically when upset signifies a lack of self-control and an incorrect belief that being more out of control equates to having more control over others?
- ☐ Do I refuse to believe I can garner empathy from others by losing it emotionally, as a strategy, since their initial response is one of shock and awe, not empathy, over my meltdown?
- ☐ Whereas earlier in life I might have jarringly overstated reality as a ploy to gain empathy and coerce a change in another person, do I reject such manipulation because it is inauthentic and ineffective over time?
- ☐ If I react and have meltdowns due to feelings of insecurity, inadequacy, shame, and a false projection of rejection and abandonment, do I return to a focus on self-care, realizing that often this reveals a personal issue in me and is not caused by others who I feel should be blamed?
- ☐ Do I avoid language not grounded in reality with verifiable facts, since it inevitably results in confusion, conflict, a discredited reputation, and

damaged relationships because it will not likely be true, kind, necessary, or clear?

- ☐ Do I communicate in such a way that others hear a kind, loving, and respectful tone that carries the necessary truth and avoids any aggressive melodrama that would only distract from the necessary truth that the listener won't hear or might dismiss?
- ☐ If I have a history of engaging in theatrics that have discredited me and damaged my relationships due to my untrue and unkind remarks, do I recognize that God may be using conflict to help me overcome this unfruitful behavior and cultivate healthier ways to express my emotions when I'm upset?
- ☐ Where I have been a verbal flamethrower, have I sought the forgiveness of those I damaged and taken steps to repair the relationship by demonstrating a responsible, matter-of-fact response during conflict?
- ☐ Do I actively work to improve my communication skills and seek feedback from others to ensure that I am conveying information accurately and effectively?

GRUMBLING VERSUS ACCEPTING

Grumbling: When I don't get what I want, I am unhappy and feel it's my right to gripe.

Accepting: When good things don't come my way, I do not give in to complaints that are unnecessary, despairing, and hysterical, but come to terms with difficulty—some of which is a normal part of life I must roll with—and give voice to constructive ways to move forward.

As a high school senior at a military school, I had the good fortune of receiving several meaningful awards at graduation. However, I did not receive a particular award that I wanted and shared my disappointment with a fellow cadet. I still remember his look of disbelief, along with his response: "Your fellow classmates just voted you most likely to succeed, and that's not good enough. You still want more."

At that moment, I embarrassingly recognized something repellent in me. I was grumbling about not getting even more of what I wanted. That natural human response was evident in me even from childhood. I recall coming down for Christmas at around age nine and seeing a life-size robot next to the tree. I was thrilled until I realized it was just a sled that my mom had wrapped in tinfoil to appear to be a robot. My grumbling began when the gift I actually got was subpar to the gift I had imagined.

Still today, more than fifty years later, I can recall the shame I felt over making the ungrateful comment to my fellow classmate, and I can only imagine how deeply I hurt my mother's feelings after she had stayed up late on Christmas Eve trying to make a memory for me.

Grumbling is the offspring of conceit. We feel that we deserve more than we already have. We go through life saying, "I deserve that, not them!" It sounds so trivial, except to ourselves.

So much of what we complain about when interacting with others is unnecessary, since it is based on us wanting more of what we already have. We end up being like the person who said, "I whined about not having a third pair of shoes until I saw a man with no feet." Truth is, much of our lives is golden, but we call it jaundiced. Many of us have more than enough goodness in our lives, but we have put on tainted glasses that only see reasons for discontent.

As a Christian, when I whine about not getting what I deserve (or think I deserve), I need to pause and remember there is another side. Truth is, I deserve God's judgment for my transgressions but am not receiving this judgment because of His grace, mercy, and love extended to me though Jesus Christ. That should stop some of my grousing and selfish, trifling, unnecessary comments about how bad I have it. And the truth is, I have it better than it should be.

SPEAK YOUR MIND ONLY WHEN NECESSARY:

Emerson's Checklist for Accepting Communication

- ☐ Do I acknowledge and accept that in life, I could have personal troubles like stress, feeling overwhelmed, uncertainty about the future, unexpected changes, burnout, a sense of inadequacy and unworth, grief, loss, or feeling as though I am without purpose or meaning?

- ☐ Do I acknowledge and accept that in life, I could have interpersonal troubles like misunderstandings, conflict, work-home imbalance, separation, disappointment, a need for healthy boundaries, decision-making struggles, or gray-area differences?
- ☐ Do I discipline myself against being a grumbler who, when I don't get what I want, is unhappy, feels I have a right to gripe, and ends up saying unnecessary and unwarranted things?
- ☐ Am I discerning enough to recognize that my grumbling about my unmet, selfish desires makes me appear self-centered and causes me to say unnecessary things about what I deserve and find wrong with others, ultimately putting people off?
- ☐ Do I adhere to the common expression of responsible people, "I control what I can control and change what I can change, but what I cannot control or change, I do not dwell on but make the best of my situation"?
- ☐ Have I taken steps so that when troubles come my way, I do not give in to needless and despairing complaints, which sometimes turn hysterical—anything but cool, calm, and collected?
- ☐ Do I welcome difficulties and troubles, as hard as that is, because I know this develops resilience, models character in front of family and friends, and deepens my faith in God to work all things together for good?
- ☐ Do I practice the discipline of giving thanks, which people in life who do not grumble practice, since it prevents a negative view of life, lightens my heart when I feel grateful for what is going well, and motivates me to be more resilient in navigating troubles?
- ☐ Do I think of what I can do to respond to my difficulties constructively, which means I explore my options, looking for creative alternatives on how best to navigate the situation, reminding myself there is nothing new under the sun?
- ☐ When stalemated on the way forward in finding a healthy solution to my trouble, do I turn to trustworthy and competent people who have successfully navigated troubled waters and can offer me guidance and encouragement?

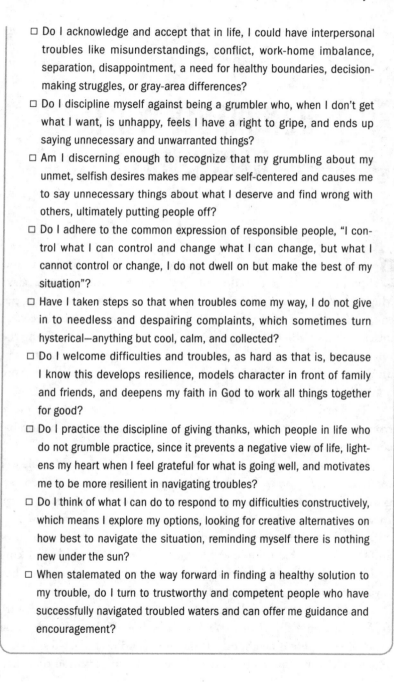

CHAPTER 13

HONORABLE WHEN NECESSARY

Do you sometimes toe, or even cross, the line on what is becoming and appropriate and, as a result, end up saying something unnecessary? Maybe you're aware of this tendency, or maybe you're not; but in the end, you do not let yourself be bothered by it, because you believe your intentions are righteous. And if by chance you are guilty of crossing the line at times, then shouldn't you be given some grace by anyone you unintentionally offended? If they have a problem with you, that's more on them than it is you, right?

To learn how to speak our minds necessarily, we must move from being someone who speaks what is improper to an honorable communicator.

When assessing our communication styles, I created a cluster referred to as *improper*. I describe improper communication as coarse, gossiping, unfiltered, and spying. People who communicate this way speak unnecessary information because they are given to off-color, crude, and vulgar comments; they are compelled to be the first to know and first to tell what is no one's business to know; they are unthinking and loose-lipped as they spout out damaging information; and they invasively question and monitor to gather private information.

On the other end of the spectrum, I created a cluster of necessary communication called *honorable*. I describe honorable communication as wholesome, good neighborly, thoughtful, and boundary-respecting. Honorable communicators share only necessary information that their grandmother would find acceptable to people who have invited them to comment on their private business, and they do so mindfully, carefully, usefully, and only after gaining that information through ethical, moral, and legal means.

Whether one's intentions are good or not, we are called to a higher standard of communicating to one another. It should be our daily goal to speak in correct, becoming, and respectful ways—to everyone, at all times—and not give in to coarseness, gossip, loose lips, and meddling.

Ultimately, this boils down to having self-control over the words you let fly from your lips. Let's consider the different types of communicators who have no filter on the words they say, as opposed to those who, like King David, pray daily, "Set a guard, Lord, over my mouth; keep watch over the door of my lips" (Ps. 141:3).

COARSE VERSUS WHOLESOME

Coarse: Admittedly, my words are off-color, but others shouldn't be such prudes.

Wholesome: I have committed and limited myself to speech that would not cause my grandmother to exclaim, "That wasn't necessary to say!"

I have found it strange that good and decent individuals for some unknown reason feel that they will be more popular if they can get people to laugh at their off-color comments or crude silliness. Sadly, their coarse jesting contributes nothing to the discussion other than the fact that they are trying to be funny. Most who listen find it in poor taste.

Mere silliness can be a problem. I know of one man who lost his job because he would not stop his silly talk, like imitating actors and saying lines from sitcoms. He received several formal warnings from his superiors that such frivolous talk was unbecoming in his professional position, and they instructed him to stop. When he did not heed their counsel, they released him of his duties. Sadly, he was a Christian who knew this scripture: "There must be no filthiness and silly talk, or coarse jesting, which are not fitting, but rather giving of thanks" (Eph. 5:4).

Why do some folks continue to use coarse communication when it isn't needful? And worse, why do they claim others are prudes when all the facts show them as lacking prudence? Some of us need to remember Ephesians 4:29, which we referenced earlier, and take God up on His challenge to "let no unwholesome word proceed from [our] mouth, but only such a word as is good for edification . . . so that it will give grace to those who hear."

I love a good joke as much as anyone, and humor is certainly needed in the world. The smartest comedians are those who observe life and are strategic about crafting a joke, story, or experience. The easiest laughs often come from sarcastic or dirty humor simply because it makes audiences uncomfortable or shocked. It's also why that kind of humor is often referred to as "a cheap laugh" and usually isn't the funniest or most remembered content of a show.

When considering what I think to be humorous or what I might share with others, an easy litmus test can be Ephesians 4:29. The word *grace* means "gift," so if what I'm about to share would not be a gift that edifies them or God, it might be best (and wise) to keep it to myself.

SPEAK YOUR MIND ONLY WHEN NECESSARY:
Emerson's Checklist for Wholesome Communication

- ☐ Do I communicate at a PG (parental guidance) rating, having committed and limited myself to speech and humor that falls within the lines of what is appropriate and necessary to most audiences?
- ☐ Do I ask myself, *Will this sound wholesome and honorable as I share what is accurate and necessary, whether on a lighthearted or controversial issue*?
- ☐ Do I have a litmus test that I apply to my communication, such as, "Would my grandmother tell me, 'That was unnecessary to say!'"?
- ☐ Do I avoid rude and crude communication that is vulgar, explicit, sacrilegious, demeaning, prejudicial, or humiliating?

- ☐ Do I see my humor, given I have a little bit of a comedic trait in me, surfacing from the ability to be imaginative, clever, relatable, and playful but never offensive or compromising my innocence?
- ☐ Do I aim to build people up with encouragement and appreciation in my conversations, and when required to address tensions, do I do so with constructive and gentle feedback?
- ☐ Because Jesus said that the mouth speaks out of that which fills the heart (Matt. 12:34), do I pray that my words reflect and honor my deepest values and faith?
- ☐ Do I steer clear of defending my unnecessary language that is rude and crude by labeling someone a prude to justify my expressions?
- ☐ When my conversation or humor is inappropriate or offensive, do I seek forgiveness and refrain from that kind of speech next time?

GOSSIPING VERSUS GOOD NEIGHBORLY

Gossiping: I must be first to know and tell, though I suppose some of it isn't my business.

Good Neighborly: I believe it is not necessary to discuss problems that are none of my business, as that can be gossip among my network of relationships; however, if asked for help and input, I am willing to offer any necessary solutions to the issue.

A TV show had a returning character who regularly gossiped to her neighbors, and she ended each story with "Now, listen, I ain't one to gossip so you ain't heard that from me!"

While this is humorous, some gossip can turn malicious. While discussing the failed marriage of a mutual friend, one man says to another buddy, "Well, you probably weren't aware of this, but the reason he was always late to dinner, which his wife hated, was because he would stop off for a drink on the way home. He felt he needed some 'liquid courage' before he could manage being with his family." The buddy now wonders, *Does my friend have loose lips? Can I trust him with confidential information if I start having family problems too? If he tells me things that I should not know, will he tell others things about me that they should not know?*

All of us have heard, "Some things are best left unsaid." To assist us in discerning what is best unsaid, a good rule of thumb is "Do not repeat any information you won't sign your name to." I have a pastor friend who carries around an index card, and when people begin to gossip, he starts taking notes on what they're saying and then tells them he's going to go to the person about whom they are talking to tell that person what's being said. People who gossip stopped coming to him because they would not put their names to the gossip.

Another rule of thumb: Be part of the solution, not part of the problem. This pastor friend also tells people who gossip, "We are going to this person about whom you are talking to ask if this is true and, if so, what we can do to help. We are going to be part of the solution here." He's humorously highlighting for them that they may not really want to be part of the solution.

SPEAK YOUR MIND ONLY WHEN NECESSARY:

Emerson's Checklist for Good Neighborly Communication

- ☐ Do I resist the reasons people gossip in their network of relationships: to feel important, to spark a thrill due to boredom, to be entertaining, to bond with the listener, to belittle people they don't like, or to control the perception of the listener about others?
- ☐ Do I see gossip as spreading rumors, usually unverified facts, but even if true, the listener has no right to know, and I have no right to tell?
- ☐ When pulled into the gossip of others, usually from people who seek to be the first to know and first to tell, among other reasons, do I disengage, since neither they nor I are part of the problem or part of the solution?
- ☐ Have I shut the door on gossip because I have no interest in being the first to know and first to tell so that I can be the neighbor in-the-know or the go-to person on private, confidential information?

- ☐ Do I believe that being a gossip damages relationships rather than improves them and discredits me as a person rather than improves my reputation?
- ☐ Do I believe that the people with whom I gossip eventually wonder if I gossip about them, creating suspicion and distrust, since why would I not talk about them behind their backs when I have talked to them about others behind their backs?
- ☐ When misunderstandings with neighbors arise, do I engage the person by communicating what is true, kind, necessary, and clear and stay engaged until there is mutual understanding and resolution?
- ☐ Do I seek to be responsible and respectable when addressing concerns among friends and neighbors?
- ☐ Do I refrain from saying anything about a person that I could not say to that person and from lying about that as some do ("And I'd say that to their face if they were here!")?
- ☐ Do I seek forgiveness and make amends when I have failed to be a good neighbor?

UNFILTERED VERSUS THOUGHTFUL

Unfiltered: I unthinkingly speak unwarranted words, but there's no ill will.

Thoughtful: I value contemplative, cautious, and purposeful communication, since I do not like the damage my mindless, careless, and useless words cause to other people.

In a board meeting of twelve people on Monday at the ABC Printing Company, Patti shares, "Cindy isn't at work today. She's taking a vacation day because she found out on Friday night that her husband is having an affair with his secretary."

That information is true, clear, and spoken out of empathy and kindness toward Cindy, who is Patti's good friend. However, that information is unnecessary. Not only does that information have nothing to do with the business of that meeting, it is none of those folks' business.

Sadly, this becomes fuel for gossip and discredits her husband, who could be repenting at that very moment.

Later in the year, Patti wonders why she doesn't get outside assignments. Someone tells her, "Management can't trust you with inside information! They view you as a loose cannon."

In battle or a storm, when a cannon breaks loose from its moorings, it does severe damage to ship and crew. It is uncontrolled and unpredictable.

Such people defend themselves, saying, "I am not trying to hurt anybody. I am just being honest or expressing concern. I can't always help myself." But a lack of tongue-control is a sign of lack of self-control. The Bible refers to this as an unbridled tongue (James 1:26). The tongue is unrestrained like the unhinged flapping sail that suddenly snaps back and slaps you across the face. When a person does not control his lips, people get hurt.

Just because you are full of goodwill does not mean you should say or write whatever you want. Good intentions do not always produce good words or outcomes. What comes out of the mouth isn't always the same as that which is in the heart. Goodwill and good sense are not synonymous. As the expression goes, "Loose lips sink ships."[1]

SPEAK YOUR MIND ONLY WHEN NECESSARY:

Emerson's Checklist for Thoughtful Communication

- ☐ Do I understand that I can be filled with goodwill—not evil intent—yet be a loose cannon verbally?
- ☐ If I am the type of person who speaks my mind, have I committed myself to think about framing my immediate thoughts into questions to get feedback, allowing me to wholly understand before I give feedback that might be untrue, unnecessary, unkind, and unclear?
- ☐ Do I avoid filling in silence with endless and mindless chatter, which over time causes others to view me as unthinking, self-centered, and insecure?
- ☐ Have I developed an aversion to the potential damage to my relationships and reputation from mindless, careless, and useless words?

- ☐ Do I refuse to make excuses like the person who said, "You know that little thing in the back of your head that tells you not to say something before you say it? Well, I don't have that little thing"?
- ☐ Do I subscribe to the exhortation that, since I have two ears and one mouth, I should use them proportionately, especially reminding me to listen first?
- ☐ Since communication is a two-way street, before I communicate, do I first aim to tailor my tone and talk by asking, "What will my listener or reader hear me saying?"
- ☐ Do I value a contemplative, cautious, and purposeful approach to communication, which means I am thoughtful, careful, and on guard against unintentional and unnecessary comments?
- ☐ Do I think about communicating information that is hopeful and helpful to another, while acknowledging what contributes to this person feeling despair and seeing themselves as unsalvageable?
- ☐ Because I want to be thoughtful, am I willing to empathetically listen to others' problems, ask clarifying questions, discern root causes of the concerns, research possible solutions with practical steps to take, and support them moving forward always from the perspective that I do not exceed my knowledge or qualification?
- ☐ When I put my foot in my mouth, do I quickly apologize for my unnecessary comment to keep relationships healthy, my conscience clear, and my reputation good?

SPYING VERSUS BOUNDARY-RESPECTING

Spying: I don't see it as snooping but as monitoring their mistakes to help them improve.

Boundary-Respecting: I have resolved not to spy by secretly watching and listening, since that is a disrespectful invasion of privacy; instead, I operate within appropriate boundaries and I ask God to show me if there is anything I need to know.

To spy is to secretly gather data on the activities of others without their consent. Unless we work for a governmental agency, it is unnecessary to spy. On a personal basis, we may have the best of intentions and seek only the truth. But the others don't know, and if they knew of our spying, it would undermine the trust in our relationships. It crosses the boundary into unwarranted territory. But more so, why are we spying? Most of us spy to catch others in wrongdoing.

Think of parents. There is no debate that parents must act responsibly toward their children and supervise them against wrongdoing. But some parents have confessed that they seek to be the Holy Spirit to their children. Because of their yearning to prevent their kids from encountering what they experienced at that age, they have an obsessive compulsion to track everything their teen is doing. The thought is, *If I catch them doing something wrong, this will motivate them to do what is right when I am not watching.* These moms and dads spy to confront and correct and, yes, control.

This does not mean there should not be any accountability where the child knows up front about the monitoring. For instance, putting protective software on the computer is a good thing. What *is* wrong is spying on the teen boy who talks to a girl in the park. That's undisclosed monitoring and will break trust in the event he finds out.

For the believer, this can be a crisis of faith. Sarah has told mothers of teenagers, "Tell the Lord, 'Lord, if there's anything I need to know, would You let me know?'" At some point we must trust God. We cannot spy 24/7.

Beyond parenting, some of us convince ourselves we spy or eavesdrop because we care. For example, we wonder if our neighbors are having money problems. Is that why they pulled their kids out of private school? So we try to look for other clues that might support or refute that idea. After all, we need to know if we should bring them a meal, right? At least that's how we try justifying our snooping around.

Or we wonder if the youth pastor at our church is considering leaving for another job. Could that be why he hasn't planned the spring break mission trip yet? We might need to start asking some questions to a few specific people in the church, to see who knows what. Our kids love the youth pastor! We need to know now if we might need to start considering another church option. There's no problem with asking appropriate questions to the right people, given that we're not doing so behind anyone's back. What frightens and offends is when we do something that appears to be spying.

How do we know if we are spying? Are we surveying secretly and fearing exposure? When we fear getting caught by those we seek to catch, we're a spy.

SPEAK YOUR MIND ONLY WHEN NECESSARY:

Emerson's Checklist for Boundary-Respecting Communication

- ☐ Do I recognize that spying on others without consent is excessive, violates healthy and respectful boundaries between adults, and destroys trust when discovered?
- ☐ Even though I genuinely care about another's improvement, do I refuse to use that compassion as justification to resort to the disrespectful and excessive tactics of surveillance?
- ☐ Do I recognize that though I do not spy by invading another's privacy, I could coerce another to divulge information by threatening or bribing, which may not be illegal but is unethical and not only violates others' rights but could cause them to confess falsely?
- ☐ Do I know that I am not responsible for monitoring other adults who make their own choices, and apart from tough love that requires intervention with experts and authorities, I am not to monitor others without their consent?
- ☐ Do I recognize that letting go of controlling other people 24/7 and allowing them to make their own choices does not mean abandonment, but that there are necessary limits to what I can do to prevent them from experiencing the negative consequences of their choices?
- ☐ Am I boundary-respecting in not invading others' privacy, since they will distrust me when they discover I deceived them by jumping over a necessary wall into the area of the covert activity of spying?
- ☐ When unsolicited information comes to my attention about secret and unbecoming behaviors in another, do I kindly and clearly confront this person about whom I care deeply, like an adult son, on what is true and necessary for them to hear about their secret and unbecoming behaviors?

- ☐ When others ask me to mentor and monitor them because they have a problem they wish to remedy, do I have an honest discussion about the necessary boundaries and communication (i.e., the game plan) that permit me to act in their best interests when they may not want me to inquire?
- ☐ If a person has a severe addiction or problem that could lead to harm, do I pursue the wisdom of those who understand the situation, like Alcoholics Anonymous members understand alcoholism and intervention?
- ☐ As a person of faith, I accept that spying is immoral and illegal—a form of espionage—but that does not eliminate my concern that someone may be doing something harmful to themselves. With that in mind, do I pray, "Lord, if there is anything I need to know, let me know"?

CHAPTER 14

RESTRAINED WHEN NECESSARY

Do you sometimes struggle with being a little too indiscreet and a bit wordy at times? "I've never met a lull I didn't love to fill up," you may joke about yourself. But might it be too much at times? If your conversations with others were transcribed and put into a book, would the pages be almost entirely filled with your words?

To learn how to speak our minds necessarily, we must move from verbose communication to restrained communication.

Verbose communicators tend to speak unnecessarily. I refer to verbose communication as oversharing, rehashing, rambling, and piling on. Such individuals inundate others with excessive data that overwhelms; repetitively and exhaustingly repeat the same points; can't stand silence, so they drone on incessantly; and see certain conversations as an opportunity to add, "And one more thing," which is not required.

However, I refer to the positive cluster on necessary speech as *restrained*. Restrained communicators are judicious, succinct, reserved, and focused. They limit what they say to what the other person needs to hear; they make their point once, stop talking, and ask for feedback; they are not afraid of silence and refrain from being a motormouth prattling on about nothing; and they stay centered on the issue, prompting interaction instead of using this as a chance to throw in the kitchen sink.

Wise people try speaking less and thinking more. They learn to limit their words because they know that fewer words can be weightier than many, especially when they end up saying what is unnecessary, untrue, and unkind. They have seen people they love be hurt unintentionally by the shrapnel from their words, like a hand grenade going off. They have vowed to be more restrained and intentional with every word they utter.

Let's discuss those who think "the more, the merrier" when it comes to their words, compared to those who realize the power of the tongue, agreeing with what James 3:8 says about it being a "restless evil, full of deadly poison."

OVERSHARING VERSUS JUDICIOUS

Oversharing: I think I provide helpful information but some feel overwhelmed, so they say.

Judicious: I want to be sure not to share too much information that ends up being unnecessary and unhelpful, so I err on the side of caution and restraint as I use my best judgment in thoughtfully and purposefully communicating.

Over the years, I have received hundreds of e-mails from spouses who share a truckload of information. They tell me that they have a bad marriage, but then they tell me about their mother's health, the landlord's unresponsiveness, the dog running away, the mechanic overcharging, the doctor not seeing them for three more months, putting on extra weight, needing a better health plan, and so on. Though I know their hearts are in the right place, I stop reading. I cannot absorb all the unnecessary information. It is classic TMI—too much information.

Oversharing communicators are usually smart but overly insecure. The insecurity drives them to get the other person to fully understand. For this reason, oversharing communicators ask, "How much information is necessary to make my point?" And if not sure, they give a little information and ask if the other person needs more. The best thing for people who tend to overshare is to remember that less is more.

Others are not insecure but still give too much information. At board meetings at the organizations I led, I would sometimes overprepare on a proposal and present way too much information. My desire for the board members to see my reasoning and position for the purpose of debate would eventually backfire because the avalanche of information became too much for them to absorb all at once.

Here's a clue to determine if you are oversharing. When you talk, do you notice people looking at their watches or phones? Do you hear people saying, "Good, that's enough. I get it. Thanks"? Do people get up and leave the room when you talk? Does your boss say, "Just begin with a one-page summary, and if I want more, I'll ask"?

One person who wrote me had an awakening to oversharing and made a commitment to reform. He said, "My new unspoken motto to strive to live by: K.I.S.S. (Keep It Simple, Stupid)." Maybe a better slogan is "Keep It Short, Stupid." This is not bad advice to think about before communicating.

SPEAK YOUR MIND ONLY WHEN NECESSARY:

Emerson's Checklist for Judicious Communication

- ☐ Do I strive to communicate with good judgment and wisdom, not saying too much and not saying too little to help others?
- ☐ Do I ensure I do not share unnecessary information when communicating so I do not overwhelm, distract, or confuse the audience, lowering their retention and wasting their time?
- ☐ To be a judicious communicator who avoids oversharing, do I keep working on my editing skills to say only what is pertinent and suitable?
- ☐ To counter my tendency to provide too much information, do I consciously ask questions as an active listener to draw the other person out so the conversation can be fair and balanced?
- ☐ Do I ask myself if my information is morally unsuitable because it is inappropriate, confidential, unverified, prohibited, illegal, or cruel?
- ☐ Do I ask myself if my information is contextually impertinent because it is irrelevant, redundant, excessive, too technical, too detailed, or untimely?
- ☐ When I wonder if the information is unnecessary to broadcast, in light of my proclivity for oversharing, do I err on the side of caution and restraint?

- ☐ When preparing to communicate, do I consider what my audience feels they need to know and what I feel they need to know and strive to strike a balance between the two?
- ☐ When I communicate, do I stay on point (keeping the goal of what I need to say the priority), not get derailed from that main concern, and continually work at being clear and concise?
- ☐ Am I in tune with why I might share too much information—a lack of self-awareness, grabbing attention, trying to be important to others, having no boundaries, or thinking I am helpful?

REHASHING VERSUS SUCCINCT

Rehashing: I've got to go over it again. I won't drop it and move on until I feel okay.

Succinct: I know when to state my exact concern once or twice and then stop the unnecessary repetition, since rehashing the issue wears out the listener and is unproductive.

A guy told me once, "She began . . . rehashing years of things that I did wrong, making me feel like I was stupid." A woman also told me, "He spends all of our time rehashing everything I ever did wrong."

In many cases, the rehashing communicator is feeling insecure more than trying to condemn the other. One woman recognized this in herself. She needed to talk to resolve things. Unless she talked things through, she didn't feel right or secure and kept rehearsing in her mind and rehashing with others. But people were shutting down on her. She turned to her dad for advice. He said, "Honey, the question you need to ask is this: 'Will I remember this in a day, a week, a month, or a year from now? Will they?' If not, it is okay to let it go. That doesn't mean you shouldn't talk it through with the other person, but it may not be necessary." She told me this liberated her, since no one had ever said that to her. All her life, she had felt everything was necessary to talk through whenever she felt bothered.

When I counsel couples, I share that certain chemicals in a woman cause her to stew for a twelve-hour period after a conflict. She rehearses the whole episode, finding it impossible to shake it. Whereas a man's chemical makeup differs, and he can stop stewing over the specifics after one hour. This is why when a couple has a fight in the morning, that evening she needs to talk about what happened nine hours earlier, whereas he replies, "What are you talking about?" He honestly can't remember why she's upset. He has thought about a hundred things at work, and their flare-up earlier that morning is now in his rearview mirror. Two mature people need to decide whether to drop it, as he has, or talk about it because she still has a need to talk about it. Neither is wrong, just different.

Some things need to be overlooked, not written on a ledger to rehash every day until we feel secure as a person. Love "keeps no record of wrongs" (1 Cor. 13:5 NIV), especially when the other person has understood that he or she came across poorly and apologized. We need to forgive and move on. Rehashing can shame the other, who now complains, "Is this necessary, again? What else can I say or do?"

Some of us need to give these matters to God, as Peter wrote, "casting all your anxiety on Him, because He cares for you" (1 Peter 5:7). A person wrote, "I still have times of weakness when I doubt [their] intentions. I seem to have a hard time stopping myself from thinking in the past and rehashing those feelings. I've been relying on prayer to help me through those issues."

Jesus said, "Come to Me, all who are weary and heavy-laden, and I will give you rest" (Matt. 11:28). Sounds like a great avenue to take! Before speaking your mind, maybe you should hit your knees and first communicate with God.

SPEAK YOUR MIND ONLY WHEN NECESSARY:

Emerson's Checklist for Succinct Communication

- ☐ Do I recognize that I am rehashing information when the repetition does not move the conversation forward meaningfully and productively?
- ☐ Do I repeat myself unnecessarily because I lack confidence in conveying clearly what I think and feel the first time, so I assume I need to say it again so the other person will understand?

- ☐ Do I rehash information because I lack confidence in my ability to communicate succinctly and my listener's ability to hear and understand?
- ☐ When someone sighs and asks me, "This again?" do I realize I am addressing something that either cannot change or has already been resolved, which is pointless and unproductive?
- ☐ Given I have said what was true, kind, necessary, and clear and the other person "gets it," do I realize how annoying and useless rehashing the same thought or feeling is to the other person?
- ☐ If I say the same thing several times and my audience does not understand, do I realize then that saying the same thing again with the same results is not the way forward, but instead I must communicate differently by using new words, better examples, and allowing for questions?
- ☐ Do I realize that I can reduce rehashing by asking, "Would you tell me what you heard me say and does it make sense?" and if they do tell me and it makes sense, then I don't need to say it again?
- ☐ Do I work at being clear and concise in my communication, since this is prized on the personal and professional level, then go quiet to see if the person understood?
- ☐ Do I understand that halting the unnecessary repetition of information does not mean ceasing providing new, vital, and required input?
- ☐ Do I realize that effective communicators who grasp complex ideas know how to distill that information in bite-size portions and use words and examples based on the audience's level of knowledge and understanding?

RAMBLING VERSUS RESERVED

Rambling: I dislike silence, so I fill it with whatever I am thinking at the time.

Reserved: I am comfortable in the silence and don't need to fill the air with chitchat to compensate for my nervousness and insecurities, since that has nothing to do with being friendly or setting others at ease.

Some of us have nothing to say, but we talk anyway.

For example, Rhonda is in the workroom of a company with five others, sorting and preparing documents for distribution, and the six of them make small talk with one another while doing their work. But rambling Rhonda talks about the new wastebasket in the ladies' room that reminds her that she needs to get a wastebasket for her freshly painted bathroom at home, which took three weeks to paint because she couldn't get the color correct. That then reminds her of her grandmother, who had only an outhouse but lived to ninety-two and died in the local hospital, which she learned just added a new wing for drug addicts. She is off and running, saying a lot about nothing, and at a certain point, no one cares and everyone stops listening.

Rambling communicators feel compelled to talk when nothing needs to be said. One person who admitted to rambling communication said she was on the phone and suddenly became aware that she felt as if she had no control over what she was saying. She felt like she was on autopilot, going on and on. What amazed this person at her point of self-illumination was that she knew that she was thinking of something else while her lips were moving on this topic. It concerned her that she had nothing to say but kept talking anyway, not even engaged in her own conversation. That takes talent.

Men have told me they refuse to include certain guys on their hunting expeditions because they don't stop talking. Instead of continuing to tell the fellow, "Put a sock in it!" because his incessant chatter is causing the animals to flee—they stop inviting him to go hunting.

If you think you might be a rambling communicator, ask yourself these questions:

- Do I talk even though I don't need to say anything?
- Why do I feel I must be the one to talk when no one is talking?
- Upon reflection, do others listen when I talk?
- If not, is that because I drone on like white noise that puts others to sleep?
- Does it bother me when I am interrupted and later no one asks me to resume what I was saying?

- Do I even care to resume what I was saying?
- Do I or anyone else even remember what I was saying?

If the answers to these questions are unfavorable, you are talking unnecessarily.

SPEAK YOUR MIND ONLY WHEN NECESSARY:

Emerson's Checklist for Reserved Communication

- ☐ Despite seeing myself as a friendly person, as an incessant talker, have I unintentionally sabotaged the formation of genuine friendships due to the one-sided nature of the conversation, since without reciprocity, deep friendships will not form?
- ☐ Have I been a rambling communicator because I was self-focused, insecure, and unrestrained instead of deciding to be interested in other people and finding out what is going on in their lives?
- ☐ Do I feel another's silence means they expect me to carry the conversation, since they find me interesting and want me to keep talking and talking still more?
- ☐ Given I tend to use rambling communication, do I interpret silence between myself and another to mean I am not making a good impression, so I need to talk to win their favor?
- ☐ Do I become anxious and insecure when silence comes into a conversation or group setting, which compels me to talk no matter how irrelevant, uninteresting, and unrestrained I am?
- ☐ When I realize I'm talking a lot, do I coach myself to be more reserved and restrained without feeling I am unkind, unsociable, or unpleasant in order to honor others by allowing them to share their thoughts and feelings?
- ☐ In adjusting to not using mindless, rambling communication, do I see that being more reserved in my silence gives another person a chance to talk so there can be a dialogue, not a monologue?
- ☐ To talk less, do I ask questions of the other person so they will share on what they have been doing, reading, or watching related to their interests and responsibilities?

- ☐ After asking others a question about themselves and they answer with a "not much" and go quiet, do I draw them out by asking something about them like, "Well, I heard you took a trip to Mexico. What was your favorite part of the trip?"
- ☐ As a recovering rambling communicator, do I remind myself of what I have learned about why I should be more reserved and restrained: It keeps me more self-aware, allows others to share their thoughts, and keeps conversations more substantive?
- ☐ Do I spend time alone in silence, or must I always have noise?

PILING ON VERSUS FOCUSED

Piling On: When upset, I think of additional stuff and say it; it's not off topic to me.

Focused: I no longer say, "And one more thing" when in conflict but state my single concern and let the truth about that one point carry its weight instead of piling on with other and unnecessary accusations, even though I have other unrelated burdens and the person is attentively listening.

I have a friend who, when he gets going on things that bother him, will humorously exclaim, in imitation of what others say, "And one more thing!" I laugh because we know this is what people do in heated conversations.

This add-on sentence keeps the fight going. For example, a woman criticizes her husband for failing to remember to pick up her clothing at the cleaners and uses this to drive home the point that he doesn't care. But she piles on. "And one more thing, you care about your mother more than you care about me. You call her a couple of times a week but never call me like that. And you mismanage money like your mother mismanages money. Like mother, like son."

It is too much. He feels punched and pummeled, and he shuts down.

My dad would pile on when arguing with my mother. If upon

returning home from work he saw debris in the bottom of the swimming pool from a storm, he would often yell, "Why did you not cover the pool during the storm? Now I have to clean all that up!" And when his anger caused her to exit the scene, he would pile on more. "There you go again, leaving the house to run around doing whatever you do, spending money on whatever." Forget that there were times when a storm would come up unexpectedly and even Dad would not cover the pool. Or that he, too, enjoyed having extra money to spend from the income Mom earned by teaching swim lessons in that pool every day. But he repeatedly piled on as though this would solicit empathy and bring about the changes he deemed crucial.

People who realized their tendencies to use piling-on communication have shared with me that they pile on stuff in an argument that has been disturbing them about the other person, even though it has nothing to do with the issue on the table. They also admit that they often speak what is unnecessary because they do not believe it is enough to speak only what is necessary. And many have shared that they never realized how their constant criticisms were affecting the other.

Are you guilty of saying, "And one more thing"?

SPEAK YOUR MIND ONLY WHEN NECESSARY:

Emerson's Checklist for Focused Communication

- ☐ Am I consistently aware in heated exchanges of the importance of staying focused on the main concern so my listener can also zero in on the root issue; otherwise, we will end up on irrelevant rabbit trails that end up frustrating both of us?
- ☐ Do I value keeping the main thing the main thing, since that keeps the conversation concise and clear, allows us to achieve more and more quickly, without digressions during problem-solving, and maintains harmony and teamwork, decreasing the amount of conflict moving forward?
- ☐ Am I restrained during emotional conflicts to stay on track, keeping the main issue the main issue, instead of getting triggered and sidetracked on concerns unrelated to the reason for the conflict?

- ☐ To avoid piling on during a conflict, do I refrain from blurting out, "And one more thing!" even if I believe the tangential comment is necessary and my right, since such a comment can derail us from the heart of the issue?
- ☐ Do I discern that piling on unnecessary information tends to be accusatory and emotionally floods others, puts them on the defensive, escalates the conflict with more items to argue about, takes us off-topic from the main concern, and delays getting to a win-win resolution?
- ☐ Do I refuse to pile on additional topics during a tense conversation, since it lacks restraint, order, reasonableness, and resolution, like asking where the car keys are and then adding, "Oh, did you pay that bill I left on the car seat, and by the way, why didn't you return my call today? And that reminds me, did you call your mom? If not, this is another example that you never listen to me"?
- ☐ During conflict, do I keep the main issue the main issue by being clear in my own mind what that is, communicating that idea clearly, and returning to that main idea when distracted?
- ☐ Though I focus on the main issue and do not pile on, do I still maintain an openness to new information surfacing that is more important to address and requires my understanding, empathy, and willingness to shift topics, like going from "Where are the car keys?" to "Did you know my high school football coach was killed in an automobile accident?"
- ☐ If another attentively listens on the main topic at hand, do I refrain from seeing this as my chance to bring up other stuff I have wanted to talk about, since this is unfair, disrespectful, and potentially provocative?
- ☐ Even though I have valid burdens that I wish to surface, when these have nothing to do with the topic being discussed, do I refrain and save those concerns for another time?

CHAPTER 15

OTHER-CENTERED WHEN NECESSARY

It's safe to say that everyone struggles, at least at times, with the natural tendency to "make it all about me" when it comes to dialoguing with others. Perhaps you find yourself saying that which is unnecessary out of a preoccupation with yourself and what is important to you. "I need to find out more so that I can advance my agenda." Or "These people are so boring. I need to bring some life into this conversation!" Or "I need to say what is on my mind, even if it means taking the microphone away from you."

To combat this requires a daily intentionality to become other-centered—to work at skillfully sharing only what is necessary for another's benefit or withholding what is unnecessary because of another's privacy. But in doing so, you will experience a sense of satisfaction in serving the person to whom you are speaking that cannot be achieved when you are consumed only with yourself. Each of us needs to make the transition from "It's all about me!" to "How can I make it more about others and their needs?"

To learn how to speak what is necessary, the shift occurs when you decide to cease being egocentric and work at being other-centered.

To refresh your memory, *egocentric* communication is a cluster that includes the following types of unnecessary words: prying, interrupting, distracting, and limelight-seeking. Some egocentric communicators seek to advance their selfish agendas and nose around for information they have no right to know by eavesdropping. (By the way, prying is different than spying. A spy will pry but not all who pry are a spy.) Some butt in because they think what they have to say is necessary, whereas the other person's information is unimportant; some fear exposure of a wrongdoing, so they sidetrack others with tangential information; and some wish to be center stage, so they dominate conversations with their interests, not with what serves and supports others.

By contrast, the *other-centered* communication cluster is considerate, listening, transparent, and supportive. These are individuals who, though curious, are caring, so they allow the other to share what is needed without meddling; who pay attention to what concerns the other person without interfering to insert something unneeded; who speak the necessary truth kindly even if self-incriminating, since this best ensures the long-term health of the relationship; and who ask questions to learn what uplifts the other and best serves another's heart-concerns.

In this final section on speaking your mind only when necessary, let's go against the grain of our natural tendencies to be "me-focused" and learn what it truly means to put others ahead of ourselves in our communication.

PRYING VERSUS CONSIDERATE

Prying: Not knowing the details, I have to meddle to enable me to advance my cause.

Considerate: Though curious and caring, I do not probe and meddle by asking intrusive questions to unearth confidential information that is unnecessary for me to know. Therefore, I have committed to being a courteous person, honoring others' privacy and acting only in beneficial ways.

A caring interest in the daily activities of others is good, but being too inquisitive can get out of hand when it comes from an unhealthy intrigue.

The problem is that some who pry don't see themselves as prying. They see themselves as caring. Sarah, my wife, talks about the twenty questions she would ask our son David every day after school when he was in the fifth grade. About a week into this regimen, David said, "Mom, it's the same every day. If anything changes, I'll let you know." Like every mother, Sarah wanted to connect with her son's heart. She cared, and from her vantage point, connection could happen only through talking. Since David did not talk to Sarah as she longed for, she felt compelled to keep asking more and more questions to draw him out. In my book *Mother & Son*, I address what a mom can do in this situation. A mother who isn't getting the communication she wants might consider asking herself: *Is this prying or connecting? Will my son feel uncomfortable because it doesn't feel friendly but more like an investigation to find out information about him in order to correct him?* I coach a mother to reassure her son that this is not her motive.

Some of us pry because we cannot stand not knowing. In doing so we push others beyond the boundaries with which they feel comfortable. Whenever strife is in the air on issues that matter to us, we feel compelled to meddle (Prov. 26:17). We "snoop for the scoop" to advance our interests. For example, we send an e-mail with questions that we cloak in innocent-sounding ways, but that we intend to use for our own agenda. We ask people questions that sound as if we are truly concerned about them or a situation when really we are just collecting data. The Bible refers to us as "a troublesome meddler" (1 Peter 4:15). This type of person is not conducting themself in an aboveboard manner but has improperly crossed the line into a covert operation. It is necessary to debate, not deceive.

At times when you find yourself wanting to ask someone a barrage of personal questions, why not first ask yourself, *Why am I asking so many questions?*

Is prying connected with your fear of missing out? Tiffany Bloodworth Rivers said, "Because we *can* be so connected, many feel that they *have to be* connected at all times. In fact, there is a real psychological condition, fear of missing out (or FOMO), which is growing among members of our society, in which people feel a compulsion to know what is happening, communicate with, or share information with any and all people, places, and things."[1] This feeds the prying proclivity.

Do you pry? Let me ask: If a single neighbor of yours suddenly had a second car in the driveway for over a week, would this drive you nuts until you knew why?

SPEAK YOUR MIND ONLY WHEN NECESSARY:

Emerson's Checklist for Considerate Communication

- ☐ Apart from a life-and-death situation, do I take the position that there is no justification for prying?
- ☐ Do I have a moral compass that enables me to detect when I am digging to unearth confidential and private information that I have no right or need to know?
- ☐ Do I see social and emotional prying as a form of home invasion and coercive, albeit metaphorical?
- ☐ Though I can be motivated by my honest curiosity and genuine caring, do I hold back on intrusive questions meant to pry confidential information that is none of my business, since that is meddling and a line I should not cross?
- ☐ If I am tempted to pry unnecessarily, is this due to inappropriate curiosity, seeking to control another with embarrassing information, a sense of entitlement and right to know, or a lack of emotional intelligence in establishing healthy boundaries?
- ☐ At times when I feel I "need to know" information that I have no right to know, do I resist because of my commitment to honor others' privacy courteously and act only in beneficial ways?
- ☐ Given I think there is information I should know, instead of prying in misleading ways, do I speak openly and honestly about my concern, like, "I have noticed some things recently going on with you, and because I care, I wanted to check in to see how you are doing and to let you know I am here for you"?
- ☐ If I have openly asked questions about what is true and necessary in a kind and clear way, yet the other person is not forthcoming with information I need to know, do I refuse to pry?

- ☐ Do I acknowledge the common-sense conclusion that the risk of prying far outweighs the reward, since unless someone wishes for me to know private information about them, it is not my responsibility to know, and that it typically damages trust and discredits me as a loving and respectful person?
- ☐ Do I reject the hypocritical idea that if someone is not honest with me, I can pry in dishonest ways to find out where they have been dishonest?
- ☐ When others invite me into their confidential private lives, do I let them know I am honored but not cross over from probing into prying, from inquisitiveness into invasiveness, or from inquiring into interrogating?

INTERRUPTING VERSUS LISTENING

Interrupting: People tell me I interrupt them unnecessarily, but what I say is important for them to hear and understand.

Listening: Since I am other-focused, I first attentively listen to understand the concern.

Several wives have communicated to me their frustrations similar to the one expressed in this e-mail: "He interrupts me when I try to speak; then I feel disrespected, unheard . . . I then react to him by raising my voice and telling him to listen to me. I try to continue, but he interrupts to tell me what I'm feeling or what he thinks I should do. I get even more offended."

All of this is unnecessary.

All of us must recognize that when we think what we want to say is the most important thing that needs to be said, we are tempted to interrupt.

For instance, two people are discussing a project in the conference room, and an individual enters to tell them that he just got tickets to an NFL game. That's nice information, but it's irrelevant to their discussion and interrupts their flow of thought. Furthermore, his real point in interrupting is to brag that the boss just gave him the tickets.

Some interruptions are innocent but annoying nonetheless. My daughter, Joy, told me, "I usually stumble upon the last few episodes of *The Bachelor/ette* with friends who are very engrossed in the TV program. But they get annoyed as I interrupt constantly about the editing and acting, not to mention cries of 'Are you kidding me?'"

What about the work arena? A manager or owner is in charge of everyone in the room and has the authority to speak their thoughts at any time, right? To this argument, I would say that the most effective leaders are not authoritarian. They are strong but gracious in asking, "Would this be a good time to describe a situation to you, or would later be better?" Most folks will immediately defer to the leader and will be appreciative of the sensitivity. People know that a leader has the greater responsibility and with that come certain rights, one of which is the right to interrupt. However, the leader need not be rude. They can say, "Sorry to interrupt, but I have a couple of important items to cover that just came to my attention. Again, I apologize for taking you away from what you are doing, so thank you for allowing me to do this."

Learning to listen better is not just for the married and office workers, though. It is a fundamental skill necessary for the health and benefit of all relationships. Joy recently reminded me of a statement I would often say to her that applies in every relationship we have: *Win the right to be heard*. In effect, that's what this book is about. Over time, when you establish a reputation for communicating what is true, kind, necessary, and clear, people view you as competent and trustworthy. You've won the right to be heard. But the first step toward earning this reputation is listening, so that you know not only the right words to say but also the right time to say them. Your words carry a great deal of weight, and if you have taken the necessary time to listen fully, when the time is right to finally speak into the current situation, your words will put you in the best position to influence the situation because you've won the right to be heard.

It comes back to the Golden Rule. Just do what you would want done to you.

SPEAK YOUR MIND ONLY WHEN NECESSARY:

Emerson's Checklist for Listening Communication

- ☐ Do I first focus on the other, listen to understand, and not interrupt or allow myself to be distracted when they share?
- ☐ Do I detect that sometimes what is necessary is for me to simply listen instead of offering a solution?
- ☐ Do I nonverbally let them know I am present and engaged by nodding, leaning in, and maintaining eye contact?
- ☐ Do I mirror back to let them know I understand by summarizing or paraphrasing what they shared?
- ☐ Do I remain silent when they are processing and presenting, ensuring I do not offer my thoughts before they have told me all of theirs?
- ☐ Do I resist the tendency to interrupt when I think I understand the issue and what they should do before I have listened and enabled them to feel I understand?
- ☐ Do I clarify by repeating back what I heard and asking, "Did I hear you correctly, or is there more I should know so that I can fully understand what you mean?"
- ☐ Do I draw them out when I know there is more, like saying, "It sounds like you are hurt and frustrated with what happened when you said (XYZ)"?
- ☐ Do I ask questions for clarification so I will not presume I know or speak from ignorance?
- ☐ Do I empathetically listen not only to what they said, like "My dog died yesterday," but also empathize with the emotions behind their face-value comment with "Oh, you loved that dog, and I cannot imagine your sorrow"?
- ☐ Before I speak, do I ask myself: *Is this relevant and helpful information in serving them with their problem?*
- ☐ Even though I disagree and disapprove of some of what they tell me, do I hold off on why I think that is not in their best interests until they are confident I understand their perspective and why they feel as they do?
- ☐ Do I apologize when they feel I did not listen or understand and ask for another chance to listen well?

DISTRACTING VERSUS TRANSPARENT

Distracting: I refuse to be put on the hot seat, so I sidetrack others with unrelated stuff.

Transparent: I strive to be straightforward about myself and what is true, since this is necessary for the health of relationships, so I set aside the insecurities that tempt me to sidetrack the conversation with tangential and misleading information to keep me off the hot seat.

When a four-year-old asks us how babies are made, we distract them by saying, "Hey, look at the bird in that tree. What kind of bird is that? Let's look in our bird book, and then let's make cookies." That kind of distraction is appropriate and necessary. But when a friend asks us why we haven't been at church in a few weeks, we can't get away with the same type of distraction—though we may try.

Many times we act like the politician refusing to be put on the hot seat when being interviewed. The politician skirts around the issue, refusing to answer the question. Occasionally that can be a good thing, but most times it is a tactic to avoid releasing any unpopular information. When questioned, the politician often employs the distraction techniques they learned at the beginning of their career: They either ask a question in return, attack the question, attack the questioner, plead ignorance, or jump to another topic.

But the discerning person is not fooled by the politician's techniques, and neither is our friend who has our best interest in heart when asking us the uncomfortable questions we try to avoid. Though being a distractor does not necessarily mean we are being untruthful per se, we are still trying to keep away from subjects we prefer not to address. As with the politician, that can be a wise thing at certain times, but when we refuse to talk to our concerned and goodwilled friend, pastor, or family member about a problem area we know we should be seeking counsel for, and instead try to distract them with another topic, this can be interpreted by others as our unwillingness to address an important topic that is necessary for them to gather information about. We talk about the unnecessary to avoid the necessary.

This does not mean that we need to be an open book to anyone and everyone, obligated to answer fully every question they have for us. But when we are asked questions that either we are not prepared to answer at the moment or we feel were unnecessary to have even been asked in the first place, can we respect the one questioning us enough not to try distracting them with unnecessary information and nonanswers and simply say, "This is not the right time for me to get into that for you. Can I get back with you on that after I have some time to think further on this issue?"

SPEAK YOUR MIND ONLY WHEN NECESSARY:

Emerson's Checklist for Transparent Communication

- ☐ Though I can distract and deflect from what is true and necessary to know about what I said or did, am I a person of integrity who refuses to sidetrack people with unrelated topics but faces the music to resolve the concern?
- ☐ Do I avoid tangents or unnecessary details that could distract from the main point or lead to confusion, and am I straightforward about events and feelings?
- ☐ Do I live by the simple truth that to be a credible person, I must be competent and trustworthy?
- ☐ I do not like being on the hot seat to answer probing questions from someone intensely scrutinizing my past actions, but when that happens, do I stay calm and answer the questions with what is true and necessary from a cooperative spirit?
- ☐ When I have been less than trustworthy, do I recognize how this causes others to feel that I might not be responsible, authentic, and dependable (R.A.D.)?
- ☐ When I fall short of being the competent person others rightly expect me to be, do I own up to that, since it demonstrates my accountability, personal growth, and transparency (A.P.T.)?
- ☐ Has there been a time when I accepted a conversation about the unpleasant consequences of what I had said or done, acknowledged the report's accuracy, took responsibility for those things, and made the necessary changes humbly and maturely?

- ☐ When I have not measured up to being a competent and trustworthy person and have lost credibility, do I seek forgiveness and make amends for the sake of the relationship?
- ☐ On the heels of acknowledging my errors, with full disclosure and transparency, do I make changes that reestablish my honor and create mutually beneficial solutions to the original problem I sidestepped?

LIMELIGHT-SEEKING VERSUS SUPPORTIVE

Limelight-Seeking: Other people are quiet or boring, so I take center stage with my interests.

Supportive: I have no desire to upstage anyone, especially when their needs are unheard. I ask questions and contentedly focus on their calling, interests, and burdens.

Returning from summer vacation, Susan, a university professor, saw her colleague in the hall and asked, "So, Fred, how was your summer?" Fred launched into a thirty-minute description of all he did during summer vacation, entertaining Susan with his numerous stories, to which she laughed. When Fred finished, he looked at his watch and said he had to go, to which Susan replied, "Well, Fred, it would have been nice for you to ask how *my* summer went." With a twinkle in his eyes, Fred replied, "Frankly, Susan, I don't care."

Storytellers grab center stage. Some are quite entertaining. I have a friend who tells the same hilarious stories in social settings, but everyone, along with me, loves to hear the episodes again and again. In fact, her friends hold up fingers to show how many times they've heard this particular episode, but they let her continue because she has them crying again with laughter. But few have this endearing ability. Almost every limelighter is egotistical, wishing to hear only his own voice, since he views others as relatively unimportant. We observe this with ego-driven intellectuals or extroverts who talk on and on about what they prize. Or as comedian Brian Regan perfectly described them, "Me-Monsters."[2]

I came across this person's words, which capture the pain of being in the shadows when a limelight-seeking communicator shows up:

> Once or twice a week I find myself having lunch with coworkers, or dinner with friends of friends, at which there is someone who just won't shut up, or who talks too loud, or who has little to say but takes forever to say it, or who always talks about the same topics. It's exhausting, and frustrating for others who wouldn't mind chiming in with their own thoughts every now and again. Why do they do this and what's the best way to handle them? I'm a quiet person. I enjoy a good chat, but I like it to be mellow and relaxed, and always make an effort to bring other people in where I can. Some people just completely lack this social skill. They think they are fun and that their energy livens things up, when actually they are stopping other people from enjoying themselves.[3]

Are you a Me-Monster? Do you tend to use limelight-seeking communication? Is this how you wish to be as a person? Try turning the spotlight off yourself and put it on someone around you. If you struggle making deep, quality friendships, shifting the focus to others will endear others to you.

SPEAK YOUR MIND ONLY WHEN NECESSARY:

Emerson's Checklist for Supportive Communication

- ☐ Do I avoid being center stage and self-promoting by humbly sharing the spotlight, highlighting and praising others' contributions, and crediting the success of working as a team to achieve various goals?
- ☐ When I dominate conversations, I can offer helpful and necessary information, but when I do that all the time, do I realize I inevitably shift from thinking about serving others to trying to impress others because my ego has taken over?
- ☐ Do I realize that I can inadvertently not hear what others are saying about what they need or feel is necessary to benefit the situation because I am a motormouth who does not listen?

- ☐ In conversations, do I ask more questions than I answer? Do I focus on others' interests, needs, and burdens and value their perspectives?
- ☐ Do I actively collaborate with others, welcome their input, and fulfill a supportive role in their lives by valuing their thoughts and feelings on what is true, kind, necessary, and clear?
- ☐ Do I avoid upstaging others by welcoming their input, focusing on their thoughts and efforts, allowing them their rightful place, and empowering them to achieve their goals?
- ☐ Though I may have experience and expertise in various areas, do I downplay that I have a corner on the truth and genuinely ask others what they think and affirm their beneficial ideas?
- ☐ When others succeed, whether in my area of interest or not, do I celebrate their success by affirming them and telling others?
- ☐ Do I work on word choice in the sense that I do not say, "Let me tell what I have accomplished due to my genius," but look for ways to credit others, like "This was a team effort" or "I could never have accomplished this without three people who influenced my early life"?

PART 4

SPEAK YOUR MIND CLEARLY

Is your true, kind, and necessary communication also clear to others?

When I was a boy, I went through the neighborhood one day calling out, "Fire! Fire! Fire!" My neighbor, Mrs. Lintz, came running to her front door, yelling, "Where?" I shouted back, "I don't know." She said, "Where's the fire?" Again, "I don't know. I am looking for him." She asked, "Him? What are you talking about?" I told her my dalmatian, Fire, had escaped from our yard and was lost. Shortly thereafter she called my parents, clearly with a demand for something to be done. So we changed the dog's name to Flyer.

Is my communication clear to me? A fellow said, "I may not be funny or athletic or good-looking or smart or talented . . . I forget where I am going with this."

Though we laugh, this represents the daily speech of some. They forget where they are going. We need to be clear in our own minds as to where we are headed in what we are saying; otherwise, those on the receiving end will be more confused. As pastors, we say, "If there is a mist in the pulpit, there's a fog in the pew."

Anthony Hope Hawkins commented, "Unless one is a genius, it is best to aim at being intelligible."[1] And even if one is a genius, one learns ways of communicating clearly to various groups. It is one thing to talk to a group of academics about what we do. It is something else when explaining to our grandmothers what we do. They may not grasp the academic side, but every expert comes up with examples that enable laity to understand at a certain level. A good-hearted genius is sensitive about talking over the heads of others and making them feel stupid but uses his intelligence to come up with stories and analogies that paint a clear picture that an elementary student can appreciate.

The point I am making is that we can and must be clear based on the different audiences with whom we communicate. The truth another needs to know can and must be clear, and we can and must convey it kindly.

THE HEART OF COMMUNICATING WHAT IS CLEAR

Clarity starts in our hearts. Proverbs 15:28 states, "The heart of the righteous ponders how to answer." And we read in Proverbs 16:23, "The heart of the wise instructs his mouth and adds persuasiveness to his lips."

When our hearts are not in it, we do not ponder or self-instruct. We lack a heart of diligence to be organized, specific, precise, articulate, and coherent. On the other hand, when it is in our hearts to communicate what is true, kind, and necessary, it will be in our hearts to make sure we do so clearly.

As I stated earlier, I practiced the first three of kindly speaking what was true and necessary but realized that not everyone understood me because I was not clear. I had to make a decision to figure out better ways to answer. I needed to teach myself how to persuade better than I had been.

When the people in our world are saying, "I did not quite understand your point. What exactly did you mean?" then we need to sharpen our skills related to clear communication.

Even the best communicators fall short. I watched a well-known editor ask a famous author, "What did you mean here in what you wrote?" The author then explained what he meant. The editor shot back, "Then why in the world didn't you say that?" That scene, which I observed from another room, stuck with me for decades.

If even a great communicator must keep improving his skills, what about the rest of us? Are we hazy communicators because we are lazy communicators? Do we need to work harder at being clear about what we mean? Do we need to put more of our hearts into this? We need to care enough to be clear.

THE GOLDEN RULE OF CLEAR COMMUNICATION

None of us likes it when people are unclear with us about what is true. We dislike wondering, *Did they mean to say that in such an unloving and disrespectful manner?* And for those who ramble, we find ourselves frustrated, trying to figure out the essential point they seek to make.

We get annoyed by hazy and lazy communicators. We do not favor those who lack the discipline to enunciate well, write legibly, and use grammar appropriately. When reading e-mails or social media posts that upset us, we are taken aback when we realize had the person reread what he or she wrote before speaking their mind, this would not appear so unintelligent.

We do not enjoy having to keep asking, "What did you mean by what you just said? Where did this happen, and when? Who was involved? Why are we just now hearing about this, and how did this happen? You provided no reasons. How do you expect us to respond?" We expect others to think well enough to clearly answer the what, when, where, who, why, and how.

But this raises the question: Do we have the same standard for ourselves?

BACK TO THE ASSESSMENT

Let's return to the self-assessment one final time to consider in greater detail the twenty types of clear communication that were introduced. Which of these rang familiar for you? Which ones stood out to you as reasons why you might be unintentionally communicating your true, kind, and necessary words in ways that are not clear to others?

In part 4, we will examine each of these twenty descriptors by looking at their clusters:

- Those who consider themselves fuzzy in their struggle to communicate themselves clearly should make better effort to use *intelligible communication* (chapter 16).
- Those with the bad habit of looking to find fault in others when they are not understood should take responsibility for their part in the miscommunication and intentionally seek *improved communication* techniques (chapter 17).
- Those who struggle with sending mixed messages and flip-flop in their beliefs should strive to use *authentic communication* so their every action and word flows naturally from their convictions (chapter 18).
- It is certainly not wrong, or even a weakness, to be emotional, but for those who allow this to affect their communications, they should learn how to use *poised communication* when sharing that which they have strong feelings about (chapter 19).
- Disjointed and unclear communicators should make an effort to use *organized communication* in their thoughts and speaking style (chapter 20).
- Finally, those who suppress what they should communicate need to gain the skills and confidence to realize their knowledge on a matter and use *open communication* with others about that helpful information (chapter 21).

CHAPTER 16

INTELLIGIBLE COMMUNICATION

Do others sometimes struggle with understanding you because you tend to be vague when attempting to express your thoughts and you are unable to fully explain yourself well? Perhaps you're not aware of your struggles to explain yourself, or maybe you know this about yourself quite well but have never taken steps to amend it. You may have no ill intent in your lack of clarity, yet your communication style doesn't leave others fully informed and thus has caused many problems that could have been avoided.

To learn how to speak our minds clearly, each of us needs to make a concerted effort to be far less fuzzy in what we communicate and say things in intelligible ways so others more easily understand. We must eliminate ambiguity so others can grasp what we say.

The cluster of *fuzzy* communication involves communicators who are unaware, mystical, incomplete, and indecisive. In other words, they wrongly assume others have the same level of knowledge they do and end up leaving folks in the dark; are not diligent in saying plainly and unmistakably what they mean because they don't know themselves; are prone to omit crucial details due to slackness and inattentiveness; and dawdle and stall due to apprehension and procrastination so others remain uncertain about options and conclusions.

On the other hand, clear communication is *intelligible*. I describe the intelligible cluster as clarifying, articulate, thorough, and decisive. That is, such communicators frequently solicit feedback by asking,

"Does this make sense?"; work hard at figuring out what they mean so they can say it sensibly; make sure they comprehensively express all that needs to be heard; and resolve issues in an informed and timely manner so people are correctly apprised.

The good news is that this may be one of the easier "fixes" when it comes to learning how to more effectively speak your mind. There are simple adjustments fuzzy communicators can make that will help them clearly, thoroughly, and promptly explain better what they mean.

In this first chapter on speaking your mind clearly, we will discuss how to best clarify what you mean to communicate, be more articulate and purposeful about what you say and write, and confidently become a more complete and decisive communicator.

UNAWARE VERSUS CLARIFYING

Unaware: At times when communicating, I'm unaware that others don't know what I know.

Clarifying: I do not assume I am always clear or people are tracking with me, so I purposefully ask, "Does that make sense?"

I met with fifteen professionals to get their feedback on this book. I recorded the meeting and had the content transcribed. When I went back over the transcripts, I found myself amazed at what I had missed. Also, there were moments various people recommended I do this or that, and I could tell they thought I knew how to do this or that like I knew the back of my hand. I remember thinking when first hearing them, *I'm not sure I would know how to do what you are suggesting.* Interestingly, during that time, I didn't stop any of them and say, "I don't know what you are talking about, not exactly," or, "That is unclear to me." We just continued talking. They were not aware that I did not know what they knew. They just assumed I knew what they knew. No one asked, "Emerson, we threw a lot of information at you. Is anything unclear?"

A friend of mine, a great negotiator and builder, would engage clients and people by talking about his proposal, but he did so in short spurts. He would then ask, "Does this make sense?" He would continually solicit feedback. When his projects cost tens of millions of dollars and townships and organizations needed to sign off, he knew it was crucial not to assume the other was buying what he was selling or understood what he was saying. Even when people said it made sense, he'd ask, "In what ways does this make sense for you?"

When we are talking to others, many will appear as though they know what we know, but because most of us are insecure and no one wishes to look stupid, few put themselves in a position to say, "I don't know what you are talking about." People will even nod their heads and the presenter can assume they are tracking and agreeing, while later learning it went over their heads. Metaphorically, we were talking about multiplication and division, but they hadn't learned to add and subtract. Though everything we kindly communicated about multiplication and division was true and necessary, earlier we should have kindly communicated what was true and necessary about addition and subtraction. We got ahead of ourselves and confused the others.

In all of our communications with others, we must ask, *Is this person on the same page with me?* When I am unaware of another's ignorance but talk to that person as though he or she knows what I know, I will be unclear.

SPEAK YOUR MIND CLEARLY:

Emerson's Checklist for Clarifying Communication

- ☐ Do I assume the other person should "get it" by totally tracking with me and blame them for not listening intelligently?
- ☐ Do I recognize that I can wrongly assume the other person understands or should understand the information I communicate?
- ☐ Do I seek to use simple, concise, and clear language to be intelligible instead of using jargon and complex technical terms?
- ☐ Do I actively listen and look for cues to help determine if the other person understood what I said?

- ☐ Do I account for factors that make it difficult for a person to understand, like their emotional state (i.e., fatigue) or physical conditions (i.e., loud noises)?
- ☐ Do I ask two basic questions: "Can you tell me what you heard me say?" and "Does that make sense?"
- ☐ Do I adjust my words based on those two answers to make me more intelligible?
- ☐ Do I seek clarification on what another understands because I feel the responsibility to be clear and intelligible?

MYSTICAL VERSUS ARTICULATE

Mystical: I know what I mean. I just don't know how to say it.

Articulate: Instead of saying, "I know what I mean, I just can't say it," I write or process my thoughts with someone until I have clarity about what I mean, and then I speak coherently.

When we say, "I know what I mean; I just don't know how to say it," we really don't know what we mean. We think with words. If we do not have the words in our brains, then we do not know what we mean in our brains.

Admittedly, trying to figure out exactly what we feel or think takes reflection. We need to think about what we are thinking and feeling. For example, *Why am I discouraged? Am I disheartened mostly because my sick child has the flu, or am I distressed mostly over the fight I had with my spouse?* Some of us do not pause long enough to ask these questions or have wise counsel in our lives to help us make sense of what we are feeling.

There is a powerful episode in season 6 of *The Crown* in which teenage Prince William yells at his father, Charles, and essentially blames him for the death of his mother, Princess Diana. He unloads everything he is feeling, but it's not until later in the episode when he plays a game of chess with his grandfather that he begins to reflect that his real anger may actually be the unwanted attention he is getting on the heels of his mother "leaving him." Instead of being able to clearly express that to his father, he chose to assume his feelings were *at* his father. Not until his grandfather asked him clarifying questions was he able to articulate his feelings and mend his relationship with his father.[1]

When we seek to inform, we either know the information or we do not. When we seek to persuade another, we either know the goal of our persuasion or we do not. When we seek to affect the heart of another with words of love or hurt, we either know what we wish to convey about our emotions or we do not.

"But, Emerson, I can say what I mean, but it still comes out poorly." As long as you say what you mean, you are halfway there. Now you just need to develop the skill of communicating better what you mean. You need to take the time to organize your thoughts and communicate them in an orderly fashion. Taking a moment to write out what you want to say or practice saying it beforehand has typically only ever benefited a communicator.

When blogging was in its early stages, many people would hit "publish" immediately with no hesitation or fear of backlash or need for editorial accuracy. For many, the goal was to get as much content out there as quickly as possible. There were no journalistic rules or checks and balances, and as a result the desire to share information quickly led to a massive amount of misinformation.

Even the apostle Paul worked at conveying what he meant. We read comments such as "I mean this" or "I did not at all mean" or "What do I mean then?" (1 Cor. 1:12; 5:10; 10:19). He would explain in clear language.

Paul himself said in 1 Corinthians 14:9, "Unless you utter by the tongue speech *that is clear*, how will it be known what is spoken? For you will be speaking into the air." He even asked for prayer. To the Colossians he wrote, "Praying at the same time for us as well . . . that I may *make it clear in the way I ought to speak*" (Col. 4:3–4).

When communicating with others, avoid saying or writing something along the lines of "I know what I mean; I just can't say it." Figure it out first. Then and only then should you move forward with the communication.

SPEAK YOUR MIND CLEARLY:

Emerson's Checklist for Articulate Communication

- ☐ To be an articulate communicator, do I recognize that I need knowledge of the issue, an undistracted mind, and basic language skills to communicate clearly?
- ☐ Do I avoid saying, "I know what I mean; I just don't know how to say it," because I subscribe to the basic truth that "If I don't know how to say it, I don't know what I mean"?
- ☐ Do I try to figure out the best words to describe my feelings and thoughts?
- ☐ Do I have the discipline to figure out what I think and feel by getting in tune with those thoughts and feelings?
- ☐ To better communicate, do I first write down my main thoughts to ensure I have figured out what I want to say?
- ☐ Do I take the time to rephrase the information to be clearer and more precise?
- ☐ Do I rehearse out loud to hear myself say these things to make sure I like what I hear and how I say it?
- ☐ If I cannot write down my main thoughts intelligibly, do I wait until I do to make sure I know what I am trying to say?
- ☐ Do I ask a friend to hear my thoughts and arrangement and ask for feedback to determine if what I want to say makes sense?

INCOMPLETE VERSUS THOROUGH

Incomplete: Occasionally I leave out vital information, since I fail to answer who, what, when, where, why, and how.

Thorough: To be completely clear, I ask, "What needs to be said and why?" "Who needs to hear this, and when and where?" and "How do I best deliver the message?"

Do people ask you questions like "What or who are you talking about? Why are you talking about this? When and where did this happen? How do you expect me to respond?"

If so, you need to be clearer.

Early on, most of us learned about the five W's and H: who, what, when, where, why, and how. Though we need not answer these in all communication, they serve as a great reminder and guide for being more comprehensive. When they are essential and we ignore them, we leave people scratching their heads.

For instance, we e-mail a fellow manager in another department: "Hey, Teresa, sometime in the next several days, I want to talk to you about David." Well, there are two Davids in the two departments, so to whom do we refer? Who is responsible to set up the meeting in several days, and when exactly, and where, and why the meeting? Is this a good or bad talk about this "David"? This e-mail doesn't answer the why, the who, or the when. Teresa is left to wonder what in the world is going on.

Few among us can avoid freaking out when we receive a text that says, "Can we talk?" *Talk about what? What did I do wrong? Who and what does this concern? Is this something we need to discuss right now? How can I even begin to go about the rest of my day like normal?* After our heart rate skyrockets, we call the person only to find out that they really did just want to talk and catch up. However, the next day it happens again, but this time it's our boss telling us we are being let go. Heart rate re-skyrockets.

For these texters, or if we've texted something like this ourselves, the five W's and H remove confusion. If you take away anything from this section, apply the five W's and H as a foundational blueprint in the communication trade. And you'll help keep everyone's blood pressure down.

SPEAK YOUR MIND CLEARLY:

Emerson's Checklist for Thorough Communication

- ☐ Do I ask myself, *What do I want my audience to know and understand after communicating?*
- ☐ Do I answer the five W's and H: what needs to be said and why, who needs to hear this, when and where, and how best do I deliver the message?

- ☐ To be intelligible, do I exhaustively research the relevant information and facts related to the topic before communicating?
- ☐ Do I outline my findings clearly and concisely?
- ☐ Do I know if the best way to deliver the information is face-to-face, in writing, or over the phone?
- ☐ Do I discern when and where best to communicate my information to the other person?
- ☐ To ensure the information was clear, do I follow up by soliciting feedback on what my audience understood?
- ☐ Do I also listen and remain teachable and receptive to new and differing information, and will I change accordingly?

INDECISIVE VERSUS DECISIVE

Indecisive: When undecided, my delay leaves others uncertain about my wishes.

Decisive: I provide clear and timely information about a required decision, since when I dawdle and stall, this leaves people uncertain and confused about my view and intent.

Decision-making can be tough if the decision is a permanent one, such as whether to take a beloved grandparent off life support. All of us struggle with such decisions. But even so, a decision needs to be made. We cannot leave the medical community in the dark. They need to know clearly our wishes.

What about marriage? The classic scene revolves around two people who have been dating for a year. She believes he is the one and wishes to marry him. He does not propose marriage, though he romantically loves her. She finds herself confused and frustrated. "If he loves me, why doesn't he propose?" His quietness and indecisiveness leave her completely baffled. Eventually, she ends the relationship and starts dating another man, whom she then marries a couple of years later.

I have had both men and women tell me that they backed away, like this fellow. Getting cold feet, they delayed. Feeling confused, they confused the other person, who eventually headed in another direction. One person told me that he has deep regrets over losing the woman he feels he should have married, but his unwillingness to make certain decisions left her unclear about the direction of the relationship, and she eventually married someone else.

On the other hand, I have coached men and women who have panicked over the thought that they were making a mistake to marry a certain person. I have had them weigh that person's godliness and wisdom and appeal to them. Two such people come to mind, both of whom are happily married today to their certain person after nearly thirty years.

I am not commenting on whether a person should or should not marry. Instead, I used these examples to show that procrastination, delay, and indecisiveness are not always good things.

I might go back to school.
I might join a gym.
I might do that budgeting system.
I might volunteer.
I might put my name in for that promotion.
I might join that Bible study.
I might . . .

Our indecisiveness and do-nothing approach to life drive people nuts. Sometimes it's better to make a poorer decision, like vacation plans, and move things forward than to make no decision and leave people waiting and wondering, "Are we or are we not going to do this?"

SPEAK YOUR MIND CLEARLY:

Emerson's Checklist for Decisive Communication

- ☐ Do I grasp and care about other people's needs to know with clarity and certainty what I intend to do about the required decision?
- ☐ To clarify this decision for myself and others, have I created a pros and cons list and weighed which is more favorable in order to make the decision?

- ☐ Have I arranged my schedule to prioritize this list of pros and cons, since an indecisive person tends to manage time poorly?
- ☐ Do I make crucial decisions based on a clear timeline and date without dallying and evading?
- ☐ After a decision has been made, do I clarify the necessary information for others to hear and know about the decision?
- ☐ Do I follow through on the chosen course of action, since procrastinators are notorious for putting off what they said they would do?
- ☐ Though decision-making may be complex for me, have I accepted that I must live with the outcomes of my decisions, good or bad, as part of the risk all decision-makers incur, and will I take responsibility for the outcomes?
- ☐ After making a decision, am I willing to make changes and pursue a different course given I learn of a better way forward?

CHAPTER 17

IMPROVED COMMUNICATION

Sometimes we are so certain that we spoke "as clear as day," and we blame everyone else for failing to grasp our point. Of course, that can be true at times; people can fail to listen fully to what we're communicating. But if we continue to find ourselves in this predicament, with everyone from our spouses to our coworkers to our friends, the wise person eventually realizes the common factor in all of these unclear communications . . . is them!

To improve our communication and speak our minds clearly, we should focus on improving our clarity instead of solely faulting others for not listening correctly. The goal is to shift from being a faultfinding communicator to an improved communicator who owns up to sharpening communication skills.

Earlier, I described the cluster of *faultfinding* communication as misconstrued, snobbish, and unfunny. By that I mean these communicators blame others for misinterpreting their words, are condescending and dismissive when others don't understand their meaning, and are witty in their opinions but claim others can't take a joke and read far too much into the sarcasm.

In contrast, clear communicators are willing to take the blame, which I refer to as *improved* communication. In this cluster, improved communicators become clearer because they focus on revising, simplifying, and cultivating. They take ownership for their speech by revisiting and rewording that which is misinterpreted by others, require themselves to be the intelligent person who reduces the confusion and complexity, and are less concerned about joking when that kind of humor undermines the relationship and closes the ears of the listener.

It's time for many of us to finally take responsibility for improving our own communication failures. With humility, we should refuse to blame others for not understanding, seek to revise the information, reduce the complexity, and better the relationship. The onus is on us to find ways to improve our communication, not find any and every way to blame others, only to say, "Oh well, it's not my fault but theirs! There's nothing that can be done to speak more clearly."

Let's take a look at three types of unclear communicators who desperately need to evaluate themselves and seek to improve their ways. These people continually find themselves saying, "It's not me, it's them," when in fact it is likely them every single time! If any of these are you, it's time to improve your unclear communication.

MISCONSTRUED VERSUS REVISING

Misconstrued: I didn't mean it as they interpreted it, but yeah, those were my words.

Revising: When people misinterpret me, though I think I have been clear, I take the initiative to improve communication by revisiting the matter and explaining myself better.

We have probably all heard the expression "Say what you mean, and mean what you say."

But sometimes in the heat of the moment we bark things we do not mean. We overstate. A husband yells, "Nobody could love you!" But he doesn't mean it. He means, "I don't like you right now because I'm upset." He is hurt and angry. Of course, what wife does not personalize that statement? Feeling unloved, she retorts, "You hate me! You've always hated me. You have never loved me!" Things escalate from there.

The "never" and "always" expressions lead to trouble. During quarrels, it is best to refrain from these comments. These are thoughtless and tactless.

A wife told me, "I now understand that when I mention a material thing (like a new car, a new home, a new appliance), he takes it to heart and feels bad that he cannot *provide* me with everything I want. I explained to him that just because I remark about something, that doesn't mean that I *want* it; more likely, I just admire it."

We need to backtrack when we say things that are misconstrued. A woman introduced my daughter with "This is Joy. She's the one that does all the videos on the internet and often doesn't care what she looks like." Joy responded, "What did you say?" The lady responded, "Oh, I didn't mean it that way." Because Joy has posted childhood pictures of herself, especially during those awkward junior high days when she wore braces and weighed more than was best, many have marveled at her transparency. Most everyone relates to her but doesn't dare do what she does, since they lack the confidence. Regardless, this woman blurted out something without thinking. What she meant was more positive, but it sounded to all who heard her as a put-down about Joy.

One person wrote to me, "Before, I didn't really consider how [this person] would interpret what I said, just as long as I said what I was feeling. [Now] . . . I don't seem to shoot my mouth off as much anymore." This person thinks before they speak.

Just because we are well meaning is no reason to believe others know our meaning. If we find ourselves frequently saying, "I didn't mean it the way it sounds," then we need to work harder at being clearer. We are wasting a lot of emotional energy. Therefore, we need to ask ourselves before we speak, *What will this person hear when I say it this way?*

SPEAK YOUR MIND CLEARLY:

Emerson's Checklist for Revising Communication

- ☐ Do I have a mindset that believes the onus is on me to be clear instead of blaming others for misconstruing what I said?

- ☐ When people misconstrue what I said, do I take the time and exert the effort to make it clearer and more easily understood?
- ☐ When others misunderstand me, do I willingly, and even gladly, revisit my messaging to clarify it or provide additional and helpful information?
- ☐ Do I view the process of revising as part of my development as an effective communicator and acknowledge that such practices improve my skills, which reduces the amount of necessary revision in the future?
- ☐ Because communication can be more of a process than a one-and-done blurting out of information, do I return to those I have communicated with to ensure I was clear?
- ☐ If later it is still unclear to them, do I invite more feedback and make further corrections and revisions as I incorporate their input to serve their understanding?

SNOBBISH VERSUS SIMPLIFYING

Snobbish: Others don't understand because they're stupid. It isn't me. I'm clear.

Simplifying: When misunderstood, I do not show condescension but improve my communication by making it simpler as I strive to reduce complexity, use basic words, give examples, create visuals, and stick to the main ideas.

Lost on a back road in Florida, a couple pulled over to where a farmer stood by his mailbox. "How do you get to Sanford?" the couple asked. The farmer replied, "My brother-in-law takes me." The couple can blame this farmer for being stupid or start again with "That's great. When your brother-in-law takes you, what route does he take?"

When there is confusion, I try to refrain from attacking another for not listening carefully (which may be the case). Instead, I take a run at communicating again but more clearly. I am not worse for the wear, other than taking a little more time. After all, what good is it to display a condescending attitude toward another as though he or she is unintelligent?

In these incidents I put the onus on myself to improve my communication skills. This prevents me from feeling like a vulnerable victim to people's inattentiveness. Even if they are not fully listening, it is better for me to say, "I guess I wasn't clear. Let me run at this again. What I am trying to say is . . ." After I restate myself I might ask, "Does that make better sense?" This is just common sense, and that feedback reassures me that I was clearer. This is so simple to do, though it may take a couple more exchanges than I prefer.

Only a snobbish communicator says, "I am better and smarter than everyone else, and I am not repeating myself to people who should have listened in the first place." This attitude may explain why people aren't listening to us in the first place.

SPEAK YOUR MIND CLEARLY:

Emerson's Checklist for Simplifying Communication

- ☐ Do I recognize that the smarter and wiser a person is, the harder they work at communicating their content clearly and simply to their audience?
- ☐ Do I avoid complex or technical words that only a few understand and instead use simpler terms?
- ☐ Am I resolved to be a clear communicator rather than someone impressing people with big words and vast knowledge with no concern for being plain and user-friendly?
- ☐ Do I let my main point stay the main point, which requires me to avoid unnecessary details?
- ☐ Do I ask others if they understand what I am communicating, and if they don't, do I work at simplifying my message so it is clear, straightforward, and uncomplicated?
- ☐ If they do not understand, do I ask them to allow me to learn how to say it better so I don't confuse them with my lack of clarity?
- ☐ During the process, am I humble and respectful as I seek to simplify, and do I never view another as a simpleton for not tracking with me?

□ Do I need more examples and non-examples to help the audience comprehend my concepts?

UNFUNNY VERSUS CULTIVATING

Unfunny: I try to be funny, but others hear it as sarcasm and misunderstand.

Cultivating: While humor has its place, being sarcastic and abrasive at the listener's expense proves and improves nothing and fails to cultivate a better relationship or ensure greater open-mindedness so others will clearly listen.

Some sarcasm is innocent and fun-loving. Parents say, "Money isn't everything in life, but it keeps you in touch with us." But other sarcasm bites. An employee says to his superior, "I work this hard for forty hours to be this poor?" Does the other person hear the joking as funny or nasty?

Should we use sarcasm to make a point? Not if the other interprets it as a put-down. If the other interprets as hurtful something by which we intended no harm, we have been unclear. We have sent the wrong message. For instance, the manager says to a new employee who botched a sale, "I am trying to envision you with a personality." Soon after, the new worker quits.

Sarcasm is rarely an effective teaching technique. Instead, it offends, like when a family member says something obvious and we remark, "How clever, Sherlock. Who would have known?" When that family member deflates and expresses hurt, the jokester snaps back, "I am just joking. Can't you take a joke?" That's not clear when it doesn't feel like a laughing matter. It is no joke when the other feels he or she is a joke.

Perhaps one of the most common mistakes people realize they have made after making a comment, either verbally or in writing, is their sarcasm. Most recipients hear it as a put-down. We need to ask ourselves, *Though I think this remark is humorous, will the other person hear it as hurtful?*

The Greek word for sarcasm, *sarkazein*, means "to tear flesh like dogs." When people do not see us as truly joking in our sarcasm, they conclude it is a disguised insult. They believe the supposed humor cloaks a deep-seated criticism. Indeed, sarcasm rips their hearts more than a direct confrontation of the issue. It eats away at them. For this reason, when we are genuinely trying to be funny, we need to clarify that when we observe a person's spirit deflate.

SPEAK YOUR MIND CLEARLY:

Emerson's Checklist for Cultivating Communication

- ☐ Do I enjoy using wholesome humor in my communications, which enables people to laugh with me and be more receptive to my message and me?
- ☐ Do I avoid sarcastic and hurtful humor at the listeners' expense, since that closes them off to me and my message?
- ☐ When speaking, am I considerate of those who listen, and do I use respectful tones throughout my presentation?
- ☐ As I have a heartfelt interest in others grasping my content, do I have a heartfelt concern for why they might struggle in grasping my message, like their painful upbringing, stressful circumstances, or future uncertainties?
- ☐ Do I avoid offending and shaming the listener but instead validate them as valued and vital?
- ☐ When engaging another person, do I politely and patiently allow them to share their perspective without rudely interrupting them?
- ☐ Since relationship determines response, do I work at not closing off others' hearts through sarcasm, which blocks them from hearing my deeper, positive, and respectful message?
- ☐ Am I aware of the importance of cultivating better relationships to ensure greater open-mindedness to me and my message?

CHAPTER 18

AUTHENTIC COMMUNICATION

Are you sending mixed messages, and is that why you struggle to communicate clearly to others? Do you straddle the fence on important issues, refusing to take a side because you fear offending someone? Or maybe you do land on a certain side of the issue . . . today. But tomorrow you may feel differently. Who knows? The truth is whatever you say it is in that moment. Maybe it's not your words that send the mixed messages but your hypocritical actions that do not reflect what you communicated. Either way, no one around you truly knows what you are trying to communicate. Perhaps you don't either!

To learn to speak our minds clearly, we must remain true to our convictions without flip-flopping for convenience, as being two-sided is insincere, confusing, and misleading. Shifting toward authentic communication means being the real deal—someone who genuinely holds to their values, having learned to communicate them humbly and honestly.

As we learned earlier, the cluster of *two-sided* communication is fence-sitting, relativistic, intoning, and hypocritical. Such personalities avoid taking clear stances, subscribe to the idea that truth is what they say it is, contradict their messaging with a severe and harsh tone, and fail to keep promises, which makes it unclear for others to know what to believe in the future.

In stark contrast, the cluster of *authentic* communication is direct, principled, congruent, and reliable. These people are respectfully forthright about what they think and believe; they are guided by a moral compass that makes clear what they sincerely and humbly believe for themselves and why; they nobly align the tone of their words—sounding kind—when speaking what is true, necessary, and clear; and they keep their promises, enabling others to trust what they say in the future.

Instrumental to learning how to speak our minds clearly is being our authentic selves in everything we do and say. It is vital that we align our beliefs and actions with our speech so as to reflect our honest opinions and moral convictions, as well as to ensure clarity and prevent misunderstandings from being two-faced. Being authentic will not always result in being the most popular person, at least in the moment, but when what you speak kindly and only when necessary is the truth, then I have found that more people will respect you for being genuine with your beliefs and convictions, even if they do not share them with you.

In this chapter, we will discuss the different ways people struggle in being true and authentic with their communications and how they may learn to boldly speak their kind and necessary truth more clearly.

FENCE-SITTING VERSUS DIRECT

Fence-Sitting: I don't land on either side of an issue to avoid trouble with both sides.

Direct: Though life has moral ambiguities in the gray areas, I strive to be honest and straightforward about my preferences when a decision is required, since as an authentic person, I need to be clear about my opinions without being demanding and unkind.

Do you have such a fear of conflict and rejection that you straddle the fence on issues? Are you willing to compromise what you believe in order to stay out of trouble? That won't work with two people who differ. We must make a choice. Lack of clarity is never permanent or permitted.

I am not referring to moments when we genuinely do not have an opinion one way or another and the matter is not all that important. Instead, I refer to the fence-sitter who seeks to have it both ways. But we cannot have it both ways, since a decision must be made and we are relevant to that decision.

I remember laughing out loud when I first heard the phrase "When you straddle a wooden fence, you're going to hurt yourself." Let's think about the pain that results for us when we straddle the fence in business. Our affirming answers on both sides of the discussion among the staff enable us to stay away from taking sides for a period of time. We have been kept from trouble by our lack of clarity on what we feel is the right decision. In our memos we have been vague and ambiguous. However, with most differences like this, a vote is called for. We can no longer remain undecided and uncommitted. When both sides realize we have been ducking and weaving, they demand that we land on one side or the other of the fence. Unfortunately, because of our deceptive avoidance, neither side respects us very much. The very thing we sought to avoid, we end up causing.

As difficult as this is, we must choose the side that best reflects our convictions. This is tough, but we must do up front what we're going to end up doing later when a vote is called for. When we put off the inevitable, we put off people. In trying to make both sides happy by not being for one side and against the other, we make both sides unhappy with us for being crafty.

SPEAK YOUR MIND CLEARLY:

Emerson's Checklist for Direct Communication

- ☐ Do I believe it is okay for me to have strong personal preferences that are at odds with others, as well as for others to have strong personal preferences that are at odds with mine?
- ☐ Do I acknowledge that in gray areas, people can have honest differences of opinion, since there is no absolute right or wrong in such areas?
- ☐ Do I accept that both sides can be valid when there is nothing immoral, illegal, or unbiblical in either position, even saying, "Neither is wrong, just different"?
- ☐ Do I carefully consider both sides of an issue, not letting my bias blind me to what is valid on the other side of an issue?

- ☐ Do I have the wisdom to speak clearly and directly about what I prefer in a considerate and respectful manner?
- ☐ Do I remain open to changing my mind and following the other's preference?
- ☐ Am I steadfast in my conviction, even when it goes against peers' and family's valid and contrary opinions?
- ☐ Do I allow others to be equally resolute in their convictions and refuse to impose my interests unduly?
- ☐ Am I resolute and clear in my perspective and stance without wavering, backpedaling, or straddling the fence even though I fear conflict and disapproval?
- ☐ Do I recognize that straddling the fence may be cowardly and send others the message that I have no genuine concern and conviction?

RELATIVISTIC VERSUS PRINCIPLED

Relativistic: I'm unmoved by my contradictions. Truth is what I say it is at the moment.

Principled: I have moral convictions as an authentic person and will not compromise these to suit my selfish wants or appease those around me; otherwise, this inconsistency confuses people on what I say I believe at my core.

Is truth relative? Not when it comes to the construction of our three-story home. Who hires a construction firm that adheres to the idea that the mathematical configurations about structural stress don't matter, since truth is relative?

On college campuses some professors wax eloquent about truth always being relative. A student told me that he raised his hand in a class when one professor lectured that there were no absolute truths. He asked, "Prof, are you saying that rape is not always wrong?" That political hot potato triggered a class discussion that ended with the class believing in absolute truth. Some things are inherently evil, wrong, or false.

What is interesting is that most relativists wax eloquent about their relativism, but in their daily lives, they hold firmly to certain beliefs in dogmatic ways and end up contradicting their claim that there are no absolutes. They say one thing over here but live another way over there. Of course, they leave people confused about what they believe because of the glaring contradictions.

When we contradict the very principles we espouse, the people who know us will say, "You can't have it both ways. Be clear. What do you really believe? Are you saying this out of selfish convenience or heartfelt conviction? Bald-headed men don't sell hair-restoration oil."

SPEAK YOUR MIND CLEARLY:

Emerson's Checklist for Principled Communication

- ☐ Do I have moral values like being truthful and kind?
- ☐ Do these values serve as a moral compass when communicating information so, for example, I will be a truth-teller and communicate with kindness?
- ☐ Am I committed to speaking my mind based on what is true, kind, necessary, and clear because these are my moral values of communication?
- ☐ Do I see the moral compass primarily housed in my conscience where I weigh right and wrong, so I must remain true to my conscience when speaking and writing?
- ☐ Do I correct my missteps when I head in a direction at odds with my moral values, like apologizing for my untruthfulness or unkindness?
- ☐ Is my identity determined by my faith and values and not by pleasing and appeasing people when to do so I must sacrifice my moral convictions?
- ☐ Though I want things in life, do I resist the temptation to lie to have these things, since by doing so I must trade my moral value of truthfulness to get what I want?
- ☐ Do I recognize that when I compromise my core moral values, others will question my sincerity about those values?
- ☐ Though I am met with disapproval and rejection, do I stand firm on my moral convictions regardless of the social pressures and negative consequences?

INTONING VERSUS CONGRUENT

Intoning: The words I speak are sincere and clear, but my stern tone puzzles people.

Congruent: I ensure that my body language and tone coincide with my words when I talk, which is what an authentic person does, to prevent confusing my listeners with an apparent contradiction.

A girlfriend asks, "Do you really love me?" The boyfriend pauses before replying listlessly, "Yes, of course." But his hesitancy and lack of enthusiasm say otherwise.

You've likely heard, "Don't look at me with that tone of voice!" I say at our marriage conferences, "You can be right but wrong at the top of your voice." When your inflection sounds contradictory to your words, those listening will be confused.

Some argue that a small percentage of conflicts are caused by the issue at hand, but the larger conflict becomes one of tones that sound unloving and disrespectful. People are left wondering, *How does this person really feel about me?*

We all know, or should know, that our tone of voice, the look in our eyes, facial expressions, the posture of our bodies, and our proximity to the other person send a message far louder than the words we speak. When there is incongruity between the verbal ("I love you") and the nonverbal (distracted and disengaged during conversations), people will eventually interpret us through the nonverbal.

Is this why people are emoji-ing their way through life? They want to make sure no one misunderstands their tone, lest their sincerely written words be misinterpreted. I guess that is a good thing, but it also reinforces the lack of confidence we have that our words clearly convey our goodwill. How lamentable that we need the protection of a smiley face. That being said, perhaps there is a lesson we can learn from this tendency of many to fill their written communications with emojis so as to better clarify tone. When speaking face-to-face with others, how should we look so that our body language matches our words? Should we smile more? Show disappointment? Should we jump up and down with excitement? Bottom line, even if someone could not hear you, would your body language match the type of response they are looking for?

SPEAK YOUR MIND CLEARLY:

Emerson's Checklist for Congruent Communication

- ☐ Do I understand that body language undermines my effectiveness as a communicator when I yawn, look at my watch, cross my arms, fidget, or avoid eye contact?
- ☐ Am I aware that my tone undermines my communication success when it is loud, piercing, shrill, or harsh?
- ☐ Do I discern that my nonverbal cues of a sour look or harshness discredit my genuine verbal statements?
- ☐ When my body language and tone do not match my words positively, do I correct myself so what I say is supported by how I look and sound?
- ☐ Is it reasonable for a person to be confused by the disparity when I tell them I love them while my negative tone and body language send the message "I hate you"?
- ☐ Do I send this contradictory message to deliberately mislead people about my hypocrisy: "Look, just listen to what I say and quit getting distracted when I am loud, angry, and throw things"?
- ☐ Do I ask others to tell me if my verbal expressions and nonverbal conduct align so I communicate clearly and helpfully?
- ☐ Do I hold myself responsible for being congruent in what I say and how I say it instead of telling offended people, "Get over it"?
- ☐ Does it matter that people see me as discredited due to my offensive body language and tone?

HYPOCRITICAL VERSUS RELIABLE

Hypocritical: My words ring hollow when my actions don't match my words.

Reliable: I do not overpromise and underdeliver, since that perplexes people, but do what I say I will do.

"He told me that he loved me, but then he left me and hasn't called me in two months. I have not seen him since." This is the classic story of jilted love. The boyfriend said one thing but did another. The talk and walk didn't match.

The manager tells the employee, "Yes, come in. I have time to chat with you." But within ten minutes the manager starts looking at his watch. The employee thinks, *Yeah, he said he had time to chat and seemed truly interested, but now he sends the message that he could not care less.*

When we send mixed messages, people believe the one that feels most negative to them. Whatever we say to counter our actions, given our actions are the more negative, will not neutralize our unacceptable behavior. Hollow words do not override pathetic and painful actions. A person told me, "I had a client who consistently was telling me that his payments would be several months late, and then he'd add 'LOL' at the end of his e-mail. I called him, and I asked, 'Do you think this is funny? I'm not laughing out loud. You are four months late with your payment, and this is unacceptable.'" The client's "LOL" was hollow in light of defaulting on his payments.

There are individuals who make promises and consistently fail to follow through. When confronted with the fact that they say one thing and do another, they defend themselves with "I intended to do it." In their way of thinking, as long as they intended to do it, they are okay. But those around them no longer feel that it is okay.

Before communicating, I need to ask myself, *Am I trying to communicate something here that cannot nullify my former conduct? If so, what must I* do *instead of* say?

SPEAK YOUR MIND CLEARLY:

Emerson's Checklist for Reliable Communication

- ☐ In my communication, do I over-promise but end up under-delivering on my follow-through?

- ☐ Do I do what I say I will do—walk my talk—so I do not have a reputation for being insincere and inauthentic?
- ☐ Do I prioritize aligning my promises with my follow-through, lest others see me as untrue, unkind, and unclear?
- ☐ As vital as it is that my words and actions align, do I refuse to cross a legal or moral boundary to accomplish that alignment?
- ☐ When necessary, do I enlist third parties as witnesses to confirm the agreement and keep me accountable to follow through?
- ☐ Do I keep good records of my contractual agreements and fulfill the contract to the letter?
- ☐ In matters involving liability, do I ensure everything I have said or written is legally accurate, clear, and understood?
- ☐ Do I go above and beyond to reasonably serve another person who is confused about what I said I would do?
- ☐ Have I built a reputation as reliable because I under-promised but over-delivered, and today people see me as competent and trustworthy?

CHAPTER 19

POISED COMMUNICATION

It is certainly not wrong to become emotional when communicating. Similar to how congruent communicators are careful that their tone matches their words, our emotions will also fluctuate depending on our communication. However, we have a responsibility to keep some of our more extreme emotions in check if we are to speak our minds clearly. Our initial reaction can oftentimes misrepresent our hearts and communicate something we did not intend.

To learn how to speak our minds clearly, we must guard against being so frazzled and overwrought that others dismiss us as too emotional and fail to grasp our rational concerns. This requires changing direction by regaining composure as poised communicators who calmly and plainly state what is behind our emotions.

Let's look at each.

Considering the cluster of *emotional* communicators, such people are unedited, provoked, and weary. They do not take the time to examine what they are experiencing and why; rather, they unthinkingly blurt out whatever they feel. They allow others to get under their skin, resulting in thoughtlessly charged comments. They also let exhaustion impair their clear thinking and, when talking, confuse the listener by saying things they don't mean.

However, the clear communicator represents the cluster of *poised* communication. Poised communicators are self-editing, temperate, and rejuvenated. These people think before they speak to censor what is untrue, unkind, unnecessary, and unclear. They recognize where they can be exasperated and realize the need to remain levelheaded to communicate truly, kindly, and clearly. And they are aware of their physical limits, so when fatigued, they rest and then revisit the issue with greater clarity.

When communicating with others, especially in emotionally charged and draining situations, do you remain composed and take the time to think well in order to communicate clearly? This does not come naturally to many and, thus, takes great intentionality, practice, and grace to learn how to be a more poised communicator in emotional times.

It boils down to your level of self-control and self-awareness. Are you aware of your tendencies and weaknesses when it comes to communicating during emotional times? What strengths do you have that you need to fine-tune? Let's discuss the different types of emotional communicators and how they can best learn to speak their minds more clearly.

UNEDITED VERSUS SELF-EDITING

Unedited: When snubbed, I react instead of calmly editing myself to be clear.

Self-Editing: I take the time to consider things carefully and share thoughtfully; otherwise, I may speak in an unedited fashion, which only confuses others.

What if we lived by this: When offended, write out the first response that comes to mind, read, edit, reread, edit, reread, wait, reread, edit, and then respond. Too exhausting? Perhaps. But this process is vital when angry or offended.

Perhaps you've heard the expression "I was so mad, I couldn't see straight." Actually, it is true. When we are really, really mad, we don't see straight, or at least pay attention to things as we should. This is readily observed when people are livid and shoot off an e-mail. They say things they do not mean and later regret. They overstate their case and conveniently leave out self-incriminating information. They attack the person instead of solely addressing the issue.

As I said earlier, and this bears repeating, the more we are upset by something, the wiser it is to let twenty-four hours pass before responding, during which time we review what we want to say. During heated moments, the potential for unclear communication increases, which runs the risk of creating worse problems.

Even when emotions are not running high, we can be careless and send the wrong message. I once received an e-mail that had brackets with the phrase [*insert name here*] at the top. No one had inserted my name, yet it was supposedly a *personal* note.

There was another time when I received an official contract from an organization expressing delight to do business with me. In the cover letter from the vice president, he expressed how special I was to them. However, when I read the contract, someone else's name was written where mine should have been. This was a template. He had forgotten to remove that name and insert mine, which then reduced the sincerity of his words and my enthusiasm.

Such mistakes as these can be innocent due to understandable distractions. One has too many forms to send out in a short period of time, and errors predictably occur. But frequently when looking back, other factors might emerge. The office worker had just had a spat with another worker. Feeling hurt and offended, she took her eyes off the ball. Steaming about the unkind and untruthful remarks, the worker shoved the contract into the envelope and sent it without double-checking the spelling of the name or if the name was actually in the contract.

We may not be lazy people, but we can act lazy when hurt, offended, or angry. We do not fully evaluate and edit what we communicate.

Before responding, I need to get in tune with my feelings. Am I so mad right now that I cannot see straight? If so, predictably I will misspeak. The more important the communication, the less I can afford to make glaring mistakes. I need to calm down, give it some time, and reread it when my hurt and anger are not controlling me and causing me to make regrettable blunders.

SPEAK YOUR MIND CLEARLY:

Emerson's Checklist for Self-Editing Communication

- ☐ Do I recognize that when upset and angry, my negative emotions can cloud my thinking and communication?

- ☐ Do I realize there are moments when my emotions can get the better of me and I say what is not best for the situation?
- ☐ In the moment, do I take enough time to think before I speak so I don't say something that should not have been said?
- ☐ Do I think beforehand if what I say is true, kind, necessary, and clear?
- ☐ Do I take responsibility for helping others understand what I am saying, since the onus is on me to clearly and kindly communicate what is true and necessary?
- ☐ Do I value working hard at reviewing and revising what I wish to express, especially when the subject matter is important personally or professionally?
- ☐ Do I work at expressing myself in ways that are easy to understand and, specifically, without ambiguity?
- ☐ Do I work at getting the facts right to ensure I am free from errors or inaccuracies?
- ☐ Do I recognize when I ramble and go off-topic and correct that by bringing things back to the main point?
- ☐ Do I weigh the urgency of the information and work at preparing and presenting the content when required?
- ☐ To communicate with clarity, conciseness, and correctness, do I take the time to edit well ahead of time?
- ☐ When I did not self-edit and said something that was not true, kind, necessary, or clear, did I seek forgiveness and make it right?
- ☐ Do I seek out wiser people to speak into my communication, given people have brought up to me that I have no filter on what I say and write?

PROVOKED VERSUS TEMPERATE

Provoked: When upset, I react in ways that appear unreasonable and confusing.

Temperate: When provoked, I remain emotionally self-controlled to avoid brash and unreasonable communication that only confuses and aggravates others and exacerbates the conflict.

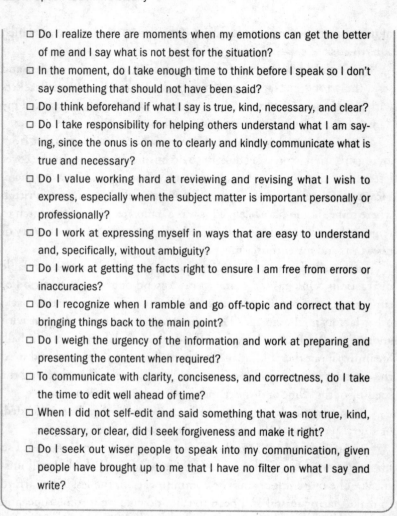

A wife e-mailed me: "My husband says that I am hostile toward him and that my anger is uncontrolled. He calls me abusive. When we argue, my physical gestures are often aggressive; I speak quickly, loudly, and dramatically. I sometimes use sarcasm and name-calling. He also feels that my anger is often unwarranted, and he never knows when I am going to blow up. Much of this is true. . . . He says he has avoided home in the past because he doesn't know what he's going to find when he gets there: Will I be happy, depressed, mad, or distant?"

In her defense, she probably felt hurt and provoked. But like her, when upset and offended, do we appear to lose it emotionally to those around us? Do we appear unpredictable and even irrational? Do the things we say make little sense? After we communicate in an excitable fashion, are things open to question? Do we leave others in doubt about our character?

For instance, at the township meeting Charlie feels ignored as a citizen and, thus, provoked because a decision has been made to put a cell phone tower near his home. Feeling impotent to persuade the township to change their plans, he threatens the council: "You leave me no other recourse than to sue you and, before that, to start a recall of every one of you on this board." Of course, neither of these things will happen; they are empty threats. But some at the meeting who are Charlie's close neighbors conclude that he intends to do both. When he does nothing, he leaves them confused. Over time his neighbors see him as emotional and unreasonable when provoked by some injustice. They know he feels indignant, but they see him as brash and knee-jerk in his reactions as he threatens litigation. He gains a reputation of being overly dramatic.

When we are slighted and hurt, do we communicate a message that causes others to see us as easily provoked and, eventually, as bad-tempered and unreasonable?

SPEAK YOUR MIND CLEARLY:

Emerson's Checklist for Temperate Communication

- ☐ Am I self-aware when feeling provoked, and because of this, can calm myself down before reacting in an unhealthy manner?

- ☐ Do I avoid brash and unreasonable retorts that are confrontational and equally provocative and only add to the chaos?
- ☐ Do I pause long enough when provoked to not only calm down but take stock of what I am about to say?
- ☐ Do I remain emotionally self-controlled when provoked, since I need to prepare my heart to say what is true, kind, necessary, and clear?
- ☐ Do I realistically accept that an intemperate reaction entails untrue, unkind, unnecessary, and unclear remarks, aggravating others and escalating the conflict?
- ☐ Do I seek forgiveness when I cross the line and say something I should not have expressed?
- ☐ Do I discern that I must understand and empathize with the other's valid underlying concerns to resolve the conflict and bring a clear way forward?
- ☐ Do I proactively focus on a win-win solution rather than the earlier provocation?

WEARY VERSUS REJUVENATED

Weary: I don't think or communicate well when I'm too tired, especially at night.

Rejuvenated: When worn out, I know my limits on trying to communicate, since I am physically and mentally fatigued; so I recharge my batteries with nourishment and rest in order to communicate clearly and kindly.

When I was a pastor, we had board meetings that would run late into the evening, pushing eleven o'clock. At that point, we most often called it quits for the night. We knew that our best thinking exited much earlier, and anger could more easily surface during heated debates.

Though believers are instructed not to let the sun set on their anger (Eph. 4:26), there are moments when two people may not be able to resolve the issue that angers them before nightfall. Two mature people agreeing to resume the discussion the next day often proves the better course to take. Minds are clearer, and so are the words.

If one claims to be a night person, then this applies to your morning. Each of us needs to get in tune with when we are at our best and when we are not. The best of communicators calls a time-out when tired and weary. It is one thing to put people to sleep by what we say; it is another to say things while we are half asleep. We can be half as civil. Before getting into an important discussion, ask yourself, *Am I tired? Can I barely keep my eyes open and my mind focused? Perhaps this would be better said tomorrow.*

If you're up late and tired but feeling the need to text someone about a concern of yours or perhaps post something on social media in response to today's big story, ask yourself, *Am I in the best frame of mind to open up that can of worms right now? Maybe I shouldn't speak my mind right now.*

SPEAK YOUR MIND CLEARLY:

Emerson's Checklist for Rejuvenated Communication

- ☐ Do I react negatively when stressed, exhausted, and hungry, and therefore I take steps to prepare against such adverse reactions?
- ☐ When I'm tired, stressed, or hungry, do I find it hard to concentrate on others' concerns and to communicate clearly?
- ☐ Am I aware of my limits when communicating while fatigued, and do I make a conscious effort to be poised and clear?
- ☐ Do I take the time to recharge emotionally and physically before communicating to avoid negative interactions due to fatigue and stress?
- ☐ Do I prioritize self-care so as to better care for others, especially when communicating information they need from me?
- ☐ Do I communicate my needs clearly when I am stressed, fatigued, or hungry so that others can understand my situation and, after getting rejuvenated, we can connect?

CHAPTER 20

ORGANIZED COMMUNICATION

For some who struggle with being clear communicators, the problem is not ill will, lack of care, or being overwhelmed by the moment; rather, their struggle is simply lacking the skills necessary to communicate clearly. Too often, they find themselves undisciplined and hurried, leading to unintentional miscommunication. Though they do not intend to confuse or mislead others, their lack of discipline, if not recognized and improved upon, will inevitably frustrate their audience, who can rarely if ever fully understand where the disjointed communicator is going with their latest rant.

To learn how to speak our minds clearly, we need to step back and ask, "Do others find me confusing due to the disjointed way I communicate, even scratching their heads and saying, 'I have no idea what you are talking about'?" If the answer is yes, we need to get organized in our thoughts, which requires some discipline so that we can be prepped, precise, and paced in our communication.

Reflecting on what I wrote earlier in the book about the cluster of *disjointed* communication, I characterized this communication as spiderwebbing, disorganized, and hasty. Disjointed communicators tend to get sidetracked by tangential thoughts, resulting in a web of unrelated ideas; they often fail to invest time and effort to convey their thoughts coherently and understandably; and they talk too fast, inundating their listeners with too much data that loses them.

On the other hand, the cluster of *organized* communication

encompasses communication that is on point, prepared, and paced. Organized communicators maintain focus on their main topic and stay on track with that information; they ready themselves to talk about significant issues logically and understandably; and not only do they choose their words carefully, but they allow people the time to process content and pause to ask whether it makes sense.

The good news is that becoming a more organized and easy-to-follow communicator is a skill all can learn, just as one can learn woodworking or gardening. But it involves patience, humility, and teachability. Becoming a more organized communicator also requires making a commitment to be concentrated, planned, and measured in your communications—both verbal and written.

Do you struggle with organizing your thoughts? Or do you have so many thoughts that you have trouble filtering your way through them when communicating, so you tend to just vomit them all out and hope that the right ones land how you intend? Or maybe your tongue is working twice as fast as your brain and you find yourself making too many regrettable, impulsive comments that come back to bite you. This chapter is about developing the skills to help limit these unfortunate, unclear moments of miscommunication.

SPIDERWEBBING VERSUS ON POINT

Spiderwebbing: I start out on one topic, but this can trigger a web of unrelated points.

On Point: I don't sidetrack others with confusing tangents and side notes but stick to the topic.

People who spiderweb could be coherent and know exactly where they are headed in the conversation, but others may get lost.

I recall a woman, a good friend of ours, who loved to tell stories. When couples would eat dinner together, she'd launch into one of her epic yarns. What I found fascinating was that the women sat on the edge of their seats as she recounted what happened to her the day before.

However, to others of us, she seemed all over the place. She was at the store, then saw an aged teacher she had in high school, which prompted a comment about her dislike for world history but also reminded her of her aging mother she had to talk to about going to the retirement center that had great medical care, which reminded her that a medical doctor worked there who she used to babysit, who still couldn't match his clothes, and that prompted her to ask, "Do you like this new outfit I have on?" As she talked, one thought triggered another thought that triggered another. Nothing was completed, and nothing seemed connected.

As I studied her, I realized she had a half dozen points all dangling out there. Most of the women laughed at her humor while tracking with everything. In the meantime, the men sat dazed and confused, with some even drifting off from mental exhaustion. Though some strings dangled, eventually she started to connect the dots into a brilliantly woven narrative that had those of us still awake laughing hysterically. On one occasion I added at the end, "Well, you finally brought it back around to the original idea that prompted this story!" She shot back, "Of course. What else did you think I was doing? Duh!" I still chuckle at that. She was a pure delight.

Some spiderwebbing communicators are entertainers. If we are not in that camp and find people asking, "Where exactly are you going with this?" then we need to control our thoughts. We need to keep whatever it is we wish to say to three simple points, especially when presenting content.

Preachers have always used three points because that's about all people can walk away remembering or follow in the first place. If we have additional points, hopefully they can work as subpoints that fall under one of the three main points. Good communicators make it as simple as possible not only to remember what we have said but to figure out where we are headed or what we just said. An old country preacher used to say, "I tell 'em what I'm gonna tell 'em. Then I tell 'em. Then I tell 'em what I told 'em."

In today's world, with easy and immediate access to so many outlets unloading information on us constantly, an individual dumping out a ton of information with no apparent connection will be mostly ignored. The brain of the listener cannot process incoherence. Spiderwebbing communicators must learn to ask themselves, *Is my point here to simply suck up all the oxygen in the room and drone on and on about every little thing, not having an actual goal with all that I'm trying to say? Or do I have a specific goal or message to communicate?* If the latter, then it is vital that they learn how to filter through and edit out anything that distracts their audience from that main point.

SPEAK YOUR MIND CLEARLY:

Emerson's Checklist for On Point Communication

- ☐ Do I have a clear purpose in speaking or writing, answering, "Why do I need to say this?" and keeping my purpose in mind both in preparation and presentation?
- ☐ Do I concisely organize my ideas and avoid vagueness and verbosity?
- ☐ Do I discipline myself to steer clear of tangents and side notes, which in turn sidetrack my audience?
- ☐ Do I avoid unnecessary information, circular reasoning, and humor unrelated to the point?
- ☐ If there is a question and answer, do I field those points germane to the topic and not get derailed from the main point by someone's marginal issue?
- ☐ Even if someone asks an irrelevant question, do I listen and then guide the conversation back to the main point?
- ☐ At the end of my presentation, do I summarize clearly and concisely the main idea, which should answer why I addressed this topic?
- ☐ Do I solicit feedback after my presentation to let others tell me if I made my point clear and stayed on point?

DISORGANIZED VERSUS PREPARED

Disorganized: My communication is not always well-thought-out and well-organized.

Prepared: Before communicating, I thoroughly plan and organize my thoughts on the topic to guarantee a clear and coherent presentation that my audience can easily understand and follow.

Many times I have been unclear because I was inattentive, not sequenced, and incomplete. An editor said to me, "This is not well-thought-out. For example, your answers don't fit the questions." Another editor recommended I title my paragraphs, since it would force me to clarify in my mind what my main point was with those sentences. All of us need to ask ourselves, *What am I trying to say here, and am I saying it?*

When writing a blog post, I like to ask myself three questions: *What is the issue? Why is this an issue? How is this issue resolved?* These questions help my brain get organized more quickly and think more comprehensively.

When writing an e-mail, I will number my points when I have more than one point. Numbering forces me to think through ahead of time the exact points but also lets the recipient clearly know there are several ideas.

On some stuff I write, Sarah tells me, "Read it out loud to yourself." Hearing what I wrote enables me to edit what sounds unclear. Sometimes I send it to others for feedback, asking, "Is this clear?" Usually, I let time pass on what I am communicating, stepping away from the content. This allows me to reread with fresh eyes. I am always amazed at what I didn't see when I first wrote out my thoughts.

When people e-mail me about their marriages, they can be emotional and overwhelmed. In that condition, they might jump right in to telling me their problems. However, sometimes it takes me a few minutes to figure out exactly what is the root issue that prompted them to write to me. I am uncertain what they want from me. They might start by saying, "We are under financial pressure like we've never experienced before, and I have health problems that add to our expenses. This is leading to a lot of arguments." I am thinking, *Is this a question about poor budgeting that is causing quarrels, and they want financial advice?* Five paragraphs later (if there are paragraphs), they'll write, "Okay, the reason I am writing is that my spouse had an affair five years ago, and I am still struggling with forgiveness." They should have said this up front in the e-mail, but some people just start writing (or talking) and expect the other person to organize their words. They expect the listener to read their minds. Since they know their main point, they expect the other person to know their main point.

When we communicate, we need to pause long enough to ask ourselves, *What is the big idea here?* State that up front, and stay on that point; otherwise, we confuse others and appear confused. Whatever it is that we intend to say is overpowered by our disorganization and incoherence.

Each of us must realize we can be like the preacher in the pulpit who started with the biblical text, departed from the text, and never returned to the text. As pastors, we all laugh because we have been guilty. We may have had a main point in mind. But when all is said and done, our thoughts were so scattered due to lack of preparation that we lost our way. And people walk away asking, "What exactly was his point?"

SPEAK YOUR MIND CLEARLY:

Emerson's Checklist for Prepared Communication

- ☐ Do I know who my audience is and why I want to communicate with them?
- ☐ Do I know their needs and interests and prepare my information to be relevant while communicating my message to them?
- ☐ Do I do the necessary homework to research the information to be accurate?
- ☐ Do I outline my main points and subpoints in the most logical arrangement?
- ☐ Do I provide examples so my audience can quickly grasp the concepts?
- ☐ In my preparation, do I review and revise to ensure the information is accurate and precise?
- ☐ Do I anticipate the questions and objections my audience might have during and after I present so I can answer those ahead of time?
- ☐ Do I know how best to present what I have prepared in writing or spoken words?
- ☐ Do I rehearse my presentation after I have prepared it?
- ☐ Do I agree that the only people who should "wing it" are those with expertise and who have been over this information countless times?

HASTY VERSUS WELL-PACED

Hasty: Yes, I'm hard to follow. I talk too fast and make impulsive remarks.

Well-Paced: I don't speak too quickly but use measured words so people can process and understand the information, because though the material is clear to me, too much information too fast gets lost for the listener.

We all have heard commercials where the professional announcer who talks faster than an auctioneer goes through a list of warnings or restrictions on a product. He talks so fast we end up ignoring what is said. Thankfully, the average person does not speak at nearly this speed. According to one source, "The average rate of speech for an American is about 125 words per minute; the human brain can process about 800 words per minute."[1] So on one hand, it is definitely a positive that the brain can listen faster than the mouth can speak. But when there is constant fast-talking, people eventually block out what is said. Pausing brings people back into focus.

If we are fast-talkers, we need to slow down. Though our intensity helps us think better, that intensity causes us to verbalize as quickly. We blurt out stuff as it comes to mind, almost on impulse. Not only is it unclear, since it is disconnected, but we also end up saying things we ought not to say.

In the court of law, witnesses are coached on not being too hasty in what they say under oath. When nervous, they can get in a hurry and be overly eager to answer, making them seem thoughtless and confusing the jury or judge. This is why a witness is instructed to take his time and, if needed, ask for a restatement of the question rather than start talking nervously.

On social media, do some of us hurry to express our opinions, for instance, on marriage, with no prior study and analysis? Forget the facts, we'll espouse our opinion quickly: "Divorce the bum!" We declare this though we heard only three sentences from a wife about her supposedly abusive husband. Though we don't know her and haven't heard from the husband or the three teenage kids, what does that matter? We are using speedy fingers to make our unresearched editorial in two tweets. After all, who has time to be quiet, slow down, think, gather all the facts, pray, and then speak?

The only redeeming thing here is that few are paying attention to our narrow dogmatism when we declare, "Divorce the bum!" since they are fixated on espousing their own hallowed, but hollow, sound bites on some other topic.

SPEAK YOUR MIND CLEARLY:

Emerson's Checklist for Well-Paced Communication

- ☐ Do I speak at a pace that enables a listener to clearly understand what I am articulating?
- ☐ Do I use language my listener can understand instead of quickly throwing out complicated vocabulary that only a few know?
- ☐ Do I pick up on bewildered looks that suggest people are not tracking with what I am saying due to my hurriedness?
- ☐ Do I present material in smaller bites to enable people to digest an idea before moving on to the next point?
- ☐ Do I slow down when covering more complex material?
- ☐ Do I provide examples and visual aids to explain complex concepts as simply as possible when I move through the material faster than normal?
- ☐ Do I use pauses and ask questions to let the audience think about the content?
- ☐ Do I provide time for questions and answers to clarify any misunderstandings?

CHAPTER 21

OPEN COMMUNICATION

The final grouping of unclear communicators we will discuss are those who are actually unclear on purpose. They know what could be communicated so as to avoid confusion, but they have their reasons to withhold saying what they know about the situation. If it helps them save face or avoid even the slightest bit of discomfort, they opt to suppress the clarifying information that would remove the confusion.

To learn how to speak our minds clearly, we must acknowledge that we may be consciously suppressing information others need to know, and we should examine why we withhold crucial and helpful details. Given that we are stifling vital information, which leaves people in the dark, we must change our communication style. We need to be clearly and courageously open with the facts and details.

Previously, when considering the cluster I call *suppressive* communication, I indicated this communication is willfully ignorant, falsely humble, and overly sensitive. Suppressive communicators deliberately avoid knowledge (external suppression by blocking out incoming information) to advance selfish interests. Some think transparency about their strengths to help others would be heard as boasting, so they withhold what is clearly true and helpful. And some fear hurting another's feelings, so they do not bring up what is true and necessary, believing if they remain vague, this will help the person.

Given one needs to adjust, I highlight here the cluster I call *open* communication. Open communicators are scrupulous, learned, and true friends. They welcome information, even if it isn't information they wish to know, since they believe in being accurately informed about what is true. They are knowledgeable about their talents and experiences and refrain from misleading silence driven by false humility, choosing instead to be transparent about how their knowledge and skills can serve others. And they are kindly clear, especially with friends, about what is true and necessary, since clarity benefits others in the long run.

In order to speak clearly and helpfully, one should choose to—after verifying the information—apply their expertise to serve others and speak up openly, knowing their silence could deprive others of what they need to clearly grasp the conversation and/or situation at hand. Though this may result in being uncomfortable, integrity is at stake here. This is about being an honest communicator as much as it is being a clear one.

Let's discuss kindly and clearly risking the uncomfortable for the sake of communicating the necessary truth.

WILLFULLY IGNORANT VERSUS SCRUPULOUS

Willfully Ignorant: I sometimes talk while knowing I'm uninformed or misinformed.

Scrupulous: When talking, I don't fake it until I make it, but I take great care to verify information so I can be accurate, which enables me to speak with confidence, truthfulness, and clarity.

I learned of an aging professor who lectured for years based on certain research, but when new research countered his earlier findings, he willfully ignored these advances. Instead of learning the new information and changing his notes, he ignored the changes in his field. It was too much work to correct his class presentations. He kept lecturing as he had for years, though he knew his students would be uninformed and, worse, misinformed because he chose to be.

In court, this is called willful blindness or contrived ignorance. For instance, to avoid legal liability one intentionally keeps himself ignorant of the facts. Those who subscribe to the tactic say, "Don't tell me the truth or facts. Leave me in ignorance so when asked by authorities, I can honestly say, 'I don't know.'" Of course, judges and lawyers try to uncover whether this person was seeking plausible deniability.

But there is another angle on knowing that we do not know. In political circles the rule of thumb is never admit a mistake or that you don't know something. Thus, keep talking in an interview to sound like an expert, all the while aware that you don't know. Feeling on the hot seat and determined never to be wrong, but fully cognizant that the information is insufficient or incorrect, keep moving your lips, weaving and ducking as best as your polemical skills permit.

The same carries over into business. Leaders can find themselves uninformed or misinformed but maintain the appearance of being in the know with the right information. However, after leaving the meeting, the CEO blurts out to aides, "Don't ever put me in that situation again."

I sometimes wonder why such people don't say, "I do not have the right information here. I have communicated incorrectly." Why is it that we say "honesty is the best policy" except when we think it is not?

If you are unsure about something, don't comment on a matter in a way that gives the impression that you know more than you do. This would be untruthful communication, and people will feel not only lied to but also confused about what is fact and what is fiction. It is better to say, "I will need to get back to you. I realize the information I have is insufficient." Of course, you need to get back to them when you have been updated correctly. The good news is that most people will give you more time to get caught up.

SPEAK YOUR MIND CLEARLY:

Emerson's Checklist for Scrupulous Communication

- ☐ Do I view myself as very careful to communicate correctly, diligently, and thoroughly and with high moral standards?
- ☐ Do I safeguard that my presentation is truthful, helpful, and clear?
- ☐ Do I respectfully present relevant, accurate, and timely content?
- ☐ Do I verify the accuracy of my information with credible resources before sharing it?

- ☐ Do I avoid presenting information based on hearsay, rumor, or speculation?
- ☐ Do I refuse to present material when uncertain of its reliability, since that is willful ignorance of potentially contrary facts and inexcusable?
- ☐ Do I refuse to succumb to deliberate blindness when I know information that contradicts my views and biases?
- ☐ Do I confess and correct inaccuracies when brought to my attention?
- ☐ Do I strive to keep learning by staying updated on my research and soliciting feedback from others?
- ☐ Do I present with confidence when I have followed the guidance of this checklist?

FALSELY HUMBLE VERSUS LEARNED

Falsely Humble: I don't wish to appear self-promoting, so I veil my competencies.

Learned: I have no interest in self-promoting to soothe my ego, but there are moments when I know what I know about what can be done, so I communicate with clarity and goodwill what I can competently do.

Liz was vague about her desire for advancement because she did not wish to be viewed as prideful and self-promoting. She was not clear on her wishes and goals lest the CEO conclude she was self-serving and wrongly motivated.

Sadly, she had no intention about being unclear and misleading the CEO. Even so, her lack of clarity left the CEO in the dark about Liz's aspirations, so he gave the promotion to Sherry, who was unambiguous about her strong interest in the position. After later hearing how much Liz had wanted this position, the CEO was in utter disbelief and deeply disappointed. He had concluded she was disinterested in the promotion.

Are you unclear because you seek to be humble but in the process mislead others? How can you let others know of your talents and passion while stating these things in a way that does not sound arrogant? Before you remain quiet due to not wanting to be self-promoting, consult with some wise people in your life who can provide input on helping you convey your goals and desires without appearing boastful.

SPEAK YOUR MIND CLEARLY:
Emerson's Checklist for Learned Communication

- ☐ Do I struggle, as most do, to maintain a balance between being humble and quiet about what I know versus confidently speaking up clearly and helpfully about what I know?
- ☐ Do I recognize that humility and confidently speaking up are not mutually exclusive but on a continuum?
- ☐ Do most people see me as one who is competent in certain areas, and when I speak, it is never with a spirit of superiority nor to attract attention by seeking the spotlight?
- ☐ Do I have a mindset about using my knowledge and skills to serve others and not to gain status and power to get what I want?
- ☐ Though I keep in front of me the potential that I could be arrogant and self-deluded about what I know on a topic, is there any evidence that, on this matter, I am inflated and delusional in my self-view?
- ☐ When I know information that can serve others—since they need it—do I humbly tell them without fear of appearing puffed up and superior to them?
- ☐ Do I communicate my knowledge with a down-to-earth attitude, avoiding a condescending and dismissive disposition?
- ☐ Do I communicate with clarity and goodwill what I can competently do to help others advance their healthy self-interests?
- ☐ Do I give credit to others for their knowledge and skills and avoid trying to take credit where credit is not due to me?
- ☐ Do I pull back from communicating unnecessary information solely to impress others with my knowledge and expertise?
- ☐ Do I detect when I talk over another, which makes me appear more significant than others, and do I then stop my unkind interruption?
- ☐ Do I continually learn from others, genuinely value their greater experience and expertise, and resist chafing at the thought that I am the lesser or giving off the air that I am their equal?

OVERLY SENSITIVE VERSUS AUTHENTICALLY FRIENDLY

Overly Sensitive: Not wanting to hurt people, I hold back on what is clearly true.

Authentically Friendly: I am loyal and trustworthy but also honest and candid—a true friend—so while I seek to be sensitive, I won't give in to fearful silence that would deprive others of hearing about what best serves them.

Most are familiar with the biblical admonition to speak the truth in love (Eph. 4:15). I especially love this verse from Ephesians because it combines two of the four checklist items we have discussed in detail throughout this book: Is it true? Is it kind? However, some of us are so loving and sensitive that we withhold the necessary truth lest it hurt the person. We need to hear Proverbs 27:6: "Faithful are the wounds of a friend, but deceitful are the kisses of an enemy." When we care about the truth and care about the person, the most loving and respectful thing to do is speak clearly about what is necessary for that person to hear. Do we believe we are helping him or her by remaining silent?

In writing this book, I came across another quote (this one extra-biblical, though still based on biblical principles) that combines two of the four checklist items. Author and researcher Brené Brown had this to say about the kindness of being clear in our communication, even when needing to share an uncomfortable truth:

> Over the past several years, my team and I have learned something about clarity and the importance of hard conversations that has changed everything from the way we talk to each other to the way we negotiate with external partners. It's simple but transformative: Clear is kind. Unclear is unkind.
>
> I first heard this saying two decades ago in a 12-step meeting, but I was on slogan overload at the time and didn't think about it again until I saw the data about how most of us avoid clarity because

> we tell ourselves that we're being kind, when what we're actually doing is being unkind and unfair.
>
> Feeding people half-truths...to make them feel better (which is almost always about making ourselves feel more comfortable) is unkind.
>
> Not getting clear with a colleague about your expectations because it feels too hard, yet holding them accountable or blaming them for not delivering is unkind.[1]

Consider this: Many would be tempted to say that the kind thing to do would be to simply remain silent and not be truthfully and lovingly clear, lest it trigger the person. Or would it, from the Lord's perspective, best serve others to clearly communicate truth to them as a caring, kind, and gracious human being, even if they do not welcome or receive the information?

In this case, our coworker and friend believed a promotion was imminent, but when she did not receive it, she blamed the company and the "bias" of management against women. They are the problem, not her, she said. However, we had reason to believe from the beginning that she would not receive the promotion, and we thought we were spot-on. However, to share this with our friend would be uncomfortable. Should we stay silent and let her continue blaming management?

Though we can talk ourselves into believing this is the kindest option, as long as we don't chime in with more ammunition against management, might this be a case of our silence communicating that we agree with our friend? Would the kind response actually be to say, "I am your friend, and I can be wrong, but my read is that your explosive anger in various staff meetings over the last year is what removed you from the running. I wish you had received the promotion, but my gut tells me it is an uphill battle for you. And my desire is to be your friend and for you to begin addressing the anger issue so you don't sabotage future opportunities."

I talked with a mother of an adult son entertaining a divorce from his wife. She told me, "I am of a mind to go to his office and confront him." I urged her to do this. Because she was soft-spoken and reserved, I told her that she of all people had a right to do this, since her son knew that she rarely spoke this way, and her grandchildren needed their parents' marriage to remain intact.

Many times such people as this mother do not want to make things worse or provoke the other person, who might be apt to act wounded, as though everyone is picking on him, and then claim, "That's the last straw. I am finished with my wife and with this family. You pushed me over the edge!" That fear does something to sensitive people. They conjure up this worst-case scenario and do not speak up. Somehow they feel they might be responsible for making things worse. But when is that ever the case? They need to see that their caring demeanor and words qualify them to speak up clearly and would never be viewed by objective people as the last straw. Encouragingly, this son called off his divorce and is working on his marriage.

SPEAK YOUR MIND CLEARLY:

Emerson's Checklist for Authentically Friendly Communication

- ☐ Might my silence, which deprives my friend of helpful truth, actually be harmful, not neutral?
- ☐ Do I see myself as loyal and trustworthy? Do my friends?
- ☐ Do I speak honestly and candidly after listening to understand what a friend is trying to communicate?
- ☐ Do I speak candidly and sensitively out of empathy, love, and respect for my friend, even though we may differ?
- ☐ Do I communicate the necessary truth kindly because my silence would deprive friends of their need to hear what best serves them?
- ☐ Do I practice sensitivity in communication with my friends by understanding the issue, being open to having misheard, and ensuring the timing of the conversation is best?
- ☐ Do I exercise sensitivity in my speech and writing from a place of wisdom, not from a place of timidity where I am controlled by a dread of rejection for speaking up?
- ☐ Do I speak with great sensitivity without sugarcoating, since that can downplay the seriousness of the concern and cause a friend to minimize the gravity of the circumstance?

- ☐ When communicating honestly and candidly with a friend, do I use language like this: "I understand your position and see where you are coming from, but I believe my view is stronger, has more merit, and is the better choice"?
- ☐ Do I consider sensitive speech with friends to mean I will not step over a line that condemns them for their honest differences of opinion?
- ☐ Do my candid and sensitive conversations convey my belief in my friend and involve positive encouragement, not shameful critiques?
- ☐ Do I accept the typical tension between remaining sensitively silent as the wisest approach in the moment versus speaking up because uncomfortable truth can trump circumstances?
- ☐ Do I celebrate my friend's success in response to my earlier input?

CONCLUSION

GO AHEAD—SPEAK YOUR MIND!

I still stand behind the necessity of the first half of my message on communication, shared in my 2017 book *Before You Hit Send: Preventing Headache and Heartache*. Look no further than the 2016 and 2020 presidential elections, as well as the COVID-19 era of 2020–22, when everyone and their grandmother had an opinion on masks, vaccines, and government mandates. Would anyone disagree that a great deal of headache and heartache could have been prevented had more people paused before they spoke their mind on whatever it was they wanted to post on social media or preach from a six-foot social distance, and asked themselves: *Is what I am about to communicate true, kind, necessary, and clear?*

I admit that a great deal of information has been thrown at you throughout this book. That was on purpose, of course. Consider this updated version more of an encyclopedia of information about many of the different types of communication struggles people have. But hopefully, somewhere in these pages, you were challenged to make some necessary adjustments concerning your communication with others. After all, I have yet to meet someone who has never struggled in some of the areas of true, kind, necessary, and clear communication introduced in these pages.

I also hope that you have been encouraged in this book when reading about your strengths as a communicator because hopefully all readers will recognize areas in which they are already doing well. Most of you, in large part because of your upbringing or the character traits you saw in older people you chose to learn from, are already on a good track overall, and I hope this book has given you confidence and momentum to keep going.

As we finish up our time together, where do you stand? What challenges are you left with? In the introduction, I shared that most reading this book fall into one of three categories. First, some have been holding back their ideas and opinions, only to regret later not speaking up. Second, some tend to blurt out their thoughts and feelings but later are sorry that they did not think before speaking. And third, some know they are fairly good speakers but have yet to become the master communicators they know they should be.

Where do you fall within these three?

I encourage you to go back to the communication self-assessment and pay special attention to the areas where you scored yourself with a 1 or 2. Then revisit the sections where we expanded on that descriptor and its positive alternative, and study once again the checklist for how to speak your mind. Do not skim over or brush any aside that might intimidate you. Really think through each of the items on that checklist. My pastor's heart would encourage you to pray for God's wisdom to help you better speak your mind in those areas.

Do you believe that God wants to help you in your communication skills? Do you believe He wants you to speak the truth—and to do so kindly, clearly, and only when necessary? I hope by now you are sure of at least that. But on top of God's instructions for us to "speak the truth in love" (Eph. 4:15 NLT), we can also be assured that He will help us do this, if we only ask Him. First John 5:14–15 tells us, "This is the confidence we have in approaching God: that if we ask anything according to his will, he hears us. And if we know that he hears us—whatever we ask—we know that we have what we asked of him" (NIV). The book of James really drives this point home when it says, "If any of you lacks wisdom, you should ask God, who gives generously to all without finding fault, and it will be given to you" (1:5 NIV).

So in this monumental challenge before us to learn how to best speak our minds truthfully, with kindness, only when necessary, and clearly, where do we begin? Whether you scored yourself with only a small handful of 1s and 2s in the assessment or the number is higher than you prefer to count right now, hopefully this book and its principles, which have transformed my own life, will give you wisdom to go ahead and confidently . . . speak your mind!

NOTES

INTRODUCTION

1. *Socrates*, Essential Thinkers Series, Collector's Library (Barnes and Noble Books, 2004).

PROLOGUE

1. Emerson Eggerichs, *Love & Respect* (Thomas Nelson, 2004), 284.

CHAPTER 1

1. Khaled Hosseini, *The Kite Runner* (Riverhead Books, 2013), 18.

CHAPTER 2

1. Fyodor Dostoevsky, *The Brothers Karamazov*, trans. Constance Garnett (Signet Classics, 1957), 49.
2. William Shakespeare, *The Tragedy of Hamlet, Prince of Denmark*, act 1, scene 3, https://www.shakespeare.mit.edu/hamlet/hamlet.1.3.html.

CHAPTER 3

1. Ralph Waldo Emerson, "The American Scholar," an address at Harvard University, 1837, in *Emerson: Essays and Lectures* (Library of America, 1983), 62.
2. "Weasel word," *Wikipedia*, updated September 7, 2024, https://en.wikipedia.org/wiki/Weasel_word.

CHAPTER 5

1. Benjamin Franklin, *Poor Richard's Almanack: Being the Choicest Morsels of Wisdom, Written During the Years of the Almanack's Publication* (Peter Pauper Press, Inc., 1986), 46.

CHAPTER 6

1. Michael Venutolo-Mantovani, "Lance Armstrong Reveals Exactly How He Got Away with Cheating for So Long," Bicycling, December 14,

2023, https://www.bicycling.com/news/a46129587/lance-armstrong-reveals-how-he-cheated-doping-drug-tests/.
2. Eileen Ogintz, "Why Modern Millennial Vacations Are All About Bragging Rights," Fox News, July 5, 2017, www.foxnews.com/travel/2016/07/29/why-modern-millennial-vacations-are-all-about-bragging-rights.html.
3. Pierre Corneille, *The Liar*, trans. Richard Wilbur (Dramatists Play Service, 2012).
4. Isabel Fonseca, *Bury Me Standing: The Gypsies and Their Journey* (Vintage, 1995), 15.

PART 2

1. *Bambi*, directed by David Hand (Walt Disney Pictures, 1942).
2. Blake Skylar, "Do Social Networking Sites Create Anti-Social Behavior?" *People's World*, August 8, 2011, www.peoplesworld.org/article/do-social-networking-sites-create-anti-social-behavior/.
3. Luma Simms, "From Salem to DC: Mary Eberstadt's Analysis of the Dangerous Religion of Secular Progressivism," *The Public Discourse*, Witherspoon Institute, June 28, 2016, https://www.thepublicdiscourse.com/2016/06/17232.

CHAPTER 7

1. Jeffrey Marlett, "Leo Durocher," Society for American Baseball Research, accessed December 17, 2024, https://www.sabr.org/bioproj/person/35d925c7.
2. Noel Sheppard, "Dr. Ben Carson Strikes Back at MSNBC's Toure Neblett: I'm No Uncle Tom," MRC NewsBusters, March 26, 2013, https://www.newsbusters.org/blogs/nb/noel-sheppard/2013/03/26/dr-ben-carson-strikes-back-msnbcs-toure-neblett-im-no-uncle-tom.
3. George MacDonald, *The Princess and Curdie* (Looking Glass Library, 1957), 80.

CHAPTER 10

1. Charles Schulz, *Peanuts*, December 15, 1964, htpps://www.gocomics.com/peanuts/1964/12/15.
2. Martin Luther King Jr., "I Have a Dream," speech delivered in 1963, in Eric J. Sundquist, *King's Dream* (Yale University Press, 2009), 14.
3. Martin Luther King Jr., *Strength to Love* (Fortress Press, 2010), 47.
4. "Distinguished Alumni Award: John Hayden Fry," University of Iowa Center for Advancement, accessed December 17, 2024, http://foundation.uiowa.edu/daa/daa-profile.php?namer=true&profileid=22.
5. Franklin D. Roosevelt, "Radio Address to the Young Democratic Clubs of America," August 24, 1935, online by Gerhard Peters and John T. Woolley, *The American Presidency Project*, www.presidency.ucsb.edu/ws/?pid=14925.

6. Audrey Hepburn in "Audrey Hepburn, Many-Sided Charmer," *Life*, December 7, 1953, 132, https://books.google.com/books?id=O0kEAAAAMBAJ&printsec=frontcover&source=gbs_ge_summary_r&cad=0#v=onepage&q&f=false.

CHAPTER 13

1. This famous slogan during World War II surfaced since family members may have known sensitive information about a son's location on a ship and told others, which could lead to enemy spies intercepting that message and sinking the ship.

CHAPTER 15

1. Tiffany Bloodworth Rivers, "Tweets, Text and Chats, Oh My! 5 Ways to Resist Workplace Distractions," *iOffice*, July 27, 2017, https://www.iofficecorp.com/blog/tweets-text-and-chats-oh-my-five-ways-to-resist-workplace-distractions.
2. Brian Regan, "Dinner Party–Me Monster" from *I Walked on the Moon*, Facebook post, October 7, 2022, https://www.facebook.com/BrianReganComedian/videos/dinner-party-me-monster-from-iwalkedonthemoon-brianregan-standupcomedy/403444688654020/.
3. "How Do You Deal with People Who Dominate Conversation?" *Quora*, accessed November 15, 2016, https://www.quora.com/How-do-you-deal-with-people-who-dominate-conversation.

PART 4

1. Anthony Hope Hawkins, "A Very Fine Day," *Collected Works of Anthony Hope* (Delphi Publishing, 2016).

CHAPTER 16

1. Peter Morgan, *The Crown*, season 6, Netflix, https://www.netflix.com/mx-en/title/80025678.

CHAPTER 20

1. "Are You Really Listening: Hearing vs. Listening," Speakeasy, June 4, 2024, https:// www.speakeasyinc.com/hearing-vs-listening/.

CHAPTER 21

1. Brené Brown, "Clear Is Kind. Unclear Is Unkind.," blog post, adapted from *Dare to Lead*, October 15, 2018, https://brenebrown.com/articles/2018/10/15/clear-is-kind-unclear-is-unkind/.

APPENDIX

SCRIPTURAL MEDITATIONS ON SPEAKING YOUR MIND

SCRIPTURAL MEDITATIONS ON SPEAKING YOUR MIND TRUTHFULLY

- **Ephesians 4:25**—Therefore, laying aside falsehood, ***speak truth*** *each one* of you *with his neighbor*, for we are members of one another.
- **Colossians 3:9**—***Do not lie*** to one another, since you laid aside the old self with its evil practices.
- **Titus 1:2**—***God . . . cannot lie.***
- **Acts 5:3–4**—But Peter said, "Ananias, why has Satan filled your heart to lie to the Holy Spirit and to keep back some of the price of the land? While it remained unsold, did it not remain your own? And after it was sold, was it not under your control? Why is it that you have conceived this deed in your heart? ***You have not lied to men but to God.***"
- **Revelation 14:4–5**—These are the ones who follow the Lamb wherever He goes. These have been purchased from among men as first fruits to God and to the Lamb. And ***no lie was found in their mouth***; they are blameless.
- **Proverbs 12:19**—***Truthful lips*** will be established forever, but a ***lying tongue*** is only for a moment.
- **Proverbs 12:22**—***Lying lips*** are an abomination to the LORD, but those who deal faithfully are His delight.
- **Proverbs 19:5**—A ***false witness*** will not go unpunished, and he who tells lies will not escape.

- **Proverbs 21:6**—The acquisition of ***treasures by a lying tongue is a fleeting vapor***, the pursuit of death.
- **Psalm 35:20**—For they do not speak peace, but they devise ***deceitful words*** against those who are quiet in the land.

SCRIPTURAL MEDITATIONS ON SPEAKING YOUR MIND WITH KINDNESS

- **Ephesians 4:15**—But ***speaking the truth in love***, we are to grow up in all aspects into Him who is the head, even Christ.
- **1 Corinthians 13:4**—Love is ***kind***.
- **Proverbs 15:1**—A ***gentle answer*** turns away wrath, but a harsh word stirs up anger.
- **2 Timothy 2:25**—***With gentleness correcting*** those who are in opposition, if perhaps God may grant them repentance leading to the knowledge of the truth.
- **Colossians 4:6**—***Let your speech always be with grace***, as though seasoned with salt, so that you will know how you should respond to each person.
- **1 Peter 3:9**—Don't pay back evil with evil. ***Don't pay back unkind words with unkind words. Instead, pay back evil with kind words.*** This is what you have been chosen to do. You will receive a blessing by doing this. (NIRV)
- **1 Corinthians 4:13**—When we are slandered, ***we answer kindly.*** (NIV)
- **Proverbs 16:21-24**—The wise in heart will be called understanding, and ***sweetness of speech increases persuasiveness.*** Understanding is a fountain of life to one who has it, but the discipline of fools is folly. The heart of the wise instructs his mouth and adds persuasiveness to his lips. Pleasant words are a honeycomb, sweet to the soul and healing to the bones.
- **Proverbs 12:25**—Anxiety weighs down the heart, but ***a kind word cheers it up.*** (NIV)
- **Proverbs 15:4**—***Kind words are good medicine***, but deceitful words can really hurt. (CEV)
- **Proverbs 19:22**—What is desirable in a man is his ***kindness***.

- **Micah 6:8**—He has told you, O man, what is good; and what does the LORD require of you but to do justice, ***to love kindness***, and to walk humbly with your God?
- **Ecclesiastes 10:12**—Words from the mouth of a wise man are ***gracious***, while the lips of a fool consume him.
- **1 Peter 3:15**—But sanctify Christ as Lord in your hearts, always being ready to make a defense to everyone who asks you to give an account for the hope that is in you, yet with ***gentleness and reverence.***
- **Colossians 3:8**—But now you also, put them all aside: anger, wrath, malice, slander, and ***abusive speech from your mouth.***
- **Proverbs 12:18**—There is one who ***speaks rashly*** like the thrusts of a sword, but the tongue of the wise brings healing.
- **Proverbs 25:15**—By forbearance a ruler may be persuaded, and a ***soft tongue*** breaks the bone.
- **Luke 4:22**—And all were speaking well of Him, and wondering at ***the gracious words which were falling from His lips***; and they were saying, "Is this not Joseph's son?"

SCRIPTURAL MEDITATIONS ON SPEAKING YOUR MIND ONLY WHEN NECESSARY

- **Ecclesiastes 3:7**—***A time to be silent and a time to speak.***
- **Proverbs 10:19**—When there are ***many words***, transgression is unavoidable, but he who restrains his lips is wise.
- **Ecclesiastes 5:3**—***Many words*** mark the speech of a fool. (NIV)
- **Ecclesiastes 6:11**—***The more the words, the less the meaning***, and how does that profit anyone? (NIV)
- **Proverbs 29:20**—Do you see a man who is ***hasty in his words***? There is more hope for a fool than for him.
- **Ecclesiastes 5:7**—For ***in . . . many words there is emptiness.***
- **Ecclesiastes 10:12–14**—The lips of a fool consume him; the beginning of his talking is folly and the end of it is wicked madness. Yet ***the fool multiplies words.***
- **Matthew 12:36**—But I tell you that ***every careless word*** that people speak, they shall give an accounting for it in the day of judgment.

- **James 1:26**—If anyone thinks himself to be religious, and yet does not ***bridle his tongue*** but deceives his own heart, this man's religion is worthless.
- **Ephesians 5:4**—And there must be no filthiness and silly talk, or coarse jesting, ***which are not fitting***, but rather giving of thanks.
- **Ephesians 4:29**—Let no unwholesome word proceed from your mouth, but only such a word as is good for edification ***according to the need of the moment***, so that it will give grace to those who hear.
- **Proverbs 25:11–12**—Like apples of gold in settings of silver is a word ***spoken in right circumstances***. Like an earring of gold and an ornament of fine gold is a wise reprover to a listening ear.
- **Proverbs 15:23**—A man has joy in ***an apt answer***, and how delightful is ***a timely word***!
- **Proverbs 17:27**—He who ***restrains his words*** has knowledge, and he who has a cool spirit is a man of understanding.
- **Proverbs 13:3**—The one who ***guards his mouth*** preserves his life; the one who opens wide his lips comes to ruin.
- **Proverbs 21:23**—He who ***guards his mouth and his tongue***, guards his soul from troubles.
- **Proverbs 17:28**—Even a fool, when he ***keeps silent***, is considered wise; when he ***closes his lips***, he is considered prudent.
- **James 1:19**—This you know, my beloved brethren. But everyone must be quick to hear, ***slow to speak*** and slow to anger.
- **Jude 1:3**—I felt the ***necessity to write***.
- **Ephesians 5:12**—For it is ***disgraceful even to speak*** of the things which are done by them in secret.

SCRIPTURAL MEDITATIONS ON SPEAKING YOUR MIND CLEARLY

- **1 Corinthians 14:9**—So also you, unless you utter by the tongue ***speech that is clear***, how will it be known what is spoken? For you will be speaking into the air.
- **Colossians 4:3–4**—Praying at the same time for us as well . . . that I may ***make it clear*** in the way I ought to speak.

- **1 Timothy 1:7**—***They do not understand*** either what they are saying or the matters about which they make confident assertions.
- **1 Corinthians 1:12; 5:10; 10:19**—Now ***I mean this . . . I did not at all mean . . . What do I mean then?***
- **1 Corinthians 14:10–11**—There are, perhaps, a great many kinds of languages in the world, and no kind is without meaning. ***If then I do not know the meaning of the language***, I will be to the one who speaks a barbarian, and the one who speaks will be a barbarian to me.
- **Ephesians 4:9**—Now this expression, "He ascended," ***what does it mean . . . ?***
- **Hebrews 12:27**—***This expression***, "Yet once more," ***denotes . . .***
- **Ecclesiastes 12:9**—He pondered, ***searched out*** and arranged many proverbs.
- **Ecclesiastes 12:10**— . . . to ***write words of truth correctly.***
- **Luke 1:3–4**—It seemed fitting for me as well, having ***investigated everything carefully*** from the beginning, to ***write it out for you in consecutive order***, most excellent Theophilus; so that you may ***know the exact truth*** about the things you have been taught.
- **Acts 11:4**— . . . proceeded to explain to them in ***orderly sequence.***
- **1 Corinthians 1:17**— ***. . . not in cleverness of speech.***
- **Ephesians 3:4**—When you read you can ***understand my insight.***
- **2 Peter 3:16**—All his letters . . . in which are some things ***hard to understand*** . . .
- **2 Corinthians 1:13**—For we write nothing else to you than ***what you read and understand.***
- **Deuteronomy 27:8**—And you shall write ***very clearly*** all the words of this law. (NIV)
- **Mark 8:32**—And He was ***stating the matter plainly.***

ABOUT THE AUTHOR

DR. EMERSON EGGERICHS is an internationally known author and speaker on the topics of marriage, parenting, communication, and more. Based on five decades of counseling as well as scientific and biblical research, he founded Love and Respect Ministries with his wife, Sarah, in 1999, which is actively impacting countless relationships all over the world.

Dr. Eggerichs has spoken to owners, coaches, players, and spouses in the NFL, PGA, and NBA. He has keynoted at national business events, professional counseling conventions, and more. He's addressed universities, megachurches, the US military, CEO groups, and the poorest of the poor in India.

After getting his undergraduate and graduate degrees at Wheaton College, he went on to be ordained at Dubuque Seminary and holds a PhD in child and family ecology from Michigan State University. He has authored several books, including the *New York Times* bestseller *Love and Respect*, which has sold over two million copies.

Prior to launching the Love and Respect Conferences, Dr. Eggerichs was the senior pastor of East Lansing Trinity Church for nearly twenty years. Emerson and Sarah have been married since 1973 and have three adult children and seven grandchildren.

Love & Respect

MINISTRIES

Join our communities on
Facebook, Instagram, and TikTok:

@loverespectinc

For podcasts, articles, videos, online courses,
books, and church resources, find us at:

loveandrespect.com